# How the Brain Learns to Read

## Second Edition

# How the Brain Learns to Read

### Second Edition

## David A. Sousa

CORWIN
A SAGE Company

**CORWIN**
A SAGE Company

FOR INFORMATION:

Corwin

A SAGE Company

2455 Teller Road

Thousand Oaks, California 91320

(800) 233-9936

www.corwin.com

SAGE Publications Ltd.

1 Oliver's Yard

55 City Road

London EC1Y 1SP

United Kingdom

SAGE Publications India Pvt. Ltd.

B 1/I 1 Mohan Cooperative Industrial Area

Mathura Road, New Delhi 110 044

India

SAGE Publications Asia-Pacific Pte. Ltd.

3 Church Street

#10-04 Samsung Hub

Singapore 049483

Acquisitions Editor:  Jessica Allan

Associate Editor:  Kimberly Greenberg

Editorial Assistant:  Cesar Reyes

Production Editor:  Amy Schroller

Copy Editor:  Melinda Masson

Typesetter:  C&M Digitals (P) Ltd.

Proofreader:  Jeff Bryant

Cover Designer:  Gail Buschman

Printed in the United States of America.

*A catalog record of this book is available from the Library of Congress.*

ISBN 9781483333946

This book is printed on acid-free paper.

SUSTAINABLE FORESTRY INITIATIVE
Certified Chain of Custody
Promoting Sustainable Forestry
www.sfiprogram.org
SFI-01268
SFI label applies to text stock

14 15 16 17 18 10 9 8 7 6 5 4 3 2 1

# Contents

# About the Author

 David A. Sousa, EdD, is an international consultant in educational neuroscience and author of more than a dozen books that translate brain research into strategies for improving learning. He has presented to more than 200,000 educators across the United States, Canada, Europe, Australia, New Zealand, and Asia. He has taught high school chemistry and served in administrative positions, including superintendent of schools. He was an adjunct professor of education at Seton Hall University and a visiting lecturer at Rutgers University. Dr. Sousa has edited science books and published dozens of articles in leading journals. His books have been published in French, Spanish, Russian, Chinese, Arabic, Korean, and several other languages. He is past president of the National Staff Development Council (now Learning Forward) and has received honorary degrees and awards for his commitment to research, professional development, and science education. He has appeared on the NBC *Today* show and National Public Radio to discuss his work with schools using brain research.

# Introduction

Most of us don't recall much about learning to talk. It just seemed to come naturally. We probably don't remember much about how we learned to read either. As adults, reading seems so effortless and automatic that we often assume it should be an easy skill for almost any child to acquire. But that is not the case. Learning to speak is an innate ability supported by specialized areas of the brain, and is automatic for almost all children raised in normal circumstances. But for many children, learning to read is a long, complicated task requiring years of conscious effort.

Have you ever thought about what your brain goes through when you read? First, your eyes have to scan those squiggly lines and curves called the alphabet and group them into the words as indicated on the page. Then, certain areas of the brain work to associate the written symbols with the sounds of language already stored in your head. As this association occurs, other neural networks decode the writing into a mental message that you understand. Incredibly, your brain can process and comprehend an entire sentence in a few seconds. It almost seems like magic. But it isn't magic. Reading is the result of an elaborate process that involves decoding abstract symbols into sounds, then into words that generate meaning. Can you remember the first time you encountered printed text and saw those letters? Just turn this page upside down and you get an idea of how alien those squiggles must have looked at first and what a struggle it was to make sense of them.

## THE BAD NEWS AND THE GOOD NEWS ⚙

### The Bad News

Educators have been well aware of the difficulties involved in learning to read and have long debated the best ways to teach beginning reading. No one method or program has triumphed, as evidenced by the lack of substantial progress in improving reading achievement scores. Unfortunately, despite all the time and resources devoted to reading programs, there have been no noticeable gains in reading achievement since the publication of the first edition of this book. The National Assessment of Educational Progress reports that nearly two-thirds of low-income fourth graders cannot read at the proficient level. Grade 8 students have made no gains in reading achievement in the past decade, and the reading scores of Grade 12 students have actually declined slightly in that same time period (NAEP, 2012). The number of students identified with reading problems, including dyslexia, is growing rapidly. No one is sure if this is because more students are developing difficulties in reading or whether school districts are getting better at diagnosing previously unidentified students. One thing seems certain: Students who are poor readers in their early years remain poor readers in their later years.

A decades-long battle over the best way to help children learn to read has only polarized the educational community though less so since the report of the National Reading Panel in 2000. Nonetheless, critics still argue that reading instruction has been out of touch with research in that too many programs minimize the teaching of phoneme-grapheme relationships. The selection of reading programs has often been fueled by debates of philosophical stances and advocacies that have little to do with what research is uncovering about how children learn to read.

## The Good News

Scientific methods are now available to study how the brain acquires reading skills. In the last two decades, brain researchers have developed new technologies for looking inside the living brain. These technologies fall into two major categories: those that look at brain *structure* and those that look at brain *function*. When aimed at the brain, computerized axial tomography (CAT) and magnetic resonance imaging (MRI) are very useful diagnostic tools that produce computer images of the brain's internal structure. For example, they can detect tumors, malformations, and the damage caused by cerebral hemorrhages.

Different technologies, however, are required to look at how the brain works. An alphabet soup describes the five most common procedures that can be used to isolate and identify the areas of the brain where distinct levels of activity are occurring. The most frequently used technologies are the following:

- Electroencephalography (EEG)
- Magnetoencephalography (MEG)
- Positron emission tomography (PET)
- Functional magnetic resonance imaging (fMRI)
- Functional magnetic resonance spectroscopy (fMRS)

Table I.1 summarizes how these technologies work and what they measure.

Using these technologies, researchers have been able to explore how different brains function when carrying out certain tasks, including reading. Here are just a few of the fascinating things that have been uncovered:

- Novice readers use different cerebral pathways while reading than skilled readers do.
- People with reading difficulties use different brain regions to decode written text than do typical readers.
- The brains of people with reading problems are working harder during reading than those of skilled readers.
- Even though dyslexia is a brain disorder, it is treatable.
- With proper instructional intervention, the brains of young struggling and dyslexic readers can actually be rewired to use cerebral areas that more closely resemble those used by typical readers.

Table I.1    Techniques for Mapping Brain Functions

| Technique | What It Measures | How It Works |
|---|---|---|
| Electroencephalography (EEG) and magnetoencephalography (MEG) | The electrical and magnetic activity occurring in the brain during mental processing | In EEG, multiple electrodes are attached to the scalp to record electrical signals in a computer. In MEG, magnetic detectors are placed around the head to record magnetic activity. EEGs and MEGs record changes in brain activity that occur as rapidly as one millisecond. When a group of neurons respond to a specific event, they activate, and their electrical and magnetic activity can be detected. This response is called an event-related potential or ERP. |
| Positron emission tomography (PET) | Amount of radiation present in brain regions | The subject is injected with a radioactive solution that circulates to the brain. Brain regions of higher activity accumulate more radiation, which is picked up by a ring of detectors. A computer displays the concentration of radiation in a cross-sectional slice of the brain regions aligned with the detectors. The picture shows the more active areas in reds and yellows, the quieter areas in blues and greens. |
| Functional magnetic resonance imaging (fMRI) | Levels of deoxygenated hemoglobin in brain cells | Any part of the brain that is thinking requires more oxygen, which is carried to the brain cells by hemoglobin. The fMRI uses a large magnet to compare the amount of oxygenated hemoglobin entering brain cells with the amount of deoxygenated hemoglobin leaving the cells. The computer colors in the brain regions receiving more oxygenated blood and locates the activated brain region to within one centimeter (half-inch). |
| Functional magnetic resonance spectroscopy (fMRS) | Levels of specific chemicals present during brain activity | This technology involves the same equipment as fMRI but uses different computer software to record levels of various chemicals in the brain while the subject is thinking. fMRS can precisely pinpoint the area of activity, but it can also identify whether certain key chemicals are also present at the activation site. |

As a result of these discoveries, it is now possible to identify with a high degree of accuracy those children who are at greatest risk of reading problems, even before the problems develop, to diagnose the problems accurately, and to manage the problems with effective and proven treatment programs (Dehaene, 2009). It is not exaggerating to say that reading is very likely the one area of school curriculum to date where neuroscience and cognitive psychology have made their greatest impact. The brain imaging studies have opened a relatively new field in neuroscience called developmental cognitive neurology (Habib, 2003). Here one observes how the developing brain reacts to various kinds of environmental constraints. Future studies will enable scientists and educators to work together to better understand both the typical brain and the causes and possible treatments for learning deficiencies, including dyslexia. The application of new discoveries in neuroscience to educational practice has spawned a very new field of inquiry called **educational neuroscience**.

## ❖ ABOUT THIS BOOK

I have been asked on many occasions to give specific examples of how the fruits of scientific research can have an impact on educational practice. That question is a lot easier to answer now than it was 15 years ago because recent discoveries in cognitive neuroscience have given us a deeper understanding of the brain. We now have more knowledge of our working (short-term) and long-term memory systems, the impact of emotions on learning, and how we acquire language and motor skills. But the greatest contribution to date, in my opinion, is the growing body of research on how the brain learns to read.

Because reading is essential for success in our society, teaching all children to read is every school district's highest curriculum priority. Although many children learn to read well, too large a number encounter difficulties. Numerous reasons are cited for this unfortunate situation, such as poor home environment, physical and psychological deficits, and inadequate reading instruction. Regardless of the reasons, teachers of reading are still faced with the awesome responsibility of getting each child to learn the difficult task of reading. The more these teachers know about how the brain learns to read, the more likely they are to choose instructional strategies that will result in successful learning. The purpose of this book is to present what scientists currently believe about how young humans acquire spoken language and then use that capability when learning to read.

### Chapter Contents

*Chapter 1. Learning Spoken Language.* Children's competence in spoken language greatly influences how quickly and successfully they learn to read. This chapter examines how the young brain detects language sounds from the background noise and begins to recognize the words, pitch, and tempo of a native language. It looks at the specialized regions of the brain that work together and manipulate sounds to build words, phrases, and sentences, and at how the brain cleverly groups words and phrases to increase the speed of spoken language comprehension.

*Chapter 2. Learning to Read.* This chapter explores the various stages that the brain must go through while learning to read, including the process of building sounds into words, words into phrases, and phrases into sentences. The alphabetic principle is introduced here as well as the roles that working (short-term) and long-term memories play in reading. Also discussed here are the most recent fascinating discoveries that brain imaging scans have revealed about the cerebral mechanisms responsible for decoding written text and the different neural pathways used by beginning, intermediate, and skilled readers.

*Chapter 3. Teaching Reading for Encoding and Decoding.* This chapter briefly reviews the history of the debate over whether phonics or whole language is the better method for beginning reading instruction. It cites the scientific studies that have gained a deeper understanding of how the brain learns to read. From these studies come valuable implications that educators can consider when deciding on the components of a reading program involving encoding and decoding, and on selecting instructional strategies in beginning reading that are likely to be more successful with more students.

*Chapter 4. Teaching Reading for Comprehension.* The ultimate goal of reading is comprehension. Yet there are students who read fluently but have little understanding of what they are reading. This chapter uses the research in reading comprehension to suggest strategies on how to teach vocabulary and linguistic knowledge, and to offer activities that help build students' comprehension skills. Reading strategies for older students and English language learners are also included.

*Chapter 5. Recognizing Reading Problems.* Because early detection of reading problems is essential for early intervention, this chapter focuses on the potential causes of reading difficulties, including what brain imaging scans have revealed about the nature of struggling readers and dyslexia. Also discussed here are the clues that teachers should look for at various grade levels to determine whether a student is having persistent difficulties with reading.

*Chapter 6. Overcoming Reading Problems.* Numerous suggestions are offered in this chapter for teachers and parents to help students overcome their reading problems. The components of early intervention programs are discussed in some detail, as are successful strategies for older students. Featured here is a discovery of great interest that came from imaging studies: Certain reading interventions can actually rewire the brains of struggling readers so that they more closely resemble the neural mechanisms used for reading in the brains of skilled readers.

*Chapter 7. Reading in the Content Areas.* This chapter discusses the major differences between developmental reading (learning to read) and content-area reading (reading to learn). It presents some tested strategies that secondary school content-area teachers can use with students who are poor readers to help them understand vocabulary and gain a more accurate and deeper understanding of the content material they are reading. It highlights the value of graphic organizers and suggests some reading patterns that are unique to different subject areas.

*Chapter 8. Putting It All Together.* Finally, this chapter examines the essential pieces that are needed to develop, select, implement, and support an effective reading program, based on our current scientific understandings of how the brain learns to read. It suggests what beginning readers need to learn, what teachers need to know about teaching reading, and what kind of professional development needs to be implemented to support the reading program. Some suggestions for closing the reading achievement gap are proposed.

Most of the chapters contain suggestions for translating the research on reading into instructional practice.

### Resources and Common Core State Standards

The Resources section contains useful information on reading, most of it available on the Internet. At the end of this section are the Common Core State Standards for English Language Arts and Literacy College and Career Readiness Anchor Standards for Reading, along with references to the chapters in this book that address each anchor standard.

The information in this book was current at the time of publication. However, as scientists continue to explore the inner workings of the brain, they will likely discover more about the cerebral mechanisms involved in learning to read. These discoveries should help parents and educators understand more about reading, reading problems, and effective reading instruction.

## ✿ ASSESSING YOUR CURRENT KNOWLEDGE OF READING

The value of this book can be measured in part by how much it enhances your knowledge about reading. This might be a good time for you to take the following true-false test and assess your current understanding of some concepts related to language, learning to read, reading difficulties, and reading instruction. Decide whether the statements are generally true or false and circle *T* or *F*. Explanations for the answers are identified throughout the book in special boxes.

| 1. | T | F | The brain's ability to learn spoken language improves for most people as they age. |
|---|---|---|---|
| 2. | T | F | Learning to read, like learning spoken language, is a natural ability. |
| 3. | T | F | There are about 200 ways to spell the sounds of the 44 phonemes in English. |
| 4. | T | F | Research studies have concluded that neither the phonological approach nor the whole-language approach is more effective in teaching most children how to read. |
| 5. | T | F | Non-English-speaking children can be taught to read English even if their spoken English vocabulary is weak. |

| 6. | T | F | Most children with attention deficit/hyperactivity disorder (ADHD) are also dyslexic. |
| 7. | T | F | Dyslexic students often have problems in other cognitive areas. |
| 8. | T | F | Many poor readers have attention problems that schools are not equipped to handle. |
| 9. | T | F | There is little that secondary school content-area teachers can do to improve the comprehension skills of their students who are poor readers. |
| 10. | T | F | The Common Core State Standards for English Language Arts include a basic curriculum and a selection of assessment instruments. |

## What's Coming?

Children must learn to speak before they can learn to read. How well they learn to speak and what prereading vocabulary they acquire can have a great impact on how quickly and how successfully they will learn to read with comprehension. Just how we acquire spoken language is the subject of the first chapter.

# 1

# Learning Spoken Language

*The richer and more copious one's vocabulary and the greater one's awareness of fine distinctions and subtle nuances of meaning, the more fertile and precise is likely to be one's thinking.*

—Henry Hazlitt, *Thinking as a Science*

How quickly and successfully the young brain learns to read is greatly influenced by the development of two capabilities: speech comprehension and visual recognition. By recognizing and trying out speech sounds, the child's brain establishes the neural networks needed to manipulate sounds; to acquire and comprehend vocabulary; to detect a language's accents, tone, and stress; and to map out sentence structure. A few years later, the brain will call on its visual recognition system to connect the sounds it has been practicing to abstract visual symbols—we call them the alphabet—so that it can learn to read.

How broad is the child's vocabulary? How many grammatical errors appear in speech? How sophisticated is the sentence structure? How well does the child comprehend variations in sentence structure? The answers to these questions help in determining the breadth and depth of the child's spoken language networks and become the starting points for assessing how well the child will learn to read. Therefore, it is important to understand what cognitive neuroscience has revealed about how the brain acquires and processes spoken words. Table 1.1 presents a general timeline for the development of spoken language and visual recognition during the first three years of growth. The table is a rough approximation based on numerous research studies with young children. Obviously, some children will progress faster or slower than the table indicates. Nonetheless, it is a useful guide to show the progression of skills acquired during the process of learning language and developing visual recognition skills.

Table 1.1    Typical Development of Language and Visual Recognition Systems from Birth to 36 Months of Age

| LANGUAGE DEVELOPMENT | | | VISUAL RECOGNITION |
|---|---|---|---|
| Hearing and Understanding | Speaking | Age in Months | Seeing |
| −Reacts to loud sounds<br>−Appears to recognize caregiver's voice<br>−Smiles when spoken to<br>−Can recognize difference between *da* and *pa* | −Makes pleasure sounds | Birth to 3 | −Able to separate out objects in visual field and track them as they move |
| −Moves eyes in direction of sounds<br>−Responds to changes in speech tone and rhythm (prosody)<br>−Notices objects that make sounds<br>−Reacts to music<br>−Broca's area already responds to caregiver's language<br>−Recognition of vowels focuses on native language | −Babbling sounds more speech-like due to phoneme recognition<br>−Sounds include onsets as *b, m,* and *p.*<br>−Uses sounds to express pleasure and excitement | 4 to 6 | −Can track objects as they move, even if briefly concealed<br>−Face recognition region of the brain becomes active |
| −Reacts and looks in direction of sounds and speech<br>−Listens when spoken to<br>−Attaches meaning to words<br>−Recognizes words for common items like *milk, cup,* or *hand*<br>−Respond to requests, such as *Want more?* or *Come here.*<br>−Difficulty distinguishing vowel sounds not in native language | −Speech contains both long and short groups of sounds<br>−Incorporates gestures with speech<br>−Attaches meaning to words, such as *mama, dada,* and *hi,* and tries to pronounce them<br>−Imitates different speech sounds<br>−Uses speech or other sounds to get and keep attention | 7 to 12 | −Can discriminate objects by their shape, texture, and structure<br>−After observing and object from difference viewpoints, can make assumptions about its three-dimensional shape<br>−Can recognize differences between concave and convex objects |

| LANGUAGE DEVELOPMENT | | | VISUAL RECOGNITION |
|---|---|---|---|
| Hearing and Understanding | Speaking | Age in Months | Seeing |
| –Left hemisphere more active when brain hears speech sounds<br>–Vocabulary growing by seven to 10 words per day | | | –Can distinguish human faces from other primates |
| –Can point to some body parts when asked<br>–Understands simple directions and questions, such as *Throw the ball,* and *Where's your cup?* | –Speech shows increasing vocabulary<br>–Shows recognition of noun/verb differences | 13 to 18 | –Can recognize a face out of context<br>–Can recognize simplified version of objects, suggesting they can abstract the basic elements of a shape from its image |
| –Points to pictures in book as they are named<br>–Listens and responds to songs, rhymes, and simple stories | –Uses phrases and questions of two or three words, such as *More milk,* and *What's that?*<br>–Uses different consonant sounds at the beginning of words | 19 to 24 | |
| –Vocabulary growing by 10 to 20 words per day<br>–Recognizes word opposites, such as *up/down, small/big,* and *in/out*<br>–Can follow two requests, such as *Get the cup and put it on the table.* | –Uses a larger vocabulary<br>–Seldom at loss for word to describe something<br>–Uses two- or three-words to talk about and ask for things<br>–Recognizes and uses other grammatical functions | 25 to 30 | –Facial recognition becomes more precise<br>–Separate brain regions begin to specialize for remembering faces, places, and objects<br>–Visual recognition system becomes more sensitive to novel visual shapes, such as lines symbols (e.g., McDonald's logo) and eventually, letters. |
| –Listens to and enjoys hearing stories for longer periods of time<br>–Most language activity moves to the brain's left hemisphere | –Uses more words with *d, f, g, k, n,* and *t* sounds<br>–Speech is comprehensible most of the time<br>–Asks for or directs attention to objects by naming them | 31 to 36 | |

SOURCES: Mehler et al. 1988; de Haan et al., 2003; Kuhl, 2004; Robinson & Pascalis, 2004; Pascalis et al., 2005; Bhatt et al., 2006; Kraebel et al., 2007; Son et al., 2008; Southgate et al., 2008; Wang & Baillargeon, 2008; Dehaene, 2009; American Speech-Language-Hearing Association, 2013

One of the most extraordinary features of the human brain is its ability to acquire spoken language quickly and accurately. We are born with an innate capacity to distinguish the distinct sounds (phonemes) of all the languages on this planet. Eventually, we are able to associate those sounds with arbitrary written symbols to express our thoughts and emotions to others.

Other animals have developed ways to communicate with members of their species. Birds and apes bow and wave appendages; honeybees dance to map out the location of food; and even one-celled animals can signal neighbors by emitting an array of different chemicals. By contrast, human beings have developed an elaborate and complex means of spoken communication that many say is largely responsible for our place as the dominant species on this planet. Spoken language is truly a marvelous accomplishment for many reasons. At the very least, it gives form to our memories and words to express our thoughts. A single human voice can pronounce all the hundreds of vowel and consonant sounds that allow it to speak any of the nearly 7,000 languages that exist today. With practice, the voice becomes so fine-tuned that it makes only about one sound error per million sounds and one word error per million words (Pinker, 1994).

Before the advent of scanning technologies, we explained how the brain produced spoken language on the basis of evidence from injured brains. In 1861, French physician Paul Broca noticed that patients with brain damage to an area near the left temple understood language but had difficulty speaking, a condition known as aphasia. This region of the brain is commonly referred to as Broca's area (Figure 1.1).

In 1881, German neurologist Carl Wernicke described a different type of aphasia—one in which patients could not make sense out of words they spoke or heard. These patients had damage in the left temporal

Figure 1.1    The language system in the left hemisphere comprises mainly Broca's area and Wernicke's area. The four lobes of the brain are also identified.

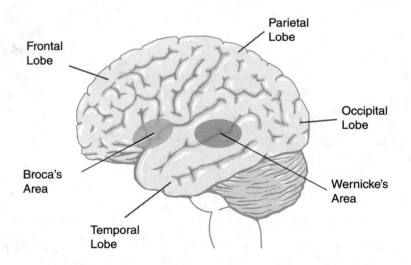

lobe. Now called Wernicke's area, as Figure 1.1 shows, it is located just above and slightly to the rear of the left ear. Those with damage to Wernicke's area could speak fluently, but what they said was quite meaningless. Ever since Broca discovered that the left hemisphere of the brain was specialized for language, researchers have attempted to understand the way in which normal human beings acquire and process their native language.

## Processing Spoken Language

An infant's ability to perceive and discriminate sounds in the environment begins after just a few months of life and develops rapidly. Recent research, using scanners, indicates that spoken language production is a far more complex process than previously thought. When preparing to produce a spoken sentence, the brain not only uses Broca's and Wernicke's areas, but also calls on several other neural networks scattered throughout the left hemisphere. Nouns are processed through one set of patterns; verbs are processed by separate neural networks. The more complex the sentence structure, the more areas that are activated, including some in the right hemisphere.

In most people, the left hemisphere is home to the major components of the language processing system. Broca's area is a region of the left frontal lobe that is believed to be responsible for processing vocabulary, syntax (how word order affects meaning), and rules of grammar. Recent imaging studies indicate that this area, in addition to helping construct language, is involved in determining the meaning of sentences (Caplan, 2006). Wernicke's area is part of the left temporal lobe and is thought to process the sense and meaning of language. It works closely with Broca's area whenever the brain is processing the elements of language. However, the emotional content of language is governed by areas in the right hemisphere.

Brain imaging studies of infants as young as four months of age confirm that the brain possesses neural networks that specialize in responding to the auditory components of language. Dehaene-Lambertz (2000) used electroencephalograph (EEG) recordings to measure the brain activity of 16 four-month-old infants as they listened to language syllables and acoustic tones. After numerous trials, the data showed that syllables and tones were processed primarily in different areas of the left hemisphere, although there was also some right hemisphere activity. For language input, various features, such as the voice and the phonetic category of a syllable, were encoded by separate neural networks into sensory memory. These remarkable findings suggest that, even at this early age, the brain is already organized into functional networks that can distinguish between language fragments and other sounds. Another study of families with severe speech and language disorders has isolated a mutated gene believed to be responsible for their deficits (Lai, Fisher, Hurst, Vargha-Khadem, & Monaco, 2001). This and subsequent studies support the notion that the ability to acquire spoken language is encoded in our genes (Graham & Fisher, 2013).

The apparent genetic predisposition of the brain to the sounds of language explains why normal young children respond to and acquire spoken language quickly. After the first year in a language environment, the child becomes increasingly able to differentiate those sounds heard in the native language and begins to lose the ability to perceive other sounds. Imaging studies show that when children grow up learning two languages, all language activity is found in the same areas of the brain. How long the brain retains this responsiveness to the sounds of language is still open to question. However, there does seem to be general agreement among researchers that the window of opportunity for acquiring language within the language-specific areas of the brain begins to diminish for most people during the middle years of adolescence. Obviously, one can still acquire a new language after that age, but it takes more effort because the new language will be spatially separated in the brain from the native language areas (Bloch et al., 2009; Hernandez & Li, 2007).

## Gender Differences in Language Processing

One of the earliest and most interesting discoveries neuroscientists made with functional imaging was that there were differences in the way male and female brains process language. Male brains tend to process language in the left hemisphere, while most female brains process language in both hemispheres (Burman, Bitan, & Booth, 2008; Clements et al., 2006). Of even greater interest was that these same cerebral areas in both genders were also activated during reading.

Another interesting gender difference is the observation that the large bundle of neurons that connects the two hemispheres and allows them to communicate (called the corpus callosum) is proportionately larger and thicker in the female than in the male. Assuming function follows form, this difference implies that information travels between the two cerebral hemispheres more efficiently in females than in males. The combination of dual-hemisphere language processing and more efficient between-hemisphere communications may account for why young girls generally acquire spoken language easier and more quickly than young boys.

There is still debate among scientists and psychologists over what these differences really mean. Some researchers suggest that the gender differences are minimal and that they decline in importance as we age (e.g., Sommer, Aleman, Somers, Boks, & Kahn, 2008; Wallentin, 2009). Others maintain that these differences continue to affect the way each gender uses and interacts with language, even as adults (e.g., Guiller & Durndell, 2007; Jaušovec & Jaušovec, 2009).

---

### Answer to Test Question #1

**Question:** The brain's ability to learn spoken language improves for most people as they age.

**Answer:** *False.* Numerous studies show that the brain's ability to acquire spoken language is best during the early adolescent years. Of course, people can learn a new language anytime during their lives. It just takes more effort and motivation.

# STRUCTURE OF LANGUAGE ✿

Considering that there are almost 7,000 distinct languages—not counting dialects—spoken on this planet, one might consider talking about the structure of language as an impossible task. Surely, the structures of these thousands of languages vary widely, but there are some surprisingly common elements. Obviously, all spoken language begins with sounds, so we start this discussion by looking at sound patterns and how they are combined to make words. The next step is to examine the rules that govern how words are merged into sentences that make sense and communicate information to others.

## Learning Phonemes

All languages consist of distinct units of sound called *phonemes*. Although each language has its own unique set of phonemes, only about 170 phonemes comprise all the world's languages. These phonemes consist of all the speech sounds that can be made by the human voice apparatus. Phonemes combine to form syllables. For example, in English, the consonant sound "t" and the vowel sound "o" are both phonemes that combine to form the syllable *to-*, as in *tomato*. Although the infant's brain can perceive the entire range of phonemes, only those that are repeated get attention, as the neurons reacting to the unique sound patterns are continually stimulated and reinforced.

At birth, or some researchers say even before birth (e.g., Porcaro et al., 2006; Voegtline, Costigan, Pater, & DiPietro, 2013), babies respond first to the prosody—the rhythm, cadence, and pitch—of their caregiver's voice, not the words. Around the age of six months, infants start babbling, an early sign of language acquisition. The production of phonemes by infants is the result of genetically determined neural programs; however, language exposure is environmental. These two components interact to produce an individual's language system and, assuming no abnormal conditions, sufficient competence to eventually communicate clearly with others.

Infants' babbling consists of all those phonemes, even ones they have never heard. Here the baby's brain is developing a competence called *phonemic awareness*. Within a few months, the baby's brain calculates which bits of speech are occurring more frequently than others. Pruning of the phonemes begins, and by about one year of age, the neural networks focus on the sounds of the language—or languages—being spoken most often in the infant's environment (Dehaene, 2009). In fact, it will soon be very difficult for the baby to pronounce sounds not spoken in the environment, such as the four-letter consonant combinations found in Russian but not in English, or the guttural sounds in Dutch. The brain cells originally sensitive to these sounds have been either recruited for the native language or pruned away.

## Learning Words and Morphemes

The next step for the brain is to detect words from the stream of sounds it is processing. This is not an easy task because people don't pause between words when speaking. Yet the brain has to recognize differences between, say, *green house* and *greenhouse*. Studies show that parents help this process along by slipping automatically into a different speech pattern when talking to their babies than when speaking to adults. Mothers tend to go into a teaching mode with the vowels elongated and emphasized, what some researchers call *parentese*. They speak to their babies in a higher pitch, with a special intonation, rhythm, and feeling. The researchers suggested that mothers are instinctively attempting to help their babies recognize the sounds of language. Researchers found this pattern in other languages as well, such as Russian, Swedish, and Japanese (Burnham, Kitamura, & Vollmer-Conna, 2002).

Remarkably, babies begin to distinguish word boundaries by the age of 8 months even though they don't know what the words mean (Singh, 2008; Yeung & Werker, 2009). They now begin to acquire new vocabulary words at the rate of about 7 to 10 a day, helping to establish their working cerebral dictionary called the *mental lexicon*. By the age of 10 to 12 months, the toddler's brain has begun to distinguish and remember phonemes of the native language and to ignore foreign sounds. For example, one study showed that at the age of 6 months, American and Japanese babies are equally good at discriminating between the "l" and "r" sounds, even though Japanese has no "l" sound. However, by age 10 months, Japanese babies have a tougher time making the distinction, while American babies have become much better at it. During this and subsequent periods of growth, one's ability to distinguish native sounds improves, while the ability to distinguish normative speech sounds diminishes (Cheour et al., 1998).

Soon, *morphemes,* such as *-s, -ed,* and *-ing,* are added to babies' speaking vocabulary. Morphemes are the smallest units of language that carry some meaning, such as prefixes and suffixes. For example, the prefix *un-* almost always means *not* or *opposite* (*unaware*), and *-ing* often indicates an ongoing action (*eating, walking*). We will see in the next chapter the valuable contribution that morphemes make when learning to read.

At the same time, working memory and Wernicke's area are becoming fully functional, so the child can now attach meaning to words. Of course, learning words is one skill; putting them together to make sense is another, more complex skill.

## Verbal- and Image-Based Words

How quickly a child understands words may be closely related to whether the word can generate a clear mental image. A word like *elephant* generates a picture in the mind's eye and thus can be more easily understood than an abstract word like *justice*. Could it be that the brain maintains two distinct systems to process image-loaded words and abstract words?

To further investigate this point, Tamara Y. Swaab and her colleagues used numerous EEGs to measure the brain's response to concrete and abstract words in a dozen young adults (Swaab, Baynes, & Knight, 2002). EEGs measure changes in brain wave activity, called event-related potentials (ERPs), when the brain experiences a stimulus. The researchers found that image-loaded words produced more ERPs in the front area (frontal lobe—the part thought to be associated with imagery) while abstract words produced more ERPs in the top central (parietal lobe) and rear (occipital lobe) areas. Furthermore, there was little interaction between these disparate areas when processing any of the words (Figure 1.2). The results support the idea that the brain may hold two separate stores for semantics (meaning), one for verbal-based information and the other for image-based information. This discovery has implications for language instruction. Teachers should use concrete images when presenting an abstract concept. For example, teaching the idea of justice could be accompanied by pictures of a judge in robes, the scales of justice, and a courtroom scene.

> **Implication for Teaching and Learning:** "Teachers should use concrete images when presenting an abstract concept to young learners."

## Vocabulary and Language Gaps in Toddlers

In the early years, toddlers acquire most of their vocabulary words from their parents. Consequently, children who experience frequent adult-to-toddler conversations that contain a wide variety of words will build much larger vocabularies than those who experience infrequent conversations that contain fewer words. The incremental effect of this vocabulary difference grows exponentially and can lead to an enormous word gap during the child's first three years.

A particularly significant two-part longitudinal study (Hart & Risley, 2003) documented the vocabulary growth of 42 toddlers from the age of 7 to 9 months until they turned 3 years old. Because parental vocabulary is closely associated with a family's socioeconomic status (SES), Part 1 of this study looked at toddlers in families from three different groups. On the basis of occupation, 13 of the families were upper SES, 23 were middle-lower SES, and 6 were on welfare. By the time the children were 3 years old, the researchers had recorded and analyzed more than 1,300 hours of casual conversations between the children and their parents. To their surprise, the analysis showed a wide gap in the number of words the children

Figure 1.2   The dotted regions represent the areas of highest event-related potentials when subjects processed image-loaded words or verbal (abstract) words (Swaab et al., 2002).

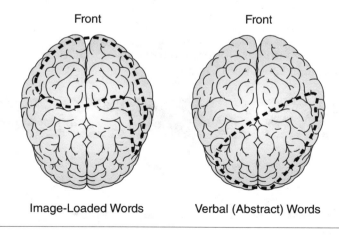

heard from their parents and in the number present in their vocabularies, based on their SES. Table 1.2 summarizes the data. Children from the welfare families heard an average of 616 words per hour and had an average recorded vocabulary size of just 525 words. Those from the middle-lower SES heard 1,251 words in an hour and had 749 words in their vocabulary, while the children in the upper SES heard 2,151 words each hour and had an average vocabulary of 1,116 words. Furthermore, the children from welfare families were adding words to their vocabulary more slowly than the other children throughout the length of the study.

Part 2 of the study was conducted six years later. The researchers were able to test the language skills of 29 of these children who were then in third grade. Test results showed that the rate of early vocabulary growth was a strong predictor of scores at ages 9 to 10 on tests of vocabulary, listening, speaking, syntax, and semantics. This study points out how important the early years are in developing a child's literacy and how difficult it is to equalize children's preschool experiences with language. These results reveal the enormous vocabulary gap that is formed between students of different socioeconomic levels. Regrettably, the gap continues to widen due to the cumulative experiences that the children have with vocabulary at their SES. In the United States, early literacy problems can be addressed successfully through the publically funded birth-to-school programs now available through the federal Head Start initiative and in several states and a growing number of school districts. In some of these programs, such as the Parents as Teachers initiative,

> *"A reliable predictor of how well youngsters will learn to read is the size of their mental lexicon."*

school district personnel meet regularly with parents of infants in low-SES households and provide them with inexpensive, age-appropriate resources to use with their children during the preschool years. The idea is to build the child's vocabulary and exposure to enriched language before they enter school. Such programs provide significant cost savings to local school districts by having fewer placements in special education, fewer grade retentions, and less remedial education. Moreover, one of the most reliable predictors of how well and how quickly youngsters will learn to read is the size of their mental lexicons. See the "Resources" section for information on Head Start and Parents as Teachers.

**Table 1.2**     English Words Heard per Hour at Home and Vocabulary Size by Three Years of Age in Various Economic Groups

| Socioeconomic Group | Average Number of Words Heard per Hour | Average Number of Words in Vocabulary |
|---|---|---|
| Upper | 2,153 | 1,116 |
| Middle | 1,251 | 749 |
| Welfare | 616 | 525 |

SOURCE: Hart and Risley (2003).

Impact of Television Viewing. Studies have found that one major reason toddlers from low-SES homes hear less vocabulary from their mothers is that they spend more time in front of television sets than toddlers in higher-SES groups. Two major studies showed that toddlers in low-SES homes spent an average of two hours per day viewing television (Christakis et al., 2009; Mendelsohn et al., 2008). More often, the mothers sat quietly and watched the programs with their child, reducing the amount of time for verbal communication between them. Placing toddlers to watch television may explain the association between infant television exposure and delayed language development.

Further support to this notion that television viewing during infancy can negatively affect language development came from a longitudinal study of more than 250 families (Tomopoulos et al., 2010). In this study, infants were assessed for cognitive and language development at 6 months and 14 months of age, and the results were compared to the average amount of time they watched television each day—from 0 to 360 minutes. Findings from the study were eye-opening: The more time the infants spent watching television between the ages of 6 and 14 months, the lower their cognitive development and language scores at the age of 14 months. Surprisingly, the type of television programing—that is, child-, adolescent-, or adult-oriented—made little difference. Similar long-range studies have found that average television viewing prior to 3 years of age was negatively associated with cognitive outcomes when children reached 6 years of age (Zimmerman & Christakis, 2005). These findings may seem to run counter to common sense. If the infant is spending so much time viewing and listening to television, shouldn't these experiences increase vocabulary and enhance language development? Obviously, not. Why? Because so much of early language learning in the infant's brain relies on other important clues to attach meaning to spoken words. The child is closely watching the parent for facial cues and listening to intonation, intensity, and rhythm. These cues are very noticeable during face-to-face communication between parent and child, but largely absent from the impersonal output of radio and television. For these reasons, the American Academy of Pediatrics recommends no media exposure prior to 2 years of age.

> "Exposing children prior to 2 years of age to media may cause significant delays in cognitive processing and language development."

## Syntax and Semantics

### Language Hierarchy

With more exposure to speech, the brain begins to recognize the beginnings of a hierarchy of language (Figure 1.3). Phonemes, the basic sounds, can be combined into morphemes, and through a set of conventions, morphemes can be combined into words. These words may accept prefixes, suffixes, and infixes (insertions), and may undergo a change of consonants or vowels. Words can be put together according to the rules of syntax (word order) to form phrases and sentences with meaning. The difference in meaning (semantics) between the sentences "The woman chased the dog" and "The dog chased the woman" results from a different word order, or syntax. Toddlers show evidence of their progression through the syntactic and semantic levels when simple statements, such as "Candy," evolve to more complex ones, for example "Give me candy." They also begin to recognize that shifting the words in sentences can change their meaning.

### The Syntactic Network

The rules of syntax in English prohibit the random arrangement of words in a sentence. The simplest sentences follow a sequence common to many languages, that of subject-verb-object (or SVO) format, as in "He hit the ball." In more complex sentences, syntax imposes a stringent structure on word order to provide clarity and reduce ambiguity. Brain areas near the front of the temporal lobe seem to concentrate on establishing the meanings that could emerge when words are combined into sentences (Vandenberghe, Nobre, & Price, 2002). Just look at what happens to meaning when writers neglect to follow the rules of syntax. The following examples are taken from actual headlines that appeared in the nation's newspapers.

- Rescue Squad Helps Dog Bite Victim
- Safety Experts Say School Bus Passengers Should Be Belted
- Dealers Will Hear Car Talk at Noon
- Sex Education Delayed, Teachers Request Training

Over time, the child hears more patterns of word combinations, phrase constructions, and variations in the pronunciation of words. Toddlers detect patterns of the SVO word order—person, action, object—so they

**Figure 1.3**    This diagram represents the levels of hierarchy in language and in language acquisition. Although the process at the beginning usually flows from the bottom to the top, recycling from the top to lower levels also occurs, as indicated by the arrows to the left. Through each step, the child's vocabulary continues to grow rapidly.

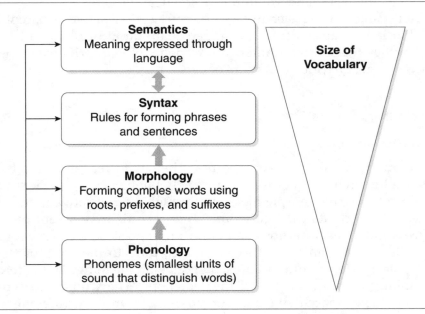

can soon say, "I want cookie." They also note statistical regularities heard in the flow of the native tongue. They discern that some words describe objects while others describe actions. Other features of grammar emerge, such as tense. By the age of 3 years, over 90 percent of sentences uttered are grammatically correct because the child has constructed a syntactic network that stores perceived rules of grammar. For example, the child hears variations in the pronunciation of *walk* and *walked*, *play* and *played*, and *fold* and *folded*. The child isolates the *-ed* and eventually recognizes it as representing the past tense. At that point, the child's syntactic network is modified to include the rule: "add *-ed* to make the past tense." The rule is certainly helpful, but causes errors when the child applies it to some common verbs. Errors are seldom random, but usually result from following perceived rules of grammar such as the "add *-ed*" rule. If "I *batted* the ball" makes sense, why shouldn't "I *holded* the bat"? After all, if *fold* becomes *folded*, shouldn't *hold* become *holded*? Regrettably, the toddler has yet to learn that over 150 of the most commonly used verbs in English are irregularly conjugated (Pinker, 1999).

Why do these common past-tense errors occur in a child's speech, and how do they get corrected? Once the "add *-ed*" rule becomes part of the syntactic network, it operates without conscious thought (Figure 1.4). So

**Figure 1.4**    These diagrams illustrate how blocking becomes part of the syntactic network. Before a child encounters an irregular verb, the "add *-ed*" rule applies. Thus *walk* becomes *walked* and *hold* becomes *holded*. After several instances of adult correction and other environmental exposures (repetition is important to memory), the syntactic network is modified to block the rule for the past tense of *hold* and to substitute *held*, a word that now becomes part of the child's lexicon (Pinker, 1999).

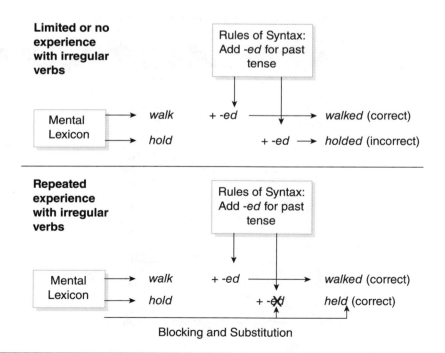

Blocking and Substitution

when the child wants to use the past tense, the syntactic network automatically adds the *-ed* to *play* and *look* so that the child can say, "I *played* with Susan, and we *looked* at some books." If, however, the child says "I *holded* the bat," repeated adult corrections, repetition, and other environmental encounters will inform the syntactic network that the "add *-ed*" rule is not appropriate in this case and should be blocked, and that a new word *held* should be substituted and added to the child's lexicon. This principle of blocking is an important component of accurate language fluency and, eventually, of reading fluency.

So how does the child eventually learn the irregular forms of common verbs? Long-term memory plays an important role in helping the child learn the correct past-tense forms of irregular verbs. The more frequently the irregular verb is used, the more likely the child will remember it. Take a look at Table 1.3, which shows the 10 most common verbs in English as computed by Brigham Young University. Known as the Corpus of Contemporary American English, the verbs are drawn from a 450 million–word database of text used in magazines, newspapers, textbooks, popular books, and other sources (Davies, 2012). Note all of these most common verbs are irregular. Interestingly enough, this tends to be true in many other languages. Pinker (1999) explains that irregular forms have to be repeatedly memorized to survive in a language from generation to generation; otherwise the verbs will be lost. He cites several infrequently used irregular verbs whose past tenses have slipped from common usage: *cleave/clove, stave/stove,* and *chide/chid.*

The ability of children to remember corrections to grammatical errors—including blocking—would be impossible without some innate mechanism that is genetically guided. No one knows how much grammar a child learns just by listening, or how much is prewired. What is certain is that the more children are exposed to spoken language in the early

**Table 1.3    Frequency of Common Verbs in English in a Million Words of Text**

| Verb | Number of Occurrences |
|---|---|
| 1. *be* | 27,880 |
| 2. *have* | 9,564 |
| 3. *do* | 5,719 |
| 4. *say* | 4,256 |
| 5. *go* | 2,558 |
| 6. *can* | 2,273 |
| 7. *get* | 2,206 |
| 8. *would* | 2,057 |
| 9. *know* | 1,983 |
| 10. *make* | 1,905 |

SOURCE: Davies (2012).

years, the more quickly they can discriminate between phonemes, recognize word boundaries, and detect the emerging rules of grammar that result in meaning.

**Syntax and English Language Learners.** Each language has its own rules of syntax. Consequently, children learning English as an additional language often have problems with English syntax. For example, unlike English, adjectives in Spanish, French, and other similar languages are typically placed *after* the noun they modify. *Blue sky* is spoken in Spanish as *cielo azul* and in French as *ciel bleu*. German verbs usually are placed at the end of a clause and rarely follow the SVO sequence so common in English.

English and the Romance languages are subject-prominent in that every sentence must have a subject in the initial position, even if the subject plays no role, as in "It is raining" or "It is possible that the sun will shine today." Other languages, like Japanese, Mandarin, and Korean, are topic-prominent in which the topic holds the initial position and there may or may not be a subject. For example, "It is cold in here" becomes in Mandarin "Here very cold." In Korean, "The 747 is a big airplane" becomes "Airplanes [topic] the 747 is big." As for Japanese, "Red snapper is my favorite fish" translates to "Fish [topic] red snapper favorite it is [note the subject-object-verb string]." Topic-prominent languages also downplay the role of the passive voice and avoid "dummy subjects," such as the *It* in "It is raining." For these beginning English language learners, special attention has to be paid to understanding how English rules of syntax differ from those of their native tongue.

## *The Semantic Network*

As phonemes combine into morphemes, and morphemes into words, and words into phrases, the mind needs to arrange and compose these pieces into sentences that express what the speaker wants to say. Meanwhile, the listener's language areas must recognize speech sounds from other background noise and interpret the speaker's meaning. This interaction between the components of language and the mind in search of meaning is referred to as *semantics*. Meaning occurs at three different levels of language: the morphology level, the vocabulary level, and the sentence level.

**Morphology-Level Semantics.** Meaning can come through word parts, or **morphology**. The word *biggest* has two morphemes, *big* and *-est*. When children can successfully examine the morphology of words, their mental lexicons are greatly enriched. They learn that words with common roots often have common meaning, such as *nation* and *national,* and that prefixes and suffixes alter the meaning of words in certain ways. Morphology also helps children learn and create new words, and can help them spell and pronounce words correctly.

**Vocabulary-Level Semantics.** A listener who does not understand many of the vocabulary words in a conversation will have trouble comprehending meaning. Of course, the listener may infer meaning based on context, but this is unreliable unless the listener understands most of the vocabulary. Children face this dilemma every day as adults around them use words they do not understand.

**Sentence-Level Semantics.** The sentence "Boiling cool dreams walk quickly to the goodness" illustrates that morphology and syntax can be preserved even in a sentence that lacks semantics. The words are all correct English words in the proper syntactic sequence, but the sentence does not make sense. Adults recognize this lack of sense immediately. But children often encounter spoken language that does not make sense to them. To understand language, the listener has to detect meaning at several different levels. Because adults do not normally speak sentences that have no meaning, a child's difficulty in finding meaning may result from a sentence having meaning for one person but not another. At this level, too, the listener's background knowledge or experience with the topic being discussed will influence meaning.

The cerebral processes involved in producing and interpreting meaning must occur at incredible speed during the flow of ordinary conversation. How it is that we can access words from our enormous storehouse (the mental lexicon) and interpret the meaning of conversation so quickly? What types of neural networks can allow for such speed and accuracy? Although linguistic researchers differ on the exact nature of these networks, most agree that the mental lexicon is organized according to meaningful relationships between words. Experimental evidence for this notion comes form numerous studies that involve word priming. In these studies, the subjects are presented with pairs of words. The first word is called the prime, and the second word is the target. The target can be a real word or a nonword (like *spretz*). A real word target may or may not be related in meaning to the prime. After being shown the prime, the subject must decide as quickly as possible if the target is a word. The results invariably show that subjects are faster and more accurate in making decisions about target words that are related in meaning to the prime (e.g., *swan/goose*) than to an unrelated prime (e.g., *tulip/goose*). Researchers suspect that the reduced time for identifying related pairs results from these words being physically closer to each other among the neurons that make up the semantic network, and that related words may be stored together in specific cerebral regions (Gazzaniga, Ivry, & Mangun, 2002).

Additional evidence for this idea that the brain stores related words together has come from several imaging studies. Subjects were asked to name persons, animals, and tools. The results (Figure 1.5) showed that naming items in the same category activated the same area of the brain (Beauchamp, Lee, Argall, & Martin, 2004; Chouinard & Goodale, 2010; Damasio, Grabowski, Tranel, Hichwa, & Damasio, 1996; Morris & Stockall, 2012). It seems that the brain stores clusters of closely associated words in a tightly packed network so that words *within* the network can activate each other in minimal time. Activating words *between* networks, however, takes slightly longer.

> **Implication for Teaching and Learning:** "Because of the brain's apparent affinity for storing related words in the same cerebral region, teachers may want to purposefully group related words into lessons aimed at acquiring new vocabulary."

How can we best represent these networks? Several different models have been proposed. One that seems to garner substantial support from contemporary neuroscientists is based on an earlier model first proposed by Collins and Loftus in 1975. In this model, words that are related are connected to each other.

Figure 1.5   This diagram is a representation of the combined imaging scan
results showing that naming persons, animals, and tools mostly
activated different parts of the brain's temporal lobe (Chouinard &
Goodale, 2010; Damasio et al., 1996).

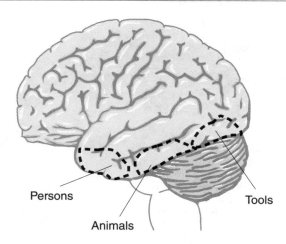

The distance between the connection is determined by the semantic relationship between the words. Figure 1.6 is an example of a semantic network. Note that the word *lemon* is close to—and has a strong connection to—the word *grapefruit*, but is distant from the word *bird*. If we hear the word *lemon*, then the neural area that represents *lemon* will be activated in the semantic network. Other words in the network such as *lime* and *grapefruit* will also be activated and, therefore, accessed very quickly. The word *bird* will not come to mind (Grainger & Ziegler, 2007; Marupaka, Iyer, & Minai, 2012).

## From Words to Sentences

We have just discussed how the brain acquires, stores, and recognizes words. But to communicate effectively, the words must be arranged in a sequence that makes sense. Languages have developed certain rules—called grammar—that govern the order of words so that speakers of the language can understand each other. In some languages, such as English, different arrangements of words in a sentence can result in the same meaning. "The girl ate the candy" has the same meaning as "The candy was eaten by the girl." Of course, different word arrangements (syntax) can lead to different meanings, as in "The boat is in the water" and "The water is in the boat."

As a child's syntactic and semantic networks develop, context plays an important role in determining meaning. When hearing the sentence "The man bought a hot dog at the fair," the youngster is very likely to picture the man eating a frankfurter rather than a steaming, furry animal that barks. That's because the rest of the sentence establishes a context that is compatible with the first interpretation but not the second.

How does the young brain learn to process the structure of sentences? One prominent model suggests that words in a sentence are assigned

**Figure 1.6**  This is a representation of a semantic network. Words that are semantically related are closer together in the network, such as *lemon* and *yellow*, than words that have no close relationship, such as *lemon* and *bird*. Similar geometric figures identify semantically related words. The lines connect words from different networks that are associated, such as *lemon* and *yellow*.

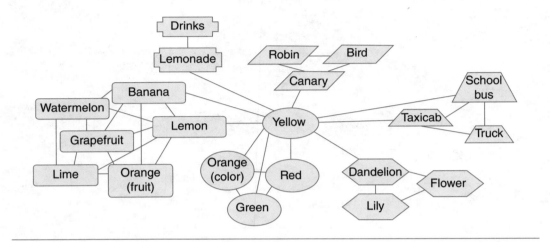

syntactic roles and grouped into syntactic phrases (Pinker, 1999). For example, the sentence "The horse eats the hay" consists of a noun phrase (*the horse*), a verb (*eats*), and another noun phrase (*the hay*). A rule of grammar is that a verb (V) can be combined with its direct object to form a verb phrase (VP). In the preceding example, the verb phrase is *eats the hay*. The combination of the noun phrase (NP) and the verb phrase comprises the sentence (S), which can be represented by the syntactic model shown in Figure 1.7.

As sentences become more complicated, each module can contain another module within it. For example, the sentence "The parent told the principal her son is ill" contains a verb phrase that is also a sentence *(her*

**Figure 1.7**  This model illustrates how the brain may process sentences to establish meaning. By grouping, or chunking, individual words into phrases, processing time is decreased.

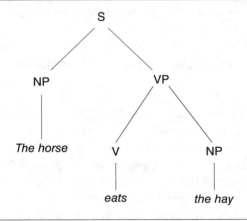

Figure 1.8    This illustrates how the brain proceeds to make additional chunks into phrases to ensure rapid processing and accurate interpretation.

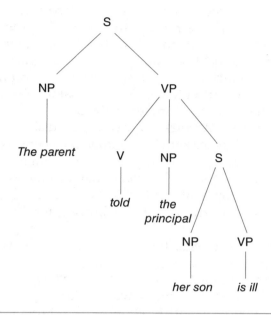

*son is ill).* To ensure rapid processing and accurate comprehension, the brain groups the phrases into the hierarchy as represented by the diagram shown in Figure 1.8.

## How Can We Speak So Rapidly?

This module-within-a-module pattern (Figure 1.8) has two major advantages. First, by rearranging and including different phrase packets, the brain can generate and understand an enormous number of sentences without having to memorize every imaginable sentence verbatim. Second, this pattern allows the brain to process syntactic information quickly so that it can meet the demanding comprehension time required for normal conversation. The efficiency of the system is amazing! The young adult brain can determine the meaning of a spoken word in about one-fifth of a second. The brain needs just one-fourth of a second to name an object and about the same amount of time to pronounce it. For readers, the meaning of a printed word is registered in an astounding one-eighth of a second (Pinker, 1999).

## Recognizing Meaning

The brain's ability to recognize different meanings in sentence structure is possible because Broca's and Wernicke's areas and other smaller cerebral regions establish linked networks that can understand the difference between "The dog chased the cat" and "The cat chased the dog." In a **functional magnetic resonance imaging (fMRI)** study, Dapretto and Bookheimer (1999) found that Broca's and Wernicke's areas work together to determine whether changes in syntax or semantics result in changes in meaning. For example, "The policeman arrested the thief" and "The thief was arrested by the policeman" have different syntax but the same meaning. The fMRI showed that Broca's area was highly activated when subjects were processing these two sentences. Wernicke's area, on the other hand, was more activated when processing sentences that were semantically—but not syntactically—different, such as "The car is in the garage" and "The automobile is in the garage."

How is it that Wernicke's area can so quickly and accurately decide that two semantically different sentences have the same meaning? The answer may lie in two other recently discovered characteristics of Wernicke's area. One is that the neurons in Wernicke's area are spaced about 20 percent farther apart and are cabled together with longer interconnecting axons than the corresponding area in the right hemisphere of the brain (Galuske, Schlote, Bratzke, & Singer, 2000). The implication is that the practice of language during early human development resulted in longer and more intricately connected neurons in the Wernicke region, allowing for greater sensitivity to meaning.

The second discovery regarding Wernicke's area is its ability to recognize predictable events. A magnetic resonance imaging (MRI) study found that Wernicke's area was activated when subjects were shown differently colored symbols in various patterns, whether the individuals were aware of the pattern sequence or not (Bischoff-Grethe, Proper, Mao, Daniels, & Berns, 2000). This capacity of Wernicke's area to detect predictability suggests that our ability to make sense of language is rooted in our ability to recognize syntax. The researchers noted that language itself is very predicable because it is constrained by the rules of grammar and syntax.

### Development of Memory Systems

Acquiring spoken language would be impossible if the brain did not have some means for remembering what it hears. While the brain is gaining competence in manipulating phonemes and morphemes, memory systems are also developing, giving the child's brain the equipment it needs to store and recall sounds, morphemes, words, and sentences and their meaning. Moreover, the brain establishes several different types of memory banks to make access to stored information faster and more accurate. It is not a perfect system, but with practice, even young children can use vocabulary and syntax with astounding accuracy. In the next chapter, we will discuss more about memory systems and their importance in learning to read.

## The Components of Speaking and Understanding Language

Any model for speaking and understanding language has to address the various stages of sound interpretation, beginning with the auditory input and ending with the formation of a mental concept represented by the word or words. Figure 1.9 shows the various neural components that linguistic researchers and neuroscientists believe are required for spoken language comprehension. It is a complex process, but the efficient organization of the linguistic networks that is built up through practice allows it to occur very quickly.

To understand the different components, let's take the word *dog* through the model. After the spoken word *dog* enters the ear canal, the listener has to decode the sound pattern. In a part of the brain referred to as the word form area, **acoustic analysis** separates the relevant word sounds from background noise, decodes the phonemes of the word (*duh-awh-guh*), and translates them into a phonological code that can be recognized by the mental lexicon. The lexicon selects the best representation it has in memory and then activates the syntactic and semantic networks, which work together to form the mental image of a furry animal that barks (concept formation). All this occurs in just a fraction of a second thanks to the extensive network of neural pathways and memory sites that were established during the early years of speaking and listening.

Notice that the flow of information in this model is from the bottom up and, thus, appears linear. However, feedback from higher to lower levels often occurs. For example, if the lexicon does not recognize the first set of signals, it reactivates the phonological coding component to produce another set before they

**Figure 1.9** This schematic representation shows the major neural components required for spoken language processing. Feedback from higher to lower levels also occurs, as indicated by the arrows on the left.

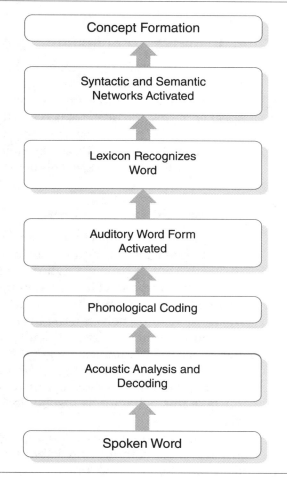

SOURCE: Adapted from Dehaene (2009); Gazzaniga et al. (2002).

decay. Likewise, if the semantic network finds no meaning, it may signal for a repetition of the original spoken word to reprime the process. It is important to understand how this process works because, as we shall see in the next chapter, the process of reading words shares several steps with this model of spoken language processing.

## LEVELS OF LANGUAGE COMPREHENSION ⚙

Parents speak differently to their children than to other adults. Elementary teachers use different language with their students than with their principal. Speech can be formal, as in the classroom, or informal, as around the dinner table. When young children use informal language, it is often context dependent; that is, the conversation focuses on the immediate situation or activities at hand. On the other hand, formal speech may be more context independent or abstract in that the child may be relating different possible endings to a story. Sometimes people say one thing but really mean something else, and they hope that the listener will catch on to the subtler meaning. These different language forms are a recognition that there are several types and levels of spoken language and of language comprehension.

## Explicit Comprehension

The most basic type of language comprehension is explicit comprehension—the sentence is clear and unambiguous. When someone says "I need a haircut," the interpretation is unmistakable. The listener knows exactly what the speaker means and does not need to draw any inferences or elaborate further. Adults tend to use explicit sentences with children to avoid ambiguity. "Eat your vegetables" and "Please be quiet" are clear statements. Whether the child complies, of course, is another story.

## Inferred Comprehension

A more sophisticated form of language comprehension requires the listener to make inferences about meanings that go beyond what the speaker explicitly said. A principal who says to a tardy teacher, "Our school really gets off to a great start in the morning when all the staff is here by 8:15," is really saying, "Be on time." The teacher has to infer the statement's real intent by reading between the lines of what the principal explicitly said.

Young children have difficulty with inferred comprehension. If the parent says, "Vegetables are good for you," the child may not pick up on the underlying intent of this statement—eat your vegetables. Consequently, the child may not finish the vegetables, and the parent may mistake this behavior as disobedience when it is really a lack of inferred comprehension.

Teachers sometimes use language requiring inferred comprehension when explicit comprehension would be much easier. A teacher who says, for example, "Do you think I should speak if someone else is talking?" may provoke a variety of responses in the minds of the children. One could think absolutely not, while another might hope she would just speak louder than everyone else so the lesson could move along. A few might get the real intent—oh, she wants us to be quiet.

Context Clues. We discussed earlier how context can be an important clue for determining the meaning of vocabulary words in a sentence. Context can also help with inferred comprehension. A first-grade teacher who is telling her spouse over dinner how crowded her class is and that there are too many students who need special help may just be seeking sympathy. But in having the same conversation with her principal, she is really saying she needs an instructional aide. She never says that explicitly; the principal must infer the teacher's intent from her statement and the context.

Children need to develop an awareness that language comprehension exists on several levels. It involves different styles of speech that reflect the formality of the conversation, the context in which it occurs, and the explicit as well as underlying intent of the speaker. When children gain a good understanding of these patterns in speech, they will be better able to comprehend what they read.

---

**QUESTIONS FOR DISCUSSION/REFLECTION**

- *Why does spoken language come so easily?*
- *How does a child's brain detect language sounds from background noise?*
- *Does a family's socioeconomic status really affect a child's vocabulary growth?*
- *What impact does television have on an infant's cognitive processing and language development?*
- *How does a child learn the irregular forms of verbs?*
- *Can children tell the difference between explicit and inferred comprehension?*

---

## What's Coming?

The child's brain has now acquired the fundamentals of spoken language. Neural networks are developing rapidly in Broca's, Wernicke's, and the word form areas, and every day brings new vocabulary and understanding to the expanding mental lexicon. How will these newly acquired language skills and knowledge help the child accomplish the next major cognitive task: learning to read? All the steps the brain must go through to progress from spoken to written language are unveiled in the next chapter.

# 2

# Learning to Read

*I wish you to gasp at not only what you read but at the miracle of its being readable.*

—Vladimir Nabokov, *Pale Fire*

Humans are by nature curious animals. From our beginning as a separate species, we constantly explored our environment, deciding what actions would enhance our ability to survive. Our brain evolved a large frontal lobe to help us process incoming information and make those vital decisions. We acquired spoken language, learned how to make tools, hunted for prey, and tilled the fields to increase our food supply. Clearly, we were born with an instinct to learn, and this instinct plays an essential role in our capacity to learn to read. In this chapter, we will explore the latest research on how scientists believe the brain learns to read. This chapter gives you a strong background in the findings from the research, and how those findings can be applied to teaching children to read will be discussed in Chapters 3 and 4.

Before going any further, it is worth noting that, as adult readers, most of us do not recall how arduous it was for us to learn to read. That may make it more difficult for us to understand why so many children struggle with reading. You may be thinking, "I did it, so why can't they?" But keep in mind exactly what is in store for these children when they enter kindergarten. Because they have already been speaking for several years, they all arrive with some degree of phonemic awareness, depending on literacy exposure at home. They likely understand the differences in some onset sounds and know that *bet* has a different meaning than *pet*, and *bat* is different from *pat*. But are they ready for our surprise? Here is the essence of it.

"Boys and girls, remember those sounds you play with in your head when you speak? Well, do we have a surprise for you! Those sounds can be matched to written symbols (which, by the way, do not exist in the real world—we made them up, and not everyone in the world uses them). You may know them as the letters of the alphabet. Well, we are going to learn them, but we have just one teensy-weensy problem. There are about 44 sounds in your head, but we have only 26 letters to represent them. So sometimes the same letter can be matched to different sounds, and sometimes the same sound can be matched to different letters. Doesn't that seem like fun?" Now the girls, many of whom are more advanced in language facility than the boys at this age, are delighted with this challenge. The boys, on the other hand, are asking themselves how they got into this mess and how they can get out of it. Given the anxiety such a situation can raise in beginning readers, it may help to keep this scenario in mind as you continue reading.

## ✿ THREE PHASES OF LEARNING TO READ

In simplest terms, learning to read involves connecting two cerebral capabilities that are already present in young brains: the spoken language networks and the visual recognition circuits. Trying to understand how this connection occurs in the brain has been a challenge for many researchers over the past decades. In 1985, British psychologist Uta Frith developed a three-phase model of how the brain acquires the ability to read (Frith, 1985). Much new research about how we read has emerged since Frith's model. Reading is far more complicated than we thought just a few years ago. Although the model's simplicity belies the complex cerebral processes that we now know are involved in learning to read, it nonetheless still provides a useful outline of what the brain experiences (Dehaene, 2009). Here is a brief summary of the three phases:

- The first phase can be considered a *pictorial* stage, when the child's brain photographs words and visually adjusts to the shape of the alphabet's letters.
- The second phase is the *phonological* stage, when the brain begins to decode the letters (graphemes) into sounds (phonemes).
- The third phase is the *orthographic* stage, when the child is able to recognize words quickly and accurately.

All of these phases activate several different brain circuits, which, over time and with practice, eventually converge in a specialized area of the left hemisphere. This area is now referred to in the scientific literature as the **visual word form area**. Let us see how this amazing process occurs.

## READING IS NOT A NATURAL ABILITY     ✿

Humans have been speaking for tens of thousands of years. During this time, genetic changes have favored the brain's ability to acquire and process spoken language, even setting aside specialized areas of the brain to accomplish these tasks, as we discussed in Chapter 1. Consequently, the brain's proficiency at hearing and quickly remembering spoken words is natural, though no less remarkable. Remember that children begin to learn words before their first birthday and during their second year are acquiring them at the rate of 8 to 10 per day. By the time they enter school, they have a well-developed language system consisting of an active vocabulary of about 3,000 words and a total mental lexicon of over 5,000 words. At some point, the child's brain encounters the written word and wonders, "Hmm . . . What are those symbols? What do they mean?"

Speaking is a normal, genetically hardwired capability; reading is not. Writing was born about 5,000 years ago in an area of the Middle East known as the Fertile Crescent. That time span is just a blip in evolutionary terms, and hardly enough time to develop specialized brain circuits for reading. Thus, reading is a relatively new phenomenon in the development of humans. As far as we know, our genes have not incorporated reading into their coded structure, probably because reading, unlike spoken language, has not emerged as a survival skill over the relatively brief time that humans have been reading. And yet we do read. How does that happen? What parts of the brain must be recruited to carry out this exquisitely complex process of matching sounds to corresponding lines and squiggles? Because no areas of the brain are specialized for reading, it is probably the most difficult cognitive task we ask the young brain to undertake. If reading were a natural ability, everyone would be doing it. But in fact, according to the National Institute for Literacy, nearly 40 million adults in the United States alone are functionally illiterate. The Canadian Council on Learning estimates that about 12 million Canadians have low literacy levels.

### The Plasticity of Neural Networks

Although Frith's model is helpful, the real question is how a brain with no innate reading center learns to accomplish this complex task. How are brain regions not designed to read coopted to undertake that challenge? Psychologists and neuroscientists have wrestled with these questions for years. Now, thanks to the growing bank of thousands of brain images and other scans, as well as a large inventory of case studies, some new ideas have emerged about how the brain adjusts to the challenge of interpreting visual signals from print into sounds that have meaning.

We already mentioned that writing appeared in our culture too recently to have made alterations in our brain through the slow process of biological evolution. Yet the fact that we *can* read must indicate that our brain makes adjustments in its capabilities that do not require changes in the genetic code. In other words, momentous events in our culture, like the invention of writing, can apparently cause important cerebral adaptations to occur as a result of cultural learning. These adaptions occur because of the brain's plasticity—that is, its ability to adapt to significant changes in its environment.

### Neuronal Recycling

Neuroscientist Stanislas Dehaene (2009) has proposed a new term, *neuronal recycling,* to describe the taking over of a brain region, initially devoted to a different function, by a cultural invention—in this case, writing. "Recycling" refers to retraining brain areas that performed an ancient function in our evolutionary past to carry out a new and more useful function in our present culture. This recycling, Dehaene asserts, does not totally undo the preexisting predispositions of these brain regions, but works around them. After all, the brain's plasticity is still constrained by its extensive cerebral networking, genetic biases, and other factors that limit its degree of adaptability.

At what age, and how, does this neuronal recycling for learning to read begin? Renewed emphasis in recent years on improving the basic cognitive skills of students has increased pressure to start reading instruction sooner than ever before. In many schools, reading instruction starts in kindergarten. Current researchers do not identify a definite age at which the brain can begin to learn to read. More important than chronological age is the degree and pace of brain development, both of which can vary widely among children of the same age. Some children make the transition from spoken language to reading with relative ease, once exposed to formal instruction. For others, reading is a much more formidable task, and for some, it definitely becomes the most difficult cognitive task they will ever undertake in their lives.

---

**Answer to Test Question #2**

**Question:** Learning to read, like learning spoken language, is a natural ability.

**Answer:** *False.* Unlike spoken language, the brain has no areas specialized for reading. The skills needed to link the sounds of language to the letters of the alphabet must be learned through direct instruction.

---

## ✿ EARLY STAGES OF READING

Intelligence generally does not play a critical role in learning to read. Three sources of evidence indicate this. First, studies of children who learn to read before entering school do not indicate a strong relationship between IQ and early reading. Second, studies have shown that IQ is only weakly related to reading achievement in Grades 1 and 2. Finally, children who have difficulty learning to read often have above-average IQs (Kortteinen, Närhi, & Ahonen, 2009; Paloyelis, Rijsdijk, Wood, Asherson, & Kuntsil, 2010; Shaywitz, 2003). It appears then that, to a large degree, learning to read is independent of intelligence. This is an important point because some teachers mistakenly assume that children with problems learning to read are of lower ability and will also have difficulty in other subject areas. Such a presumption can lead to lower expectations and less challenging work for those children.

> "To a large degree, learning to read is independent of intelligence."

Before children learn to read, they acquire vocabulary by listening to others and by practicing the pronunciation and usage of new words in conversation. Adult correction and other sources help to fine-tune this basic vocabulary. Because the ability to read is strongly dependent on the word forms learned during this period, a child's beginning reading will be more successful if most of the reading material contains words the child is already using. The phoneme-grapheme connection can be made more easily. Reading, of course, also adds new words to the child's mental lexicon. Consequently, there must be some neural connections between the systems that allow the brain to recognize spoken words and the system that recognizes written words.

**Multiple Lexicons.** We should mention here that there are several different types of lexicons in the brain of a proficient reader. The *mental lexicon* generally refers to the store of familiar words. But we also have an *orthographic lexicon* for visual recognition of letters, graphemes, and morphemes. For instance, the orthographic lexicon might deconstruct the word *island* into *is + land*. Our *phonological lexicon,* which stores how words are pronounced, would tell us that this word is pronounced *eye-land*. No doubt we also maintain a *grammatical lexicon* that contains the rules of plurals and sentence structure. Finally, to arrive at meaning, each word is associated with certain properties. For example, an island is an isolated piece of land, surrounded by water. This information is kept in a *semantic lexicon.* These various dictionaries communicate with each other to provide the information needed to make reading successful.

Learning to read starts with the awareness that speech is composed of individual sounds (phonemes) and a recognition that written spellings represent those sounds (the alphabetic principle). Of course, to be successful in acquiring the alphabetic principle, the child has to be aware of how the phonemes of spoken language can be manipulated to form new words and rhymes. The neural systems that perceive the phonemes in our language are more efficient in some children than in others. Just because some children have difficulty understanding that spoken words are composed of discrete sounds doesn't mean that they have brain damage or dysfunction. The individual differences that underlie the efficiency with which one learns to read can be seen in the acquisition of other skills, such as learning to play a musical instrument, playing a sport, or building a model. To some extent, neural efficiency is related to genetic composition, but these genetic factors can be modified by the environment. Nonetheless, being aware of sound differences in spoken language is crucial to learning to read written language.

## Phonological and Phonemic Awareness

Phonological awareness is the recognition that oral language can be divided into smaller components, such as sentences into words, words into syllables, and, ultimately, syllables into individual phonemes. This recognition includes identifying and manipulating onsets and rimes as well as having an awareness of alliteration, rhyming, syllabication, and intonation. Being phonologically aware means having an understanding of all these levels. In children, phonological awareness usually starts with initial sounds and rhyming, and a recognition that sentences can be segmented into words. Next comes segmenting words into syllables and blending syllables into words.

**Phonemic awareness** is a subdivision of phonological awareness and refers to the understanding that words are made up of individual sounds (phonemes) and that these sounds can be manipulated to create new words. It includes the ability to isolate a phoneme (first, middle, or last) from the rest of the word, to segment words into their component phonemes, and to delete a specific phoneme from a word. Children with phonemic awareness know that the word *cat* is made up of three phonemes, and that the words *dog* and *mad* both contain the phoneme /d/. Recognition of rhyming and alliteration is usually an indication that a child has phonological awareness, which develops when children are read to from books based on rhyme or alliteration. But this awareness does not easily develop into the more sophisticated phonemic awareness, which is so closely related to a child's success in learning to read, especially if such awareness begins in preschool settings (Phillips, Clancy-Menchetti, & Lonigan, 2008). Nonetheless, reading programs that emphasize phonological and phonemic awareness have proved to be successful in schools, especially with children displaying some difficulties when learning to read (Bailet, Repper, Murphy, Piasta, & Zettler-Greeley, 2011).

Phonemic awareness is different from **phonics**. Phonemic awareness involves the auditory and *oral* manipulation of sounds. A child demonstrates phonemic awareness by knowing all the sounds that make up the word *cat, /k/ /a/ /t/*. Phonics is an instructional approach that builds on the alphabetic principle and associates letters and sounds with *written* symbols. To demonstrate phonics knowledge, a child tells the teacher which *letter* is needed to change *cat* to *can*. Although phonemic awareness and phonics are closely related, they are not the same. It is possible for a child to have phonemic awareness in speech without having much experience with written letters or names. Conversely, a child may provide examples of letter-sound relationships without ever developing phonemic awareness. In fact, simply learning these letter-sound relationships during phonics instruction does not necessarily lead to phonemic awareness (SEDL, 2001).

The terms *phonological awareness, phonemic awareness,* and *phonics* have different meanings, but they can be easily confused. Table 2.1 defines these terms. In this book, I will refer mainly to phonemic awareness because many of the research studies on learning to read focus specifically on phonemes.

### Phonemic Awareness and Learning to Read

Beginning readers must learn the alphabetic principle and recognize that words can be separated into individual phonemes, which can be reordered and blended into new words. This enables learners to associate the letters with sounds in order to read and build words. Thus, phonemic awareness in kindergarten is a strong predictor of reading success that persists throughout school. Early instruction in reading, especially in letter-sound association, strengthens phonological awareness and helps in the development of the more sophisticated phonemic awareness. One thing has

Table 2.1    Definitions of Terms Related to Speech and Reading

| Term | Definition | Example |
|------|-----------|---------|
| Phonological awareness | The awareness of any size unit of sound, including the ability to separate words into syllables, to count syllables, to identify phonemes in words, and to generate and recognize rhyming words | The word *carpet* has two syllables, each one composed of three phonemes. |
| Phonemic awareness | The awareness that spoken language is made up of individual units of sound | The word dog has three phonemes, /d/ /ô/ /g/. |
| Phonics | An instructional approach for teaching reading and spelling that emphasizes sound-symbol relationships | The symbol *p* is used to represent the italicized sounds in the words *p*ot, jum*p*, and co*p*y. |

SOURCE: Yopp and Yopp (2000).

become increasingly clear. The discovery of phonemes is *neither* innate nor automatic. It results only from the explicit teaching of the alphabetic principle. Beginning readers must learn the code before they can decode written words! We have known for at least three decades that even struggling adult readers can fail to detect phonemes in words. Phoneme recognition does not arise spontaneously (Morais, Cary, Alegria, & Bertelson, 1979).

> *"Beginning readers must learn the alphabetic code before they can decode written words."*

Numerous research studies over the past two decades have established a strong positive link between phonemic awareness and success in early reading. About 70 to 80 percent of children are able to learn the alphabetic principle after one year of instruction. For the rest, additional study is needed (Shaywitz, 2003).

## Sounds to Letters (Phonemes to Graphemes)

To be able to read, the brain must memorize a set of arbitrary lines and squiggles (the alphabet). The brain does not yet know the system or logic of writing, but it begins to recognize patterns based on visual characteristics, such as curvature, orientation, and shape. For example, it notices that some symbols seem to be mirror images of each other (e.g., *b* and *d*, *p* and *q*), and that some are symmetrical (e.g., *H, M,* and *O*). It also detects that some symbols occur more often than others (e.g., *a, e, r,* and *s*), and that some letter combinations are more often at the end of the string (e.g., *-ed, -ing,* and *-tion*). This is what we referred to at the beginning of the chapter as Frith's pictorial stage. Some of this visual letter/word recognition may occur before the formal teaching of reading. How many sight words are remembered will vary greatly among children.

In the phonological stage, the brain ceases to process whole words and begins to identify which symbols, or **graphemes**, correspond to the phonemes already stored in the mental lexicon. Many European languages use abstract letters (i.e., an alphabetic system) to represent their sounds so that the words can be spelled out in writing. The rules of spelling that govern a language are called its orthography. How closely a language's orthography actually represents the pronunciation of the phoneme can determine how quickly one learns to read that language correctly. Some languages, like Spanish, Italian, and Finnish, have a very close correspondence between letters and the sounds they represent. This is known as a shallow (or *transparent*) orthography. Once the rules of orthography in these languages are learned, a person can usually spell a new word correctly the first time because there are so few exceptions.

English, on the other hand, has a poor correspondence between how a word is pronounced and how it is spelled. This is called a deep (or *opaque*) orthography. It exists because English does not have an alphabet that permits an ideal one-to-one correspondence between its phonemes and its graphemes. Consider that just when the brain thinks it knows what letter represents a phoneme sound, it discovers that the same symbol can have different sounds, such as the *a* in *cat* and in *father*. Consider, too, how the pronunciation of the following English words differs, even though they all have the same last four letters in the same sequence: *bough, cough, dough,* and *rough*. This lack of sound-to-letter correspondence makes it difficult for the brain to recognize patterns and affects the child's ability to spell with accuracy and to read with meaning. Eventually, the brain must connect the 26 letters of the alphabet to the 44-plus sounds of spoken English (phonemes) that the child has been using successfully for years. Table 2.2 illustrates the complexity of English orthography, compared to some other related languages. There are more than 1,100 ways to spell the sounds of the 44-plus phonemes in English.

Table 2.2     Language Sounds and Their Spellings

| Language | Number of Sounds (Phonemes) | Number of Ways to Spell Sounds | |
|---|---|---|---|
| Italian | 33 | 25 | Shallow orthography |
| Spanish | 35+ | 38 | |
| French | 32 | 250+ | Deep orthography |
| English | 44+ | 1,100+ | |

Looking at Table 2.2, one can easily understand the plight of students whose native language is Italian or Spanish when they are faced with reading English. Because there is such a close sound-to-letter correspondence (shallow orthography) in their native language, reading and writing unknown words is quite easy. There are very few exceptions in their language's rules of spelling. But English is rife with spelling irregularities, and this poses a significant challenge to these and other English language learners.

### Alphabetic Principle

The alphabetic principle describes the understanding that spoken words are made up of phonemes and that the phonemes are represented in written text as letters. This system of using letters to represent phonemes is very efficient in that a small number of letters can be used to write a very large number of words. Matching just a few letters on a page to their sounds in speech enables the reader to recognize many printed words: for example, connecting just four letters and their phonemes /a/, /l/, /p/, and /s/ to read *lap, pal, slap, laps,* and *pals.*

Despite the efficiency of an alphabetic system, learning the alphabetic principle is not easy because of two drawbacks. First, the letters of the alphabet are abstract and thus unfamiliar to the new reader, and the sounds they represent are not natural segments of speech. Second, because there are about 44 English phonemes (this number varies slightly, depending on the counting method) but only 26 letters, each phoneme is not coded with a unique letter. There are over a dozen vowel sounds but only five letters, *a, e, i, o,* and *u,* to represent them. Further, the child needs to recognize that how a letter is pronounced depends on the letters that surround it. The letter *e,* for example, is pronounced differently in *dead, deed,* and *dike.* And then there are the consonant digraphs, which are combinations of two consonants, such as *ch, sh,* and *ph,* that represent a single speech sound. There are also three-letter combinations, called trigraphs, such as *tch* and *thr.* With more practice at word recognition, the reader must work toward fast and accurate word recognition in order to increase reading fluency.

---

### Answer to Test Question #3

**Question:** There are about 200 ways to spell the sounds of the 44 phonemes in English.

**Answer:** *False.* Actually, there are more than 1,100 ways to represent the sounds of the 44 English phonemes. This condition, known as deep orthography, is one major reason that English is a difficult language to learn, especially for those whose native language, such as Spanish, has more reliable letter-to-sound correspondences.

---

As we discussed earlier, the human brain is not born with the insight to make sound-to-letter connections, nor does it develop naturally without the instruction needed to reassign brain regions to perform this task. Children of literate homes may encounter this instruction from their parents before coming to school. Others, however, do not have this opportunity during their preschool years. For them, classroom instruction needs to focus on making the phoneme-phonics connections before reading can be successful. If children cannot hear the *-at* sound in *bat* and *hat* and perceive that the difference lies in the first sound, then they will have difficulty decoding and sounding out words quickly and correctly. When children learn the alphabetic principle, the problems of inconsistent orthography are resolved the same way other learning challenges are— through practice. The brain's visual areas learn to break down a word into its letters and graphemes. With sufficient, effective practice, children develop a context-sensitive understanding of letter-to-sound correspondence. Eventually, they learn that -ough in the context of c_ _ _ _ is pronounced differently than it is in the context of thr_ _ _ _. Furthermore, having children simply practice letter recognition or phoneme pronunciation without teaching the letter-to-sound correspondence has been shown in studies to be of no value in helping children acquire the alphabetic principle (Castles, Coltheart, Wilson, Valpied, & Wedgwood, 2009).

## Letters to Words

### Decoding

Phonological awareness helps the beginning reader decipher printed words by linking them to the spoken words that the child already knows. This process is called decoding. It involves realizing that a printed word represents the spoken word through a written sequence of graphemes that stand for phonemes, and then blending the phonemes to pronounce the word. A child must be able to decode with accuracy and fluency in order to read proficiently. Now we are in the third, orthographic, stage. Decoding starts with learning the visual image of the letters of the alphabet and the basic sounds they represent. There has been serious discussion among researchers over whether beginning readers should learn the letters of the alphabet by their *names* (that is, *ay, bee, cee, dee,* etc.) or by how they generally *sound* (that is, *ah, beh, cuh, duh,* etc.). Some researchers believe that knowing the names of the letters of the alphabet may actually delay the acquisition of reading. Knowing that "p" is *pee,* "h" is *aitch,* "o" is *oh,* "n" is *en,* and "e" is *ee* is of little help when trying to read the word "phone." And when is "f" ever pronounced as *ef* in a word? Reading requires understanding phonemes, not letter names, they argue. It might be more helpful to learn the *common sounds* of the alphabet letters rather than their names so as to accelerate the child's ability to link sounds to letters (Dehaene, 2009). On the other hand, those who support first learning the names of the letters believe that doing so makes it easier to refer to the letter.

Early decoding most likely starts when children match symbols in their environment to concrete objects in contextual situations. For example, many children recognize the Golden Arches and the McDonald's sign as representing a place they like to eat, yet they might not be able to read the word *McDonald's* out of context. Children might also recognize the word *corn* on a cereal box, but might not recognize it in a story. This situation is called *environmental print reading.*

Exactly how the human brain developmentally makes the connections between sounds and words needed for successful decoding is still unclear. But research studies, including those using brain scans, have helped neurolinguists gain a better understanding of how written word knowledge develops in the beginning reader. One model was developed by Ehri (1998), who proposed four phases of word recognition during early reading (Figure 2.1). Psychologists continue to use this model today because it still represents what they observe in children as they become skillful in word recognition. The phases are described as follows (Morris, Bloodgood, Lomax, & Perney, 2003):

1.  *Prealphabetic phase.* In this phase, children remember words by connecting visual cues in the word (such as the two *l*s in *bell* or the curve at the end of *dog*) with the word's meaning and pronunciation. There is no systematic letter-sound connection. Consequently, the child's ability to commit new words to memory or retain old words is overwhelmed when visually similar words (such as *bell, ball,* and *will,* or *dog, bug,* and *dig*) are encountered in the text.

2.  *Partial alphabetic phase.* In this phase, the child commits printed words to memory by connecting one or more printed letters with the corresponding sound(s) heard during pronunciation. For instance, a child might remember the word *talk* by joining the beginning and ending letters (*t* and *k*) with their corresponding spoken sounds *tuh* and *kuh.* New readers enter this phase when they know some letter-sound correspondences and can separate the beginning or ending sounds from the word. Words now become easier to remember because they can be processed through a more reliable letter-sound system rather than the unreliable visual cues used in the prealphabetic phase. This phase is sometimes called *sight-word reading,* and the readers develop the ability to recognize certain familiar and high-frequency words. However, because these readers still have a limited memory, the ability to remember new words diminishes. They will confuse letters, misreading *take* or *tack* for *talk,* and usually cannot read text that has words outside their mental lexicon.

3.  *Full alphabetic phase.* As reading progresses, phonemic awareness improves, and the reader moves into this phase. Here, the child remembers how to read a specific word by making accurate connections between the letters seen in the word and the phonemes used in the word's pronunciation. For example, when reading the word *trap,* the child recognizes the initial consonant blend, */tr/,* then the medial vowel, */u/,* and then the final consonant, */p/.* This complete phoneme-grapheme connection will facilitate committing this word to long-term memory, thus leading to more accurate reading.

4.  *Consolidated alphabetic phase.* In this phase, the beginning reader begins to notice multiletter sequences that are common to words stored in memory (such as the ending *-ake* in *cake, make,* and *take,* or *-ent* in *bent, cent,* and *tent*). By forming a chunk for each common sequence, word reading becomes faster and more efficient. When encountering a new word containing the chunk (such as *dent*), the child just processes the beginning consonant and the chunk, instead of processing each letter separately. **Chunking** is particularly helpful when reading longer, multisyllable words like *practice, measurement,* and *traditional.*

As children master each phase, their mental lexicons grow dramatically. Ehri's model is consistent with current studies (e.g., Wagovich, Pak, & Miller, 2012), all of which describe an increasing degree of phoneme awareness that occurs in stages. Beginning readers focus on the initial sound of a word (*bug* = /b/ /-/ /-/). Then they progress to processing the

Figure 2.1    As word recognition develops over time from the prealphabetic phase to the consolidated alphabetic phase, the reader's vocabulary (the mental lexicon) grows dramatically (Ehri, 1998).

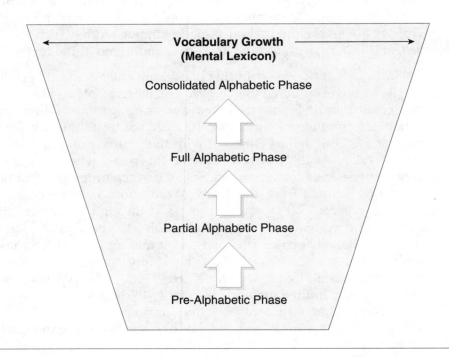

beginning and ending sounds (*bug = /b/ /-/ /g/*), and finally to each sound in the word (*bug = /b/ /u/ /g/*).

## *Morphemes*

**What Are Morphemes and Morphology?** As reading practice continues, the neural systems are no longer decoding words letter by letter, but are becoming better at recognizing **morphemes**. Morphemes are the smallest word elements that can change a word's meaning, such as the *-ing* that changes *signal* to *signaling*. They can stand on their own as a complete word (free morphemes) or exist as prefixes and suffixes (bound morphemes) that must be added to a root word. When readers understand morphemes, they can separate unfamiliar words into comprehensible parts. If the reader understands what *hate* means and also what *-ful* means, then the reader is likely to comprehend the meaning of *hateful*. This component of grammar that builds words out of pieces (morphemes) is called **morphology**.

There are two types of bound morphemes:

1.  *Inflectional morphemes.* These are suffixes that provide information such as case (*Tommy's dog*), number (*dog/dogs*), tense (*he called*), and person (*she calls*).

2.  *Derivational morphemes.* These are affixes (prefixes and suffixes) that create new words by changing the meaning of the root words. Some derivational morphemes change the root word's part of speech

(*attend* is a verb, but add *-ance* and *attendance* becomes a noun). Others, like *un-* and *re-*, change the root word's meaning but not the part of speech.

Morphology is an important component of our language, even to young brains. Research studies confirm that before they learn to read, children are more cognizant of morphology than phonology (Mann, 2000). This means they comprehend more easily that the inflectional morpheme *-s* in *dogs* represents the plural of *dog* than that the *-s* in *yes* represents a phoneme. They also understand more easily that the *-er* in *bigger* is a comparison to something that is already big than that the *-er* represents the second syllable in a word like *power*.

Morphological and Phonemic Awareness. Of course, when students first learn to read, phonemic awareness becomes all-important as the young brain tries to match letters to sounds. But morphological awareness is already starting to develop in Grade 1 (Wolter, Wood, & D'zatko, 2009). By Grade 3, morphological awareness begins to surpass phonemic awareness in the development of decoding skills (Singson, Mahony, & Mann, 2000). Morphological awareness helps these students when they encounter multisyllabic words. A word like *indisputable* will be separated into its affixes and root word: *in-, dispute, -able.* Because such words do not appear frequently in texts, the ability to understand these words will depend far more heavily on the reader's morphological awareness than on word recognition skills (Mahony, Singson, & Mann, 2000).

Other than helping to decode unfamiliar words, morphemes can also help the reader decide whether a word is an adjective (*singing*), a noun (*singer*), or a verb (*sing*), and thus assist in determining the word's meaning. The syntactic position of the word also helps determine its grammatical aspects, and this redundant information makes the sentence easier to understand and increases reading speed. At this point, word recognition is largely automatic, and the reader can understand familiar words without consciously analyzing and decoding their phonemic characteristics. When a student can recognize enough words, the next step is to read sentences and paragraphs fluently.

> *"Young readers who are exposed to direct instruction on the morphological aspects of language become more capable readers than those who are not."*

A recent review of studies on morphological instruction shows that teachers do not spend enough time on direct instruction of building beginning readers' morphological skills (Bowers, Kirby, & Deacon, 2010). But in those classrooms where teachers do devote time to explaining and demonstrating phonemic variations in word structure and other elements of morphology, students become better readers. The effects of this instruction are particularly powerful with less able readers.

## Is Spelling Crucial to Reading?

English spelling is a nightmare. We will discuss more about the problems that English spelling poses for beginning readers in Chapter 3. For now, we should recognize that, despite its difficulties, spelling becomes important almost as soon as the child has mastered phonemic awareness and begins to make the letter-sound correspondences. Now the new reader must match the variety of spellings to their sounds. Research studies have found that preschool children are sensitive to the orthographic patterns in the way words are spelled (Puranik & Apel, 2010). By Grade 1, children note that *ck* never comes at the beginning of a word, and it is always preceded by a short vowel. Older children are not likely to spell *dirty* as *dirdy* because they recognize the morpheme *dirt* and a suffix.

As children progress in mapping letters and sounds, they discover an important reality about spelling: Usually, the mapping from spelling to pronunciation is more reliable than from pronunciation to spelling—the same sound can be spelled in different ways. This fact apparently causes some hesitation in word identification during reading. Research has shown that the more ways a sequence of phonemes can be spelled, the longer it takes to read a sentence containing that sequence. For example, *shelf* is read more quickly than *sneer* because the rime unit /ɛlf/ is always spelled *elf* whereas the rime unit /ir/ can be spelled as *ere, eer, ier,* or *ear* (Andrews & Lo, 2013; Peereman, Content, & Bonin, 1998; Stone, Vanhoy, & Van Orden, 1997). The researchers suspect that the hesitation is caused by a feedback mechanism in the reader's brain that verifies whether past experience supports the pronunciation of *eer* as /ir/. This notion demonstrates at least one way in which reading and spelling may be closely related in neural network processing.

Success in reading does not automatically result in success in spelling. Reading requires recognition whereas spelling requires production—a more complex skill that utilizes additional mental processes. Indeed, many skilled readers consider themselves to be terrible spellers. This is because so many English words do not adhere to strict phonetic rules. Almost every spelling-to-sound convention has exceptions. Nonetheless, good spelling is crucial for recognizing and decoding the meaning of words. To become an expert decoder, the reader will need to learn how to correctly identify and spell the exceptions. Studies show that the accuracy of a student's spelling in kindergarten and Grade 1 is a predictor of later reading ability (Moats, 2005).

As students develop their spelling skills, they also increase their word recognition speed during reading. Word recognition becomes automatic, and skilled readers are now able to recognize new words based on their morphemes. For example, a student who recognizes the spelling of *react* in *reaction* will realize that the words are related and make connections between their meanings. This is the primary way in which students expand their lexicon in Grade 3 and beyond. In sum, good spelling skills usually lead to rapid word recognition and comprehension.

## ✿ READING COMPREHENSION

Remember that learning to read requires close coordination between the brain's language processing and visual recognition systems. Both systems are constantly searching for sound and visual patterns while they attempt to make sense and gather meaning from the written word. But patterns in the English language are unpredictable, not just in spelling, but also in syntax. As soon as the brain suspects it has detected a pattern, a change in word order or the insertion of another word can upset the pattern and alter the meaning. When that occurs, the brain must not only remember the original pattern, but also the exception it just encountered. This back-and-forth between "I think I see the pattern" and "Oops, the pattern didn't work this time" can be very frustrating for beginning readers. This is especially true for boys, many of whom tend to slightly lag behind girls in language development in their early years.

## Words to Sentences

Comprehension of reading material occurs when readers are able to place the meaning of individual words into the structure and context of an entire sentence. Furthermore, the reader's ability to *remember* the sentence's structure (syntax) relies on working memory. Let's examine first the role of syntax in sentence comprehension; we will discuss working memory later in this chapter.

### Syntax and Comprehension

When children read simple sentences, they grasp meaning mainly through simple associations that are already stored in the brain's word form area and the mental lexicon. The syntax is easy, and there is little risk of ambiguity of meaning. In the sentence "The cat is white," only one interpretation is possible. But as sentences get more complex, syntax plays an important role in comprehension. Readers are more likely to encounter ambiguity in reading than in speech because written texts tend to use complex grammatical structures more often than casual conversation.

Before beginning to read, children already have a good sense of syntax as a result of speaking and listening. They learn that "I want cookie" sounds better (and may get more results) than "Cookie, I want" or "I cookie want." Their brains soon recognize the SVO speech pattern: Who's acting? (subject), What's the action? (verb), and What's being acted upon? (object). Interestingly enough, this syntax pattern is common to many Indo-European languages. Sentence structure gets more complicated in reading, however. There are three types of syntactic structure for sentences, as follows (SLC, 2000):

- *Simple:* A simple sentence contains just one main clause, for example, "The boy rowed the boat."
- *Compound:* A compound sentence has two or more main clauses separated by a comma and joined by a connecting word, for example, "The boy rowed the boat, and his mother watched."
- *Complex:* A complex sentence contains a main clause and one or more dependent or relative clauses, for example, "The boy who rowed the boat waved to his mother."

Many syntactic changes can occur within these three categories that change the meaning of these sentences. Some clauses include negation ("The boy didn't row the boat") or contain prepositional phrases ("The boy rowed the boat to his mother") or conjunctions ("The boy and his mother rowed the boat"). Using the passive voice will reverse the relative position of the subject and the object ("The boat was rowed by the boy"). Relative clauses can further complicate the matter by being relative to the subject ("The boy who rows the boat is lost") or relative to the object ("The boy rows the boat that is leaking").

So how is a beginning reader going to deal with differences in meaning that result from variations in syntax? The following six syntactic variations can be particularly troublesome and require some basic strategies that, by the way, do not always work (SLC, 2000):

- Word order
- Minimum-distance principle
- Analysis of conjoined clauses
- Passive voice
- Negation
- Embedding

**Word Order.** As mentioned earlier, prereading children are accustomed to the subject-verb-object (SVO) sequence and rely heavily on it to decode early reading. This reliance is fine as long as the sentences are in the active voice, such as "He chased the dog." Difficulties arise, however, when sentences are in the passive voice, such as "He was chased by the dog." In the latter case, the order of the words, *He, chased,* and *dog,* is preserved, so the reader might misinterpret the sentence to mean "He chased the dog."

**Minimum-Distance Principle.** Because of the brain's pattern-seeking predisposition, beginning readers assume that words in a sentence refer to the closest related words, verbs refer to the closest preceding nouns, and pronouns refer to the closest noun of the same gender. The minimum-distance principle is easily applicable to the sentence "He rowed the boat all by himself," but not to "He rowed the boat that belonged to the fisherman all by himself." Readers are apt to rely more on the minimum-distance principle when the number of words they have to remember in the sentence exceeds the capacity of their working memory.

**Analysis of Conjoined Clauses.** While attempting to comprehend a sentence with two clauses, the young reader may assume that the two clauses are conjoined by a conjunction such as *and.* Consequently, the reader may misinterpret the sentence "The man chased the dog that ate the steak" to mean "The man chased the dog, and the man ate the steak."

**Passive Voice.** For the young reader, sentences containing the passive voice are particularly difficult to understand and learn. They violate the SVO sequence, and they can be particularly troublesome if they are reversible, such as "She was called by him," which could be mistakenly read as "She called him." Sometimes, common sense helps the reader to comprehend passive voice sentences correctly. For example, in the sentence "The window was broken by the baseball," it is clear that the window couldn't break the baseball, so only one interpretation makes sense.

**Negation.** Sentences written in the negative are usually more difficult for the young brain to comprehend. That is because the brain tends to first interpret the sentence in the positive sense, and then move to the second phase to process the negative sense. Consequently, the young reader will find the sentence "Circle the picture that shows cows and sheep" easier to understand than "Circle the picture that has cows but not sheep." Substantial practice with negation can improve a reader's comprehension and fluency with these types of sentences.

**Embedding.** Embedded clauses can lead to ambiguity or misinterpretation. In Grades 2 and 3, readers encounter the following three types of embedded clauses:

1. *The subject of the main clause is the same as the subject of the embedded clause.* Example: "The boy rowed the boat and waved to his mother." These are usually easy for young readers to understand.

2. *The object of the main clause is the subject of the embedded clause.* Example: "The man chased the dog that ate the steak." These are more difficult to comprehend accurately. The reader may incorrectly apply the conjoined-clause strategy here and read the sentence as "The man chased the dog, and the man ate the steak."

3. *The subject of the main clause is the object of the embedded clause.* Example: "The boat that the boy rowed belongs to the fisherman." Ambiguity arises because these types of sentences violate both the SVO sequence and the minimum-distance principle.

As students read more and as their working memory becomes more efficient, they gradually switch from using these rudimentary strategies to paying closer heed to the actual syntax of sentences.

## *Morphology and Comprehension*

Morphology, you will recall, studies how words are put together from pieces (e.g., prefixes and suffixes), and how these pieces can change the meaning of words or create new ones. Morphological awareness contributes to reading comprehension in the following ways (Mahony et al., 2000):

- *Meaning.* The reader is able to distinguish the difference between nouns formed by adding *-tion* and nouns formed by adding *-ive.* Thus, *operation* and *operative* are formed from the same root word but have different meanings.
- *Syntactic properties.* The reader understands that a particular suffix indicates a part of speech. For example, *-y* indicates an adjective (*noisy*) and *-ly* indicates an adverb (*noisily*).
- *Phonological properties.* The reader understands that derivational suffixes can alter the pronunciation of the root word. For example, adding *-ic* to hero involves a shift in emphasis from the first syllable of *heroic* to the second, and adding *-al* to *hymn* involves pronouncing the previously silent consonant *-n* in *hymnal.*
- *Relational properties.* The reader understands the relationship between words formed by adding different prefixes and suffixes to the same root word, as in *import* and *export* or in *operation* and *operative.* When readers use relational properties effectively, their reading fluency, pronunciation, and comprehension improve. Furthermore, they get better at distinguishing between true morphological relationships, such as *sail-sailor,* and false ones, such as *may-mayor.*

*Decoding Ability, Intelligence, and Comprehension*

Research studies have shown that phonological awareness, phonological memory, and visual-spatial skills (all part of decoding) are stronger predicators of success with reading comprehension than intelligence during the stages of early reading (Brunswick, Martin, & Rippon, 2012). As children progress, however, the research evidence suggests that decoding speed as well as intelligence (as measured by standard IQ tests) are closely related to reading comprehension. One study involving 124 children found that decoding ability was the best single predictor of how well the child comprehended the reading. The child's IQ was also a significant predictor, although not as strong as decoding ability (Tiu, Thompson, & Lewis, 2003).

## Reading Comprehension and Language Comprehension

Not surprisingly, reading comprehension is very closely related to spoken language comprehension. It reflects the degree of coordination between the brain's language processing and visual recognition systems. If that is the case, how do we explain those children who can read words but whose comprehension in reading is not as good as their spoken language comprehension? One likely explanation is that children learn spoken language in settings that are different from where they learn to read. Written language generally adheres to stricter grammatical structures and uses more formal vocabulary than spoken language. Consequently, how well a child comprehends a written text is determined by how well that child comprehends the same text when it is spoken.

## ✿ HOW MEMORY AFFECTS LEARNING TO READ

To understand how memory affects reading, we need a brief review of the brain's memory components. As researchers gain greater insight into the brain's memory processes, they have had to devise and revise terms that describe the various stages of memory. Neuroscientists now believe that we have two temporary memories that perform different tasks. It is a way of explaining how the brain deals briefly with some data, but can continue to process other data for extended periods of time. For now, *short-term memory* is used by cognitive neuroscientists to include the two stages of temporary memory: immediate memory and working memory (Gathercole, 2008). Figure 2.2 illustrates the stages of temporary and permanent memory.

### Immediate Memory

Immediate memory is one of the two temporary memories and is represented in Figure 2.2 by a clipboard, a place where we put information briefly until we make a decision on how to dispose of it. Immediate memory operates subconsciously or consciously and holds data for up to about 30 seconds. (Note: The numbers used in this chapter are averages over time. There are always exceptions to these values as a result of human variations or pathologies.) The individual's experiences determine its importance. If the information is of little or no importance within this time frame, it drops out of the memory system. For example, when you look up the telephone number of the local pizza parlor, you usually can remember it just long enough to make the call. After that, the number is of no further importance and drops out of immediate memory. The next time you call, you will have to look up the number again.

## Working Memory

Suppose, on the other hand, you can't decide whether to call the pizza parlor or the Chinese takeout place, and you discuss these options with someone else in the room. This situation requires more of your attention and is shifted into working memory for further processing. Working memory is the second temporary memory and the place where conscious, rather than subconscious, processing occurs. In Figure 2.2, working memory is shown as a work table, a place of limited capacity where we can build, take apart, or rework ideas for eventual storage somewhere else. When something is in working memory, it generally captures our focus and demands our attention. Scanning experiments show that most of working memory's activity occurs in the frontal lobes, although other parts of the brain are often called into action (Gathercole, 2008; Goldberg, 2001).

### Capacity of Working Memory

Working memory can handle only a few items at one time. This functional capacity changes with age. Preschool infants can deal with about two items of information at once. Preadolescents can handle three to seven items, with an average of five. Through adolescence, further cognitive

**Figure 2.2**   This diagram illustrates the theory of temporary and permanent memories. Information gathered from our senses lasts only a few seconds in immediate memory. Information that needs further processing moves to working memory where it usually endures for minutes or hours, but can be retained for days or longer, if necessary. The long-term storage sites (also called permanent memory) store information for years.

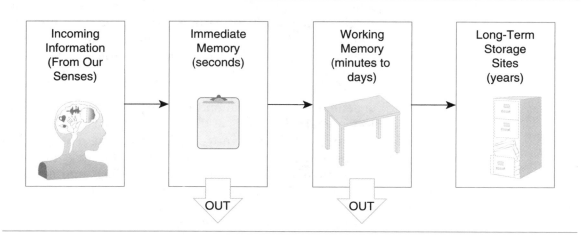

expansion occurs, and the capacity increases to a range of five to nine, with an average of seven. For most people, that number remains constant throughout life.

This limited capacity explains why we have to memorize a song or a poem in stages. We start with the first group of lines by repeating them frequently (a process called **rehearsal**). Then we memorize the next lines and repeat them with the first group, and so on. It is possible to increase the number of items within the functional capacity of working memory through a process called *chunking*. In spoken language, chunking occurs when the young child's mind begins to combine phonemes into words, such as when *can* and *dee* become *candy*.

### Time Limits of Working Memory

Working memory is temporary and can deal with items for only a limited time. For preadolescents, it is more likely to be 5 to 10 minutes, and for adolescents and adults, 10 to 20 minutes. These are average times, and it is important to understand what the numbers mean. An adolescent (or adult) normally can process an item in working memory intently for 10 to 20 minutes before fatigue or boredom with that item occurs and the individual's focus drifts to other items. For focus to continue, there must be some change in the way the individual is dealing with the item. As an example, the person may switch from thinking about it to physically using it, or making different connections to other learnings. If something else is not done with the item, it is likely to fade from working memory.

This is not to say that some items cannot remain in working memory for hours, or perhaps days. Sometimes, we have an item that remains unresolved—a question whose answer we seek or a troublesome family or work decision that must be made. These items can remain in working memory, continually commanding some attention, and can, if of sufficient importance, interfere with our accurate processing of other information. Eventually, we solve the problem, and it clears out of working memory.

### Reading Comprehension and Working Memory

Spoken language uses memory systems for meaning. Memory helps students remember a set of oral directions: "Take out your math book and do the even-numbered problems on pages 18 and 19, and then check your answers on page 237." But reading is a far more complicated skill involving a number of brain systems. When reading a word, the decoding process breaks the word into its segments, and while being retained in working memory, the phonemes are blended to form words that the reader can recognize. The ability to retain verbal bits of information is referred to as **phonologic memory**.

When reading sentences, the visual and memory systems of the brain must decode and then retain the words at the beginning of a sentence for a period of time while the reader's eyes move to the end of the sentence. In a short sentence like "See the dog run," that is no problem because the memory time-span requirement is minimal. However, reading complex sentences, such as "The boy ran down the street to tell his friend that the ice cream truck was just around the corner and would be here soon," requires much more memory time. Furthermore, the brain must pay attention to syntax and context in order for the sentence to be accurately understood. Because of working memory's limited capacity, beginning readers will have difficulty understanding long sentences or sentences with complex structure or syntax. They may be able to read the sentence aloud, but may not comprehend its meaning (Figure 2.3).

A child's ability to store words temporarily in working memory depends on several factors, such as age, experience, and language proficiency. But the code that readers of any age use to store written words and phrases is a phonological code. Consequently, phonological coding skills are crucial for using and developing the ability of working memory to store representations of written words. A reader with efficient phonological decoding skills will be able to quickly generate and retain phonetic representations of written words as well as preserve the words themselves and their sequence in the sentence. By developing these working memory skills, the reader with appropriate background knowledge can comprehend not only the sentence, but also the paragraph and the chapter.

During reading, working memory helps comprehension in the following two ways:

- *Understanding complex structure.* In complex sentences, such as "The woman who is getting into the blue car dropped her key," working memory holds the decoded results of the first part of a sentence while the visual cortex processes the words and phrases in the rest of the sentence. Working memory then puts all the pieces together to establish the sentence's meaning.

**Figure 2.3**   As a young beginning reader's eye moves across the sentence, words that were at the beginning may fade from working memory. By the time the eyes gets toward the end of the sentence, the reader may not remember the previous words and thus cannot establish meaning.

**The boy ran down the street** to tell his friend that the ice cream truck was just around…

The boy ran down the street **to tell his friend that the** ice cream truck was just around…

The boy ran down the street to tell his friend that the **ice cream truck was just around**…

- *Preserving syntax (word order).* Take the sentence "The driver of the blue car, not the red car, honked his horn." Here, working memory preserves the word order so that the reader can process the sequence, recognize negation, and correctly identify who honked the horn.

As reading progresses, the meaning of each sentence in a paragraph must be held in memory so that the sentences can be associated with each other to determine the intent of the paragraph and whether certain details need to be remembered. Working memory must then link paragraphs to each other so that, by the end of the chapter, the reader has an understanding of the main ideas encountered. With extensive practice, the working memory becomes more efficient at recognizing words and at chunking words into common phrases. As a result, the child reads faster and comprehends more.

### Forming Gists

Because working memory has a limited capacity, it cannot hold all the words of a long sentence. To deal with this limitation, working memory merges words within a clause to form a **gist** (the memory device known as *chunking*) that is then temporarily stored in place of the words. A gist essentially preserves a mental summary of the event described in what the individual just read, without the exact words (or number or pictures, for that matter). As reading continues, the brain adds new gists of clauses until the sentence is completed. Then a gist of the sentence is generated. Gists from other sentences in the paragraph are chunked to form a higher-level gist of the paragraph. Then, gists of paragraphs are chunked to form an even higher-level gist of the chapter, and eventually for the entire text. Table 2.3 shows how gists at one level combine to form gists of the next level.

Early reading makes heavy demands on both the processing and storage functions of a young working memory. Chunking the representations of word forms into gists is an efficient way of managing the competition for space and time in working memory. Gists take up less space and are retained while individual word forms are deleted. Sentence gists are then deleted when paragraph gists are formed, and so on. Clause gists endure for about 30 seconds; chapter gists can last for 15 minutes or more (SLC,

**Table 2.3**    Levels of Reading Comprehension Gists in Working Memory

| **4th Level:** | Chapter #1 gist ✚ Chapter #2 gist ✚ Chapter #3 ➜ **Text gist** |
|---|---|
| **3rd Level:** | Paragraph #1 gist ✚ Paragraph #2 gist ✚ Paragraph #3 gist ➜ **Chapter #1 gist** |
| **2nd Level:** | Sentence #1 gist ✚ Sentence #2 gist ✚ Sentence #3 gist ➜ **Paragraph #1 gist** |
| **1st Level:** | Clause #1 gist ✚ Clause #2 gist ✚ Clause #3 gist ➜ **Sentence #1 gist** |

SOURCE: SLC (2000).

2000). However, these endurance times can be extended through oral rehearsal and with written summaries when the child is able to write. Gists can remain in memory networks for extended periods and serve as cues for recall. We have all had the experience where an unexpected stimulus (e.g., an old song or the odor of a perfume) brings back a memory or an event that may have occurred years ago. We cannot quite remember the details, but the "gist" is there (Reyna et al., 2011).

Other factors affect the ability of working memory to retain or lose information during reading (Figure 2.4). New reading that the child finds interesting is likely to make it past immediate memory to working memory for conscious processing. And if the new reading activates material recently learned, **long-term storage** retrieves that information and moves it into working memory where it enhances the acquisition of the new learning. This process is called *transfer* and represents one of the most powerful principles of learning (Sousa, 2011a).

Reading information can also leave working memory if either of the following occurs:

- Too many minutes have elapsed since the information was last activated. For instance, just after reading the first sentence of a lengthy paragraph, the reader gets involved in a brief conversation not

**Figure 2.4**    Reading and memory interact in several ways. Reading that is interesting to the reader will pass through immediate memory into working memory for conscious processing. New reading may activate long-term storage to retrieve related gists already learned. Reading information can fall out of working memory by fading or by being displaced by additional information.

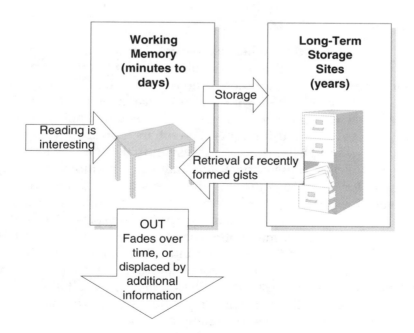

related to the reading with another child. When the reader returns to the text, the previously read material has faded, and the child must start again from the beginning.

- Additional information is placed in working memory, and its capacity is exceeded. This can happen if the child is reading faster than he can comprehend, thus giving the brain insufficient time to form the necessary gists and then clear out the individual words. In this case, the words are removed from memory before the gist is generated, and comprehension suffers.

As more demands are placed on working memory during reading, other difficulties may arise. A young child who is just learning to read using a book with advanced vocabulary words will have trouble with comprehension because so much memory capacity is being used trying to decode unfamiliar words. Research studies on the pace at which people read have offered further insights into how memory affects comprehension (e.g., Carretti, Borella, Cornoldi, & De Beni, 2009; Fedorenko, Gibson, & Rohde, 2006). For example, the studies found that readers spent more time reading the topic sentence of a paragraph. This may indicate that working memory is exerting more effort to generate and ensure the retaining of this gist because it is most useful in understanding the rest of the passage, and for creating the gist of the entire paragraph. The research studies also demonstrated, to no one's surprise, that readers remembered best those ideas and concepts that were referenced repeatedly, as well as those that were linked through cause and effect (SLC, 2000). On the other hand, readers spent the least amount of time reading the details of a paragraph and, thus, had difficulty recalling them. They were able to recall, however, details related to a humorous or vivid event, probably because such events evoke emotion, a powerful memory enhancer.

## Memory and Comprehension

Reading without comprehension is an unfulfilling endeavor. Why go through all that practice and devote all that neural energy required to rewire parts of the brain if there is no reward at hand? The magic of proficient reading is that it allows us to form visions in our head of places we haven't been or could not even exist, to discover the thoughts of those long gone, and to share our thoughts with others. Fortunately, nature has provided us with a visual processing system that allows us to create mental images as well as a memory system that can remember these images and thoughts for years to come. In what ways does reading comprehension influence the processes of memory storage, consolidation, and recall?

Gist formation is one model that helps explain some aspects of recall, but it does not account for many of the characteristics of memory recall that we all have experienced. A reader's ability to comprehend gists is largely dependent on that individual's past experiences and the mental networks that have evolved as a result of those experiences. We all use these networks to help us interpret the world and to predict situations occurring in our environment. Mental networks containing memories of our past experiences are important in helping us to comprehend text. Readers use these memories to interpret cause and effect, to compare and contrast, and to make inferences about the author's meaning. Information that does not fit into our memory networks may not be understood or may be understood incorrectly. This is one reason why readers may have problems comprehending text on a subject in which they have no experiences even though they understand the meaning of every word in the text. Memory networks are greatly influenced by an individual's culture. Thus, young readers who were not brought up in the United States may have a difficult time reading and answering questions about George Washington.

Memory networks store not just information, but also images. Our visual lexicon contains thousands of images from our past encounters. Some are vivid, and some are blurry, depending on how many times we recalled them. Recalling an image or a memory strengthens the neural pathways containing the elements of that image, thereby making it easier to recall and more intense. If I told you that I am now going to read you a story about a cat, chances are your brain instantly created a mental image of a cat, most likely one you know. You might even see its color, and hear its meows, or sense the softness of its fur. These images are not only essential to understanding language but are important components of reading comprehension.

### Modifying Our Memory Networks

Our memory networks are created through repeated experiences with events, people, and objects that we encounter in our world. When we encounter a new experience, our networks can be modified in any of the following three ways (Figure 2.5):

- *Accretion:* The learner incorporates the new information into an existing schema without altering that schema. For example, suppose I visited a public library, and all that I experienced there fit into my long-held schema of a library as a place with just print material and a card catalog. As a result, I did not alter my library schema in any appreciable way.
- *Tuning:* The learner realizes that the existing schema is inadequate to accommodate the new information and alters the existing schema to be more consistent with the new experience. For example, when I visited a modern public library and realized that the card catalog was replaced by a computer database, I had to modify my library network to accommodate this experience.
- *Restructuring:* The learner realizes that the new information is so inconsistent with the existing schema that a new schema has to be created. For example, now my ability to access the print information at the local public library directly from my computer at home any time of the day or night has forced me to create a new schema.

## WHAT DOES NEW RESEARCH ✿ REVEAL ABOUT READING?

Although studies using brain imaging and other types of scans have helped researchers understand more about how the human brain learns to read, there are still limits as to what these technologies can do. For example, they

**Figure 2.5**    This illustration shows how a stored experience from a memory network helps us to interpret new information. As the new information is processed, the experience can be returned to long-term memory unchanged or altered to accommodate the new experience. In some cases, the new information cannot be accommodated by the current network, so a new one is created.

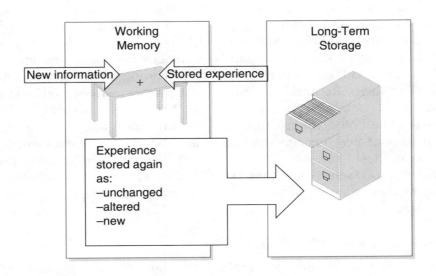

can detect which brain regions are involved in reading, but they cannot track reading progress *directly* in an individual child's brain. By examining a large collection of images and data, researchers can make educated inferences about how we *think* such development occurs. However, it is difficult to know *precisely* whether activity in a brain region is due solely to a particular stimulus. Nonetheless, much progress has been made so far, and new findings are appearing regularly. Table 2.4 describes what researchers have surmised about the brain and reading, based on the information available at the time of this printing.

## Reading Pathways

Using functional imaging scans, neuroscientists have discovered the neural mechanisms that are activated during reading. As would be expected, the scans have shown that all readers use neural circuitry dedicated to visual processing, because the curves and lines of the alphabet need to be visually analyzed to distinguish one letter from another. In addition to the visual processing area, Shaywitz (2003) and other researchers (Dehaene, 2009; McCandliss, Cohen, & Dehaene, 2003) noted that other areas of the brain were involved in reading. However, which of these areas the brain used was dependent on how skilled the person was at reading. Apparently, beginning readers use different neural pathways than skilled readers, most likely because certain brain regions need to be modified to detect the different shapes of letters and to make the sound-to-letter correspondences. Here is what the researchers found.

## Pathways for Beginning Readers

Before learning to read, when a child sees a word, the left-hemisphere language centers do not show unusual activity (Table 2.4). Rather, regions in the right hemisphere activate, most likely processing the visual picture, or snapshot, of the word. This could represent the pictorial stage that we mentioned earlier in this chapter. During this prereading time, the child's brain memorizes the snapshots from the shapes of the letters, similar to how it would recognize faces. For instance, we pointed out earlier that young children who spot and respond to a McDonald's restaurant sign are probably reacting to the Golden Arches logo and a mental picture of the word *McDonald's*, not to its phonemes. Nonetheless, the pattern-seeking capabilities of the brain are constantly at work, and there is evidence that this right-hemisphere region may visually differentiate strings of consonant letters (Maurer, Brem, Bucher, & Brandeis, 2005). At about the age of 6 or 7 years, the brain of a beginning reader responds more actively to printed words than to geometric shapes or meaningless letter strings—that is, nonwords (Maurer et al., 2006).

Visual Word Form Area. By the age of 8, the brain is aggressively recruiting areas in both hemispheres, especially in the visual recognition system, to deal with the challenge of increased reading. A clearly defined area of high activity emerges in the left hemisphere at the boundary of the occipital and temporal lobes (Parviainen, Helenius, Poskiparta, Niemi, & Salmelin, 2006; Yeatman, Rauschecker, & Wandell, 2013). That would place it slightly to the rear of the left ear. This region is officially called the left occipitotemporal area. However, scientists have suggested that it be called by a less technical term: the *visual word form area*, abbreviated as VWFA (Cohen et al., 2000). The term emphasizes its role in the visual analysis of letters and their shapes. With more reading practice, the VWFA attaches meaning directly to whole word forms, thereby allowing the reader to significantly increase fluency and comprehension (Glezer, Jiang, & Riesenhuber, 2009). Broca's area, a specialized region for language located behind the left temple (see Chapter 1), is also significantly involved in this word analysis. Studies show that the activation in the VWFA and other language areas in the left-hemisphere area is in direct proportion to the child's skill at phonemic awareness, or the ability to mentally manipulate the basic sounds of language (Turkeltaub, Gareau, Flowers, Zeffiro, & Eden, 2003). Once again, we see the impact of phonemic awareness on reading acquisition.

At this point, when the child's brain now sees the word *dog* in print, the visual word form area records the three alphabetic symbols and

Table 2.4 Comparison of Eye Movements of Novice and Skilled Readers

| Reading Skill Level | Fixation Time (in milliseconds) | Fixation Span (in letter spaces) | Percentage in Regression |
|---|---|---|---|
| Novice | 300 to 400 | 3 to 5 | Up to 50 |
| Skilled | 200 to 250 | 9 | 10 to 15 |

SOURCES: Häikiö et al. (2009); Rayner el al. (2001).

activates the left-hemisphere language centers to provide and match the *duh-awh-guh* phonemes to their appropriate letters, *duh = d, awh = o,* and *guh = g.* This developing sound-to-letter relationship is the alphabetic principle in action. Eventually, a mental image of a furry animal is conceptualized in the mind's eye, adding meaning to the symbolic representation of *d-o-g.* With more frequent exposure to the word *dog,* the VWFA will eventually attach the meaning to the word's letter string, thereby increasing reading speed and comprehension.

   **Children at Risk for Reading.** Given the substantial amount of cerebral reorganization that takes place during the acquisition of reading, it is no surprise that difficulties can arise along the way. Imaging studies of poor beginning readers show variations in the expected development of the sites responsible for learning to read. For instance, although most brain activation associated with typical beginning readers occurs in the left hemisphere, a more bilateral pattern is observed in poor readers (Bach et al., 2010; Yamada et al., 2011). It seems that both the visual recognition areas and the frontal lobe of the right hemisphere are more engaged than in typical readers. These findings may indicate that the brain recruits right-hemisphere regions to compensate for difficulties that are occurring during the modifications of the left-hemisphere reading areas.

## Pathways for Intermediate Readers

Learning to read enhances a child's spoken language capabilities. Between 10 years of age and the beginning of adolescence, Broca's and other language areas undergo significant modification in addition to the visual recognition system. Visual analysis occurs faster. With repeated encounters of the same word, the child's brain makes a neural model—called a word form—and the child can read this word far more quickly. Just seeing it activates all the necessary components at once, mostly in the left hemisphere, without any conscious thought on the part of the reader. As more word forms collect in this cerebral region, reading becomes more fluent, and reading skill levels rise dramatically. Broca's area now plays only a minor role in assisting this region. The more skilled the reader, the more quickly the VWFA responds to seeing a word—in less than 200 thousandths of a second (200 **milliseconds**), much faster than the blink of an eye (Dehaene, 2009).

## Pathways for Skilled Readers

If the intermediate reader continues to read regularly, then by early to mid adolescence, the visual form word area reaches full maturity. As the reader acquires new vocabulary and more sophisticated rules of syntax, and as semantics play a greater role in establishing comprehension, additional brain areas are required and recruited. Scanning images reveal complex interactions and connections to numerous networks, mainly in the brain's left hemisphere. Becoming an expert adult reader results in activity changes that are not present in accomplished child readers. Imaging scans reveal that there are similar but not identical patterns of regional brain activity when adult and child skilled readers perform identical reading tasks at comparable levels of performance. Children activate some neural regions during reading that adults do not activate, or may activate less, and vice versa. These differences in activity patterns probably reflect the increase in the efficiency of brain processing as the child matures into an adult (Schlaggar & Church, 2009).

Figure 2.6 reflects the most recent model of the neural networks required for skilled reading, and how researchers believe they interact. This model is considerably different from the linear model that scientists accepted until just a few years ago. At that time, scientists believed that visual input went from the visual cortex to the brain's reading center in a region called the **angular gyrus**, located in the left parietal lobe at the top left side of the head. For many years, this structure was believed to be responsible for interpreting shapes in the environment, so it made sense to assume it also interpreted the physical forms of letters. From there, according to the older model, information passed through Wernicke's and Broca's areas for interpretation, and finally to the frontal cortex for comprehension. It was a fairly simple linear route.

But more recent and extensive imaging research indicates that the process is much more complex. Letter analysis actually occurs in the VWFA, while several other word processing functions are operating in parallel. Perhaps a dozen or more neural sites are involved. The newer model helps explain how a skilled reader can acquire the visual images of words, extract their roots, determine syntax, and ultimately find meaning in just

**Figure 2.6** This model illustrates the various brain networks currently thought to be involved in reading. Visual input goes first to the visual word form area (solid dark blue areas) and is then distributed to regions spread across the left hemisphere. The medium blue areas (connected by solid arrows) are mainly used for gaining access to word pronunciation and articulation. The checkered regions (connected by dotted arrows) help in establishing meaning. All these areas (except the visual word form area) likely play other roles in processing spoken language. The diagram shows that reading results from collaboration between language and visual areas of the brain.

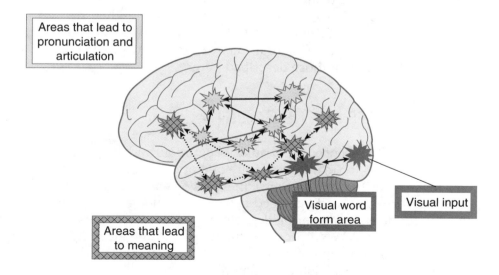

SOURCE: Adapted with permission from Dehaene (2009).

a fraction of a second. Brain regions must be operating simultaneously and constantly exchanging information with other sites.

It is important to note that most of these areas are not exclusive to reading, and may carry out other tasks. The VWFA, however, generally responds only to written words and not to spoken words. Some areas contribute to spoken language processing while others process visual information. Signals can move in both directions between sites. Learning to read tends to be linear at the very beginning, progressing from phonemes to morphemes to graphemes. However, it becomes more bidirectional as reading skills, especially comprehension, develop and expand. By showing how complex the reading process is, researchers realize that the model is not static and will probably evolve as newer findings emerge. In fact, some neuroscientists doubt whether we will ever fully understand how the reading brain truly works. Nonetheless, we have a lot of information to date, certainly enough to recognize what educational strategies are more likely to help children learn to read as well as what problems can arise during that process. We will discuss these topics in the following chapters.

**Reading Is Universal.** Surprisingly, images of an adult reading brain are substantially the same regardless of the native language or culture of the individual in the scanning device. Even for Chinese and Japanese readers who use a pictorial script, or for those who read from right to left, the location of the VWFA in the left hemisphere is virtually identical. It is genuinely remarkable to realize that despite the vast differences among the nearly 7,000 languages on this planet, and the many forms in which those languages are expressed in writing, we all still summon the same brain areas to help us identify and comprehend the written words of our language.

To summarize, beginning readers rely on visual recognition information and use both Broca's area and the developing visual word form area to slowly analyze each word. Intermediate and skilled readers, on the other hand, rely mainly on the visual word form area to process and direct information to interconnected sites, rapidly producing meaning from words, with only marginal help from Broca's area when needed. As we shall see later on, children and adults with reading difficulties, including dyslexia, show patterns of brain activation when reading that are distinctly different from those described here.

## ✿ TWO ROUTES TO READING

After mid adolescence, the visual recognition and language processing systems needed for reading are fully operational in most people. A skilled reader is born. Through practice, the VWFA is assigning meaning directly to word forms, so reading speed is increasing along with comprehension. No longer does the reader have to sound out the phonemes when reading *dog*, because the VWFM provides the word and the meaning necessary to form the mental image of a dog and not an elephant or a rabbit. And all that happens in a fraction of a second.

Other cerebral areas are recruited as needed to process more complex sentence structure and syntax. Exactly how all these systems work is still not completely understood, but researchers are making progress. By observing what happens to the reading abilities of patients who have had strokes or lesions in these brain areas, researchers conclude that written words seem to be processed by two cerebral routes. These routes coexist and support one another to provide the reader with pronunciation and meaning quickly and accurately (Dehaene, 2009; Gazzaniga, Ivry, & Mangun, 2002).

When we encounter a word that we see frequently, we use a direct *lexical* or *vocabulary-centered* route that first identifies the letters (in the orthographic lexicon), next selects the word and its meaning (in the semantic lexicon), and then uses the phonological information (in the phonological lexicon) to retrieve its pronunciation. This direct route—letters to word/meaning to pronunciation—is used for most words, as long as they occur frequently and are stored in the reader's various mental dictionaries (Figure 2.7).

However, when the word is novel or rare, we use a *phonological route* (Figure 2.8). On this route, the visual recognition system decodes the string of letters, then signals the language areas for the corresponding phonemes to help with pronunciation, and finally communicates with the frontal lobe in an attempt to find meaning in the sound pattern. Meaning may be difficult to find if the word is not in the mental lexicon, or is pronounced very differently than it is written, such as *island, colonel,* or *Wednesday.* This indirect route—letters to sounds to meaning—is helpful when we are learning new words.

Reading fluency requires that these two routes work in close coordination. Each contributes to the total reading experience depending on what type of word is being read and processed. In an expert adult reader, these routes are working so closely together in parallel that rapid

Figure 2.7    This diagram illustrates the direct processing route taken when the reader sees a familiar written word, such as *band.* The brain recovers the meaning and identity of the word through the orthographic and semantic lexicons and then uses the phonological information to pronounce it.

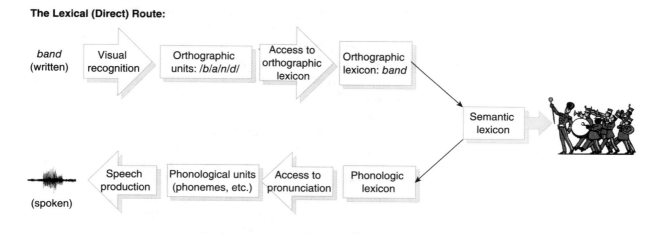

SOURCE: Adapted from Dehaene (2009); Gazzaniga et al. (2002).

**Figure 2.8**    This diagram illustrates the indirect route taken when the word is unfamiliar. The brain sends additional signals along multiple paths to determine if enough orthographic, phonologic, and semantic data are present to interpret the word, pronounce it, and find its meaning.

**Phonological (Indirect) Route**

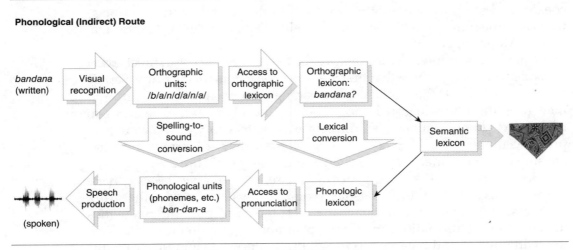

SOURCE: Adapted from Dehaene (2009); Gazzaniga et al. (2002).

comprehension may give the appearance that there is a single route. But research findings from scans and patient case studies suggest that fluent and proficient reading requires the brain regions to be organized into multiple parallel paths. Even at this printing, some researchers are suggesting that the dual-route model oversimplifies what is really going on in the brain during reading.

## Eye Movements During Reading

Only the central part of the eye, called the *fovea*, is the area on the retina of highest resolution. Consequently, when we read, our eyes make rapid movements across the page, called *saccades,* stopping for certain periods of time, called **fixations**. It is during these fixations of about 200 to 250 milliseconds that the eyes actually acquire information from the text. As you read this, your eyes are making four or five of those saccades per second in order to comprehend this text. Then the eyes take about 20 to 40 milliseconds to move to the next fixation point, a distance of about seven to nine letter spaces. This is a very small number but appears to represent the most information that our brain systems can process in one fixation.

During this time, vision is suppressed, and no new information enters the processing system. Skilled readers also move their eyes backward about 10 to 15 percent of the time in order to reread material. These **regressions** are needed when the reader has difficulty comprehending the text (Rayner, 2009; Rayner, Foorman, Perfetti, Pesetsky, & Seidenberg, 2001). It is interesting to note that in languages that are read from left to right, our span of vision detects more letters to the right than to the left of the fixation point. But in languages that are read from right to left, as in Hebrew and Arabic, the visual span reads more characters to the left than to the right. In other words, our eye movement strategies adapt to our native language's reading protocols.

Research studies on eye movements during reading lend further support to the notion that beginning and skilled readers are processing written information differently. Beginning readers fixate on every word in a text, and they often fixate on the same word several times. Their fixation points are only about three letter spaces apart, and their fixation periods run longer, from 300 to 400 milliseconds. Furthermore, up to 50 percent of their eye movements are regressions. These eye movements most likely indicate the difficulty the beginning reader is having encoding the text. The longer fixation time may also result from the slower process of word analysis that occurs in the brain's visual word form area. Table 2.4 shows a comparison of the eye movements of novice and skilled readers.

Research into how eye movements affect reading in adults has produced some interesting results (Häikiö, Bertram, Hyönä, & Niemi, 2009; Rayner, Slattery, & Bélanger, 2010). It confirms that slow readers have a smaller perceptual span than fast readers. However, there was little difference in the slow and fast readers' ability to identify the words they were reading. This finding supports earlier explanations that slow readers use more cerebral processing resources to comprehend the words they are fixated on than do fast readers.

Another finding was that the spacing of letters *within* a word and the spacing *between* words affected the reading rate. Studies showed that reducing the spacing between letters increased the reading rate, provided the spacing between words was slightly increased (Paterson & Jordan, 2010; Rayner et al., 2010). Researchers suggested that increasing the spacing between words makes it easier for the eye to demarcate the beginnings and endings of words, thereby aiding comprehension and increasing the speed of reading.

## THE IMPORTANCE OF PRACTICE ⚙

It is evident that learning to read requires significant reorganization of the visual recognition and language processing areas of the brain. New neuronal connections and broader cerebral networks need to be established. Strengthening these connections and building disparate networks comes through repetition and practice. The more frequently these pathways are activated, the faster and more consolidated they become. Consequently, for most children, reading improves with practice. Experience in reading improves several components of the decoding and comprehension processes (Joseph, 2007; Rayner et al., 2001). For example, practice does each of the following:

- Allows the mental lexicons and the visual word form area of the brain to acquire increasingly accurate representations of a word's spelling and meaning, thereby strengthening the connection between how the word sounds (the phonological form) and its spelling (the orthographic representation). This is called the *phonological-orthographic connection.* The stronger this connection, the faster one reads.
- Results in an increasing facility with words because it increases the quality of the words' representation in the lexicon, thereby enhancing comprehension.

- Turns low-frequency words into high-frequency words, improving the fluency of reading. Fluency involves developing rapid and automatic word-identification processes as well as bridging the gap between word recognition and comprehension.
- Increases familiarity with the patterns of letters that form printed words, thereby improving spelling. This is referred to as the *lexical-orthographic connection*. It is not the same as the phonological-orthographic connection. Both contribute in their own way to support the brain's ability to read words.
- Improves comprehension because the reader is exposed to both familiar and new words used in many different contexts. This helps the reader recognize that two words can have the same spelling, but have different meanings, grammatical functions, and pronunciation, such as: "I *lead* a team that tests our drinking water for *lead* and other metals."

Less able readers are likely to get less practice than more able readers. Consequently, the gap between more and less able readers increases over time. It is not surprising, then, that studies have found that reading ability in kindergarten was a strong predictor of reading ability in Grade 8 (Adlof, Catts, & Lee, 2010). This evidence contradicts a common belief that initial differences in reading ability wash out over time.

## Being a Skilled Reader

Skilled readers do not read each word individually, nor do their eyes move from word to word until they reach the end. Rather, they scan the text searching for patterns that will make the task of reading easier. To illustrate this, look at the following block of text and note any irregularities:

QQQQQQQQ

QQQQQQQQ

QQQQQPQQ

QQQQQQQQ

QOQQQQQQ

QQQQQQQQ

What did you notice? Most people will spot the letter "P" almost immediately, but miss the letter "O" in the fifth line. This illustrates the selectivity of vision. We notice something that violates the pattern but skim over something that very closely resembles it. These expectations of conformity guide our reading and allow us to increase our reading speed. This activity also shows the faster we read, the more detail we miss.

Another interesting characteristic of skilled reading is that the phonologic module becomes so adept at recognizing common words that it can do so even if the word is significantly misspelled. Can you understand the following text?

Aoccdrnig to rseerach at an Elingsh uinervtisy, it deosn't mttaer in waht order the ltteers in a wrod are, the olny iprmoetnt tihng is taht the frist and lsat ltteer is in the rghit pclae. The rset can be a total mses, and you can sitll raed it wouthit a porbelm. Tihs is bcuseae we do not raed ervey letetr by itslef, but the wrod as a wlohe.

Most skilled readers can read this paragraph despite the misspellings. Apparently, the beginning and ending letters as well as the context supply enough clues for the phonologic module to recognize the words and determine meaning. This example illustrates how reading modifies the native capabilities of our brain to acquire an amazing culture skill. Reading enhances our language, visual, and memory systems. It "literally" changes our brain forever . . . pardon the pun.

---

**QUESTIONS FOR DISCUSSION/REFLECTION**

- *What must a child be able to do in order to read effectively?*
- *What role does working memory play in learning to read?*
- *What happens in the brain when a child goes from a nonreader to a novice reader, and finally to a skilled reader?*

---

## What's Coming?

That the brain learns to read at all attests to its remarkable ability to sift through seemingly confusing input and establish patterns and systems. For a few children with exceptional language skills, this process comes naturally; most, however, have to be taught. In the next chapter, we discuss some considerations that parents and teachers should keep in mind when teaching children to read.

# 3

# Teaching Reading for Encoding and Decoding

*Reading is to the mind what exercise is to the body.*

—Joseph Addison (1672–1719)

## BRIEF HISTORY OF TEACHING READING

Reading instruction in the United States over the past 130 years has involved two general methods: an analytical method called the *phonics* approach and a global method that encompasses the *whole-word* and the *whole-language* approaches (Figure 3.1). Phonics instruction was the earliest method for teaching reading. Children were taught the letter names and simple syllables from which they then constructed words. Emphasis was on phonics drills. In this analytical approach, bits of words were used to build syllables, then words and meaningful phrases.

At the beginning of the twentieth century, the emphasis shifted to a more global approach, and choral reading emerged. Students would spell the syllable aloud together and then pronounce it. A few decades later, the pendulum swung back, and phonics drill returned. But dissatisfaction with this method arose again in the 1940s, and the emphasis shifted back

**Figure 3.1**   The timeline from 1870 to the present shows how the predominant method of reading instruction has alternated between analytical and global approaches. Today, the emphasis has shifted toward a balanced and comprehensive approach that seeks to combine phonics instruction with enriched reading text.

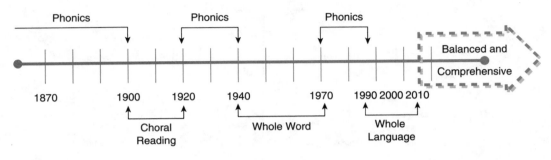

to a global approach known as whole-word instruction. The whole-word method placed little emphasis on phonics drill and more on recognizing entire words as the meaningful units of reading. The teacher showed the students a flash card with a word on it. After the teacher pronounced the word, the children would say it aloud. The small set of beginning vocabulary words was gradually expanded.

One major reason for advocating the whole-word approach was that the irregularities in the pronunciation of common words, such as *pint* (which violates the pattern of *hint, mint, tint,* etc.) and *have* (which violates the pattern of *gave, pave, save,* etc.), meant that the letter-to-phoneme correspondence was not very reliable. Therefore, emphasis should be on learning to memorize the pronunciation of whole words, not parts of words. Another argument for whole-word instruction was that it promoted comprehension early in the learning of reading: Words have meaning; speech sounds do not (Larson, 2004; Rayner et al., 2001).

In the early 1970s, concerns over the poor results on standardized reading tests prompted a shift in emphasis back to phonics drill. At the same time, a psycholinguistic approach to reading was emerging, based on the work of Smith and Goodman (1971). Psycholinguistic advocates suggested that reading was like a guessing game in which readers determined meaning through a variety of redundant cuing systems present in rich literature. This approach, which became known as the whole-language method, also suggested that phonics not be taught separately because the drills could be boring and failed to show the child that learning to read could be enjoyable. The proponents of phonics, however, were not convinced that the whole-language method (now also called the literature-based method) was effective. Thus, the so-called reading wars began in earnest and continued through the 1990s.

The reading wars are essentially over, although remnants of them still linger. In recent years, experience has taught us that no one mix of instructional strategies and curriculum materials will work for every child. As a result of the reports of the National Research Council (Snow,

Burns, & Griffin, 1998), the National Reading Panel (NRP, 2000), and the development of the Common Core State Standards for English Language Arts (NGA & CCSSO, 2010), many educators now recognize that the teaching of reading should use a balanced and comprehensive approach that includes a phonics component as well as enriched text. Furthermore, school districts in the United States need to consider whether their reading program is based sufficiently on scientific research to meet the requirements of the No Child Left Behind Act of 2001, although the act had not been reauthorized at the time of publication.

## Basic Rationale for the Balanced and Comprehensive Approach

The balanced and comprehensive approach is based on the following considerations:

- No one reading program is the best program for all children.
- Children need to develop phonemic awareness in order to learn to read successfully.
- Children need to master the alphabetic principle.
- Phonics are important but should not be taught as a separate unit through drill and rote memorization.
- Phonics should be taught to develop spelling strategies and word analysis skills.
- An important component is learning to read for meaning (**comprehension**).
- At the appropriate time, introducing enriched literature helps students develop a positive disposition toward reading and develops their ability to think imaginatively and critically.

There is still some debate about what constitutes a balanced and comprehensive reading program. For instance, although many states have adopted the Common Core State Standards for English Language Arts, some groups are already expressing concern over what types of assessment and evaluation components will accompany them. Regardless of their biases and perspectives, educators, parents, and policy makers must now recognize that scientific research has given us important insights about how the brain learns to read that cannot be ignored. We know it is a complex process, and science certainly does not have all the answers. But the information we have to date can help teachers of reading make curricular and instructional choices that are more likely to result in their students becoming successful readers.

In this chapter, we look at three aspects related to the teaching of reading. First, we examine what research is saying about the factors that enhance early literacy skills during a child's prereading period. We address what kinds of interventions can improve early literacy. Second, recognizing that reorganizing the brain to read means acquiring certain skills, we explore the research findings on what teachers can do to make skill acquisition successful. Finally, we discuss those strategies that help beginning readers become fluent readers through decoding and encoding.

# ✿ EARLY LITERACY SKILLS

After reading the first two chapters, it is clear that the more exposure to and practice with spoken language and print materials prereaders have, the more likely they are to be successful at learning to read (see Figure 3.2). These early literacy skills begin to develop and organize the cerebral networks needed to manage phonemes and morphemes, and to tackle the challenge of the alphabetic principle. This reasoning seems logical, but what research evidence exists to support it? The task of answering that question was undertaken by the National Early Literacy Panel (NELP) convened by the U.S. Department of Education, which issued its report in 2008.

The panel was charged with examining four questions: (1) What skills and abilities can predict later success in reading, spelling, and writing? (2) Which instructional approaches and interventions are linked to later success in these areas? (3) What family environments and other settings are linked to better results in later literacy? and (4) What characteristics of children are related to improved skills and abilities in later literacy? (Shanahan & Lonigan, 2010). After reviewing hundreds of research studies involving thousands of preschool and kindergarten children, the panel found the following:

**Figure 3.2**   This diagram shows the factors that research studies have found can predict success in later literacy skills. Note that factors such as socioeconomic status, race, and ethnicity are not included here because they were not reliable predictors.

**Factors Affecting a Pre-reader's Later Literacy Skills**

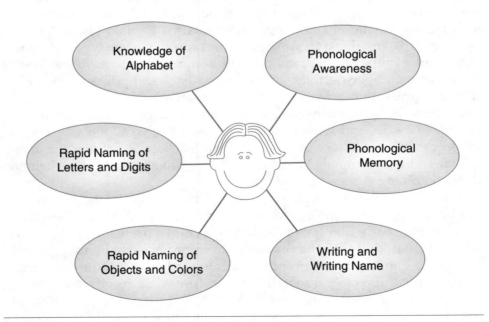

## Predictors of Success

Six variables emerged that strongly predicted later success in literacy. These variables showed a strong correlation to later skills (i.e., in first and second grade) in decoding, comprehension, and spelling:

- Knowledge of the alphabet: Knowing the names and sounds of letters.
- Phonological awareness: The ability to detect, manipulate, or analyze the sounds and auditory aspects of spoken language independent of meaning.
- Phonological memory: The ability to remember spoken information for a short period of time.
- Rapid automatized naming of letters and digits: The ability to rapidly name sequences of random letters or digits.
- Rapid automatized naming of objects and colors: The ability to rapidly name a sequence of repeating random sets of pictures of objects or colors.
- Writing and writing name: The ability to write letters in isolation or to write one's name.

Several other variables appeared, such as print knowledge and visual processing, but their predictive power was weak.

## Successful Instructional Approaches

Five categories of instructional approaches and interventions revealed positive results in helping these students with later literacy skills:

- Code-focused interventions: Interventions designed to teach skills related to cracking the alphabetic code. These involve getting children to detect and manipulate the sounds that comprise words, usually though rhyming activities.
- Shared reading interventions: Interventions that involved reading books to children. The degree of student participation in the shared reading varied, although the more interactive interventions yielded better results in later literacy.
- Parent and home programs: Interventions by parents, some of whom were taught instructional techniques to use at home with their children. The biggest impact of these interventions was on vocabulary development.
- Preschool/kindergarten programs: Studies evaluating any aspect of a preschool or kindergarten program, including educational programs, curricula, and policies. These studies showed that the greatest impact was on readiness.
- Language enhancement interventions: These studies looked at instructional strategies designed to improve young children's language development. Most were successful at improving oral language skills, including frequency of word use, and the average length of their statements.

These results demonstrate that there are strategies and interventions that parents as well as preschool and kindergarten teachers can use to improve the literacy development of young children.

### Family Settings and the Child's Characteristics

Surprisingly, the research review could not find specific family or child characteristics, such as socioeconomic status, age, race, or ethnicity, that altered the effectiveness of the instructional approaches and interventions. The results here are important signals to teachers to resist the common notion that these family and child characteristics can impede or enhance a child's *ability* to acquire literacy skills. Although their *opportunities* for exposure to literacy may have been fewer, their capacity to fill that gap is not diminished.

## ⚙ BRAIN RESEARCH AND LEARNING A SKILL

Reading is a *learned* skill, and the curriculum programs selected to teach reading must reflect what science continues to learn about how we acquire skills. Research in cognitive neuroscience indicates that learning any skill, including reading, requires some basic elements if such learning is to be successful. These elements include the following:

- *Motivation and attention.* Motivation is the key to successfully learning a skill because it keeps students interested in paying attention and in practicing the skill. Getting students' attention these days is not easy because so many other things in the environment are competing for it. Even beginning readers have already become accustomed to interacting with electronic tablets and similar devices at home. Young children have difficulty focusing on one thing for an extended period of time because their brain's attention systems are still very immature. Yet those children in preschool who are persistently inattentive during literacy instruction perform more poorly in phonemic awareness and letter naming in kindergarten one year later (Walcott, Scheemaker, & Bielski, 2010).

Naturally, interest levels and preferences vary among children. Remember, too, that learning to read requires not only focus but also considerable mental effort to sustain it. Teachers of reading can include a variety of motivational strategies, especially those that use technology. However, we need to take care that the technology becomes a means to achieving a reading goal and not an end unto itself. Children do not recognize this difference, but teachers do.

- *Intensity.* Learning a new skill requires focus and concentration. Intense focus on a new skill allows the learner's brain to build more neural support for that skill in a short period of time. If you are planning on running a marathon, occasional jogging will not have sufficient intensity to prepare and train your body. To become a skilled reader, the learner must first focus intently on the basic skills needed to learn the correct letter-to-sound relationships.

- *Practice.* For the brain to build and strengthen the neural pathways required to learn a new skill, the learner must be repeatedly exposed to, and process, the material being learned. But the practice cannot be haphazard. Remember, practice makes permanent, so it is important that the activities associated with practice be carefully planned to ensure that the learning being stored is correct. Practice does not have to be boring, either. One of the major criticisms of the total phonics approach was the repetitive and monotonous drills of the phoneme worksheets. Several publishers now have phonological practice lessons on interesting and appealing computer programs. As for reading, practice brings about true accomplishment. Studies show that the more a person reads, the better that person will be at reading at any age and at any level of proficiency.

- *Cross-training.* Learning any skill is easier if it can be supported by other skills the student already knows or is learning at the same time. Cross-training involves bringing together a wide range of skills that reinforce overall comprehension of the material. Doing so allows seemingly unrelated neural networks to establish connections, expanding the learner's ability to decode unfamiliar words and comprehend more material. Accomplished reading requires that the learner be simultaneously proficient in many different skills, such as spoken language fluency and comprehension.

- *Adaptivity.* When teaching a new skill, the teacher needs to assess the student's current skill level and adapt the new instruction accordingly. If the instructional skill level is too low, the learner may get bored and lose interest. If the skill level is too high, the learner may get frustrated and lose motivation. The secret is to differentiate instruction by finding that in-between level where the learning challenge is sufficient to motivate but not seemingly unattainable. Reading instruction should include constant monitoring of the learner's progress so that the teacher can adapt the instructional strategies as needed.

- *Awareness of skill level.* As readers gain competence in the alphabetic principle, they begin to realize that they can read and pronounce many words that they have never seen or heard before. Of course, they will make mistakes when encountering a word like *choir*, whose onset pronunciation is very different from more common words like *chair*, *chicken*, and *cheese*. Nonetheless, their success in decoding unfamiliar words empowers them while giving them the confidence to continue to practice and raise their skill level.

None of the elements mentioned above will come as a surprise to any person who has taught. Nonetheless, they are worth reviewing. With so many reading programs available, these elements become important measures that teachers can use to assess the effectiveness of materials designed to support the teaching of reading.

## MODERN METHODS OF TEACHING READING ✿

Over the past decade, trying to determine the components of a successful reading program has not been easy. First came the reports of the National Research Council (Snow et al., 1998) and the National Reading Panel (NRP,

2000). Both reports concluded that, based on scientific evidence, reading programs that included a strong phonics component were more likely to be successful with more beginning readers than programs lacking this component. The reports were met with some criticism but gained support from the No Child Left Behind legislation of 2001, which required districts to use scientifically based reading programs. To this day, some educators and politicians are not clear about what "scientifically based" means.

Meanwhile, the research using fMRI and other scanning technology continues to offer new insights into how the brains of beginning, skilled, and struggling readers differ. Furthermore, intensive interventions with struggling readers (described in Chapter 6) changed their fMRI images to resemble those of typical readers.

Educators need to make important recommendations regarding the type of reading program that is most likely to help young children learn to read successfully. Accordingly, let's consider what the major research studies have revealed about how the brain learns to read. Also included is research related to how writing improves reading. The evidence presented here comes from the following sources:

- *The National Reading Panel (NRP, 2000).* Issued in 2000, the NRP report was the result of two years of effort that included reviewing thousands of research studies on reading, interviewing parents and teachers, and recommending the most effective and scientifically proven methods for teaching reading. The NRP report took into account the report of the National Research Council and focused on the specific topics of alphabetics (phonemic awareness and phonics), fluency, vocabulary and text comprehension, teacher preparation, and the use of computer technology in reading instruction. Many of the recommendations of the NRP were translated into teaching strategies in a publication developed by the Center for the Improvement of Early Reading Achievement and funded by the National Institute for Literacy (NIFL, 2001).

- *The National Early Literacy Panel Report (NELP, 2008).* As we discussed earlier, this panel looked at hundreds of research reports involving preschool and kindergarten children to determine what skills and abilities can predict later success in reading, spelling, and writing. It also determined which instructional approaches and interventions are linked to later success in these areas.

- *Writing to Read: Evidence of How Writing Can Improve Reading* (Graham & Hebert, 2010). This report looked at research showing that writing about material enhanced students' reading comprehension, that teaching writing strengthens students' reading skills, and that increasing writing improves how well students read.

- *Laboratory Studies.* Experimental studies conducted in laboratories are also providing new information about the reading process. Using brain imaging and mapping technologies, scientists are learning more about the brain regions associated with the different stages of learning to read. More than 70,000 articles written between 2003 and 2013 can be found in scientific journals worldwide dealing with reading and the brain. Many of them include looking at the brains of people with reading problems. Findings from some of these studies offer valuable insights for teachers of reading to consider.

- *Best Practices Research.* Best practices research on reading conducted in schools involved case studies that assessed whether certain instructional practices were more effective than others. These studies examined the practices of exemplary teachers to sort out what they were doing differently than others that resulted in greater student achievement. Several of these reports have been published recently, and they offer valuable insights into the effectiveness of various strategies for teaching reading. Although some of the studies involved a small sample of students, their results cannot be dismissed.

- *Evidence-Based Practices.* Other research studies have looked at the effectiveness of practices in longitudinal and multilevel designs rather than just at exemplary teachers. Results from these types of studies are particularly valuable because they generally involve a large sample of students whose achievement is monitored for a year or more.

In this and the following chapters, we will discuss the findings of research studies and reports as they apply to the teaching of reading to children who do not display reading difficulties. Diagnosing children with reading problems, and how to address those problems, will be discussed in subsequent chapters. Figure 3.3 reminds us that reading involves the two major processes of decoding and comprehension. Successful decoding includes phonemic awareness, phonics, and fluency. Comprehension requires a developed vocabulary, interaction with the text, and a teacher whose training provides strategies for advancing the learner's ability to understand what is read.

## RESEARCH FINDINGS ON READING ✿ INSTRUCTION—DECODING

### Phonemic Awareness Instruction

Phonemic awareness, you will recall, is the ability to manipulate individual sounds in *spoken* language. Children have phonemic awareness when they can (1) recognize words beginning with the same sound, (2) isolate

Figure 3.3     Successful reading is the result of the interaction between the decoding and comprehension processes. Decoding includes phonemic awareness, phonics, and fluency. Comprehension requires adequate vocabulary and linguistic knowledge, and interaction with text to capture meaning.

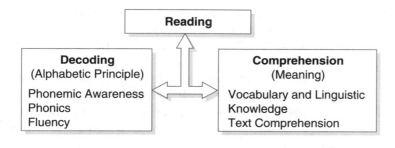

and say the first and last sounds in a word, (3) combine and blend sounds in a word, and (4) break a word into its separate sounds. Phonemic awareness and letter knowledge are the two best predictors of how well children will learn to read during their first two years of instruction. Even for middle and high school students, phonemic awareness is a good predictor of their ability to read accurately and quickly (Shaywitz, 2003). Phonemic awareness can be taught and learned.

The findings in the research (NIFL, 2001; Shankweiler & Fowler, 2004) show that phonemic awareness instruction

- helps children learn to read. Phonemic awareness is the first step in mastering the alphabetic principle, the ability to map letters onto the spoken sounds of language. As children's mapping skills get better, they can read faster and with greater comprehension;
- helps children learn to spell. Children who have phonemic awareness understand that letters and sounds are related in a particular way, and that these relationships are important in spelling;
- is most effective when children are taught to manipulate phonemes while handling cutouts of the letters of the alphabet that represent those phonemes. This allows children to see how phonemic awareness relates to their reading and writing. Learning how to blend letters with phonemes helps them to *read* words, and learning to segment letters with sounds helps them to *spell* words;
- is most effective when it focuses on only one or two types of phoneme manipulation, rather than several types. Teaching too many types at once confuses children and may not allow enough time to teach each type well. Another possibility is that it may inadvertently result in teaching more difficult types before the children have learned the simpler ones; and
- is effective under a variety of teaching conditions with a variety of learners across a range of grade and age levels. Furthermore, the improvements in reading lasted well beyond the end of the phonemic awareness training, indicating mastery in most children.

Recent brain imaging studies have also shown the following:

- Effective practice can build new neural circuits. After children are introduced to new letter-sound relationships, additional practice is necessary to ensure that the learning is committed to long-term memory.
- Learning to read depends critically on mapping the letters and the spellings of words onto the sounds of speech and speech units they represent in order to develop the visual word form area.
- Explicit instruction in the phonological structure of speech and of phonemes and their spellings helps children acquire the alphabetic principle and use it appropriately when they encounter unfamiliar words in text. Neural circuits help to map these new graphemes onto known phonemes.

## How Do I Teach Phonemic Awareness?

- Assess each child's phonemic awareness capabilities before beginning instruction. This will help identify which students should start with simple manipulation and which can move on to more advanced manipulation activities.
- A complete phonemic awareness program provides activities that include matching, isolating, substituting, blending, segmenting, and deleting sounds in words (Yopp & Yopp, 2000).
- Teach one or two types of phoneme manipulation to produce a greater benefit rather than teaching several types at once.
- Teach students to manipulate phonemes along with letters to enhance their mental lexicon. Have them say the whole word aloud and then the individual phonemes. Then write each letter on the board as they sound out its phoneme. This helps the students acquire the alphabetic principle.
- Remember that phonemic awareness instruction can benefit *all* children, including preschoolers, kindergarteners, first graders, and even less able readers.
- Avoid spending too much time on phonemic awareness activities. The whole program should average out to about 10 minutes per day. Obviously, some students will need more time than others, perhaps up to 30 minutes per day.
- Small groups are usually more productive for phonemic awareness instruction. Children can benefit from hearing their classmates and receiving feedback from the teacher.
- Preschool (and parental) instruction should focus on
  - developing an awareness of rhyme; and
  - separating words into syllables and syllables into phonemes.
- Kindergarten instruction should focus on
  - practicing the sound structure of words;
  - the recognition and production of letters; and
  - knowledge of print concepts.
- Grade 1 instruction should provide
  - explicit instruction and practice with sound structures that lead to phonemic awareness;
  - familiarity with sound-spelling correspondences and common spelling conventions and their use in identifying written words;
  - sight recognition of frequent words; and
  - independent reading, including reading aloud.
- Remember that phonemic awareness instruction is only one important part of a reading program. How well students learn to read and comprehend will depend not just on phonemic awareness but also on the effectiveness of the other components in the literacy curriculum.
- Keep in mind the importance of practice. When children learn new letter-sound correspondences, they should practice them in isolation and then in reading aloud simple sentences and books. With every bit of practice and corrective feedback, the word form that will be stored in the brain's memory is likely to be accurate in pronunciation, spelling, and meaning. Through additional practice in spelling-sound patterns, a precise replica of the word form will be established in the neural circuits, and recognition of that word again in the future becomes easier.

## Phonics Instruction

Phonics instruction teaches the relationship between phonemes of spoken language and the graphemes of *written* language, and how to use these relationships to read and write words. It includes helping children use the alphabetic principle to recognize familiar words automatically and accurately, and to decode unfamiliar words. Critics of phonics say that English spellings are too irregular for phonics instruction to be of any value. Nonetheless, phonics instruction teaches children a system for remembering how to read words. For example, when children learn that *ghost* is spelled this way and not *goast,* their memory helps them to remember the spelling and to recognize the word instantly. Although many words are spelled irregularly, most of them contain some regular letter-sound relationships that help children learn to read them. Moreover, students at risk for reading failure, such as those in special education and Title I programs, benefit the most from phonics-based programs (Foorman, Francis, Fletcher, Schatschneider, & Mehta, 1998). An examination of 22 studies showed that phonics instruction resulted in significantly higher achievement for elementary students, especially minority students (Jeynes, 2008). Phonics instruction that is systematic and explicit does all of the following:

- Makes a bigger contribution to a child's growth in reading than little or no phonics instruction.
- Significantly improves kindergarten and Grade 1 children's word recognition and spelling when compared to children who do not receive systematic instruction. It should be noted that the effects of phonics instruction on students in Grades 2 through 6 are limited to improving their oral text and word reading skills. Explicit phonics instruction beyond Grade 6 is not generally productive for most students.
- Significantly improves children's reading comprehension. This is because their increased ability for automatic word recognition allows them more time to focus on and process the meaning of text. Contrary to what some believe, research studies indicate that phonics instruction contributes to comprehension skills rather than inhibiting them.
- Is effective for children from various economic and social levels.
- Particularly helps children who are having difficulty learning to read and who are at risk for developing future reading problems.
- Is most effective when introduced in kindergarten or Grade 1.

### How Do I Teach Phonics?

Systematic instruction is characterized by the direct teaching of the letter-sound relationships of both consonants and vowels in a clearly defined sequence. Such programs give children substantial practice in applying these relationships as they read and write, as well as opportunities to spell words and write their own stories. Several approaches to teaching phonics exist, depending on the unit of analysis or how letter-sound combinations are presented to the student:

- *Analogy-based phonics*—using parts of word families to identify unknown words that have similar parts
- *Analytic phonics*—analyzing letter-sound relationships in previously learned words
- *Embedded phonics*—learning letter-sound relationships during the reading of connected text

- *Onset-rime phonics*—identifying the sound of the letter or letters before the first vowel (the *onset*) in a one-syllable word and the sound of the remaining part of the word (the *rime*)
- *Phonics through spelling*—learning to segment words into phonemes and to make words by writing letters for phonemes
- *Synthetic phonics*—learning how to convert letters or letter combinations into sounds, and then how to blend the sounds together to form recognizable words

Effective programs for phonics instruction

- include knowledge of the alphabet, phonemic awareness, vocabulary development, the reading of text, and systematic instruction in phonics;
- help teachers systematically and explicitly instruct students in how to relate sounds and letters, how to break words into sounds, and how to blend sounds to form words;
- help children understand why they are learning relationships between sounds and letters;
- help children apply their knowledge of phonics as they read text;
- help children apply what they learn about sounds and letters to their own writing; and
- can be adapted to the needs of individual students.

Systematic programs in phonics introduce the child to different letter-sound pairings, starting with the simplest and most frequent combinations and then progressing to more complex and unusual ones. One approach (Carnine, Silbert, & Kame'enui, 1997) suggests these steps:

- *Start with one-to-one letter-sound relationships.* Introduce consonants that are predictable in their relationships between the letter and their sounds. A possible sequence could begin with *m, t, s, f, d,* and *r,* and end with *k, v, w, j, p,* and *y.*
- *Continue with vowel sounds.* Vowels are needed to help make up words, but they can be more difficult for young children to pronounce than consonants. Identify long vowels that say their name, as the /a/ in *made,* the /e/ in *be,* the /i/ in *mine,* the /o/ in *row,* and the /u/ in *used.* Short vowels do not say their name, such as in *dad, tell, kid, top,* and *run.*
- *Introduce phonic units.* These usually contain six to eight consonants and two vowels. As the children master more phonic units, they should be able to pronounce a larger number of words.
- *Finish with complex letter-sound combinations.* Introduce common digraphs, such as *sh-* in *should, ch-* in *chip, th-* in *thing,* and *wh-* in *what.* Later, the children will recognize larger phonetic combinations, such as *-tch* (*witch*), *-dge* (*fudge*), and *-ough* (*cough, rough*).

Practice materials should include stories that contain words using the specific letter-sound correspondences the children are learning (often called decodable texts). Students should also have practice writing letter combinations and using them to write their own stories.

- Phonics instruction can be taught effectively to individual students, small groups, or the whole class, depending on the needs of the students and the number of adults working with them.
- Phonics lessons should last typically from 15 to 20 minutes a day, but should also be reinforced during the remainder of the day with other activities in the child's reading program, including opportunities to read and write.
- Phonics instruction should be taught for about two years for most students, usually kindergarten and Grade 1. If begun in Grade 1, it should be completed by Grade 2.

*(Continued)*

(Continued)

- Phonics instruction is but one of the necessary components of a comprehensive reading program, including phonemic awareness, fluency, and text reading and comprehension skills.
- Role reversal can be an effective strategy for helping children acquire the alphabetic principle. Ask the students to make up vocabulary words for you to write down. They should be nonsense words that the children create. Ask them to clearly enunciate each sound so that you can write the word down accurately (SEDL, 2001).
- Pay close attention to how children write. To assess their understanding of the alphabetic principle, it is not necessary for them to write accurately. It is important, however, that they write one symbol per sound; that is, a word with three phonemes should be represented in writing by three symbols.

## Spelling and Invented Spelling

In Chapter 2, we discussed the challenges of English spelling, especially compared to the transparent orthography of other common European languages, such as Spanish and Italian. Learning to spell in transparent languages requires only a modest set of brain regions to detect letters and morphemes. Although there are some rules of spelling in English, it takes more brain areas to remember and encode complex exceptions—that is, words whose pronunciation strays far from the expected. Examples are words containing the fragments *-tion, -ough,* and *-ould.* Spelling is closely linked to reading because it involves breaking apart a spoken word into its sounds and encoding them into the letters representing each sound. While learning to read words, children also learn how to spell those words. As children try to represent words with the alphabet, they often encode words by their initial consonants, followed by their ending sounds. Middle sounds, usually vowels, are omitted at first. Thus, *horse* might be written as *hrs,* and *monster* as *mstr.* The pronunciation of this invented spelling is very close to that of the intended word. Invented spelling allows children to practice applying the alphabetic principle and gain in phonemic awareness. It serves as a transitional step and assists in the development of reading and writing.

Studies on early literacy development have shown that invented spelling is a reliable measure of early reading achievement. One study found that preschool and kindergarten children who were inventive spellers performed significantly better on word reading and on storybook readings. In a literacy study of four Grade 1 classrooms, two teachers encouraged invented spelling while the other two teachers encouraged traditional spelling. The inventive spellers scored significantly better than the traditional spellers on several measures of word reading that were administered during the second semester in Grade 1 (Ahmed & Lombardino, 2000). Invented spelling was the best predictor of how well kindergartners could match, through finger-point reading, spoken words to printed words in reading a sentence—a skill known as *concept of a word in text* (Uhry, 1999). In a study of kindergarteners, the invented-spelling group learned to read more words in a learn-to-read task than groups trained in phonological awareness or drawing pictures (Ouellette & Sénéchal, 2008). The researchers suggested that invented spelling encourages children to use an analytical approach to spelling and facilitates the integration of pho-nological and orthographic knowledge.

When their invented spelling is accepted, children feel empowered to write more and with purpose, communicating their messages from the very beginning of school. Writing slows down the process of dealing with text, allowing children more time to recognize and learn about sound-letter relationships. For some children, writing may be an easier way to literacy than reading. In reading, the process involves changing letter sequences to sounds, whereas in writing the process is reversed—going from sounds to letters. Accordingly, writing may be a simpler task because it involves going from sounds in the child's head, which are already known and automatic, to letters, rather than from the unknown letters in reading to what is known (Dehaene, 2009).

Some researchers in the past have raised concerns about whether the persistent use of invented spelling leads to confusion and the formation of bad spelling habits. But research studies indicate that, with appropriate teacher intervention, the invented spellings gradually come closer to con-ventional forms. Consequently, spelling errors should be seen not as an impediment to writing but as an indication of the child's thought pro-cesses while making sense of letter-sound relationships. From that per-spective, the errors could yield important information about a child's internal reading patterns (Sipe, 2001). On the other hand, remember that practice eventually makes permanent. The consistent repetition of incor-rect spellings will, in time, lead to their storage in long-term memory. Therefore, teachers should use strategies that will help children transform invented spelling into conventional spelling.

## Does Texting Lead to Poor Spelling?

With so many young children having access to texting devices in recent years, parents and educators are wondering whether the spelling short-hand used in texting, often called "textese," will cause children to become poor spellers. It seems like a sensible fear, but recent research studies do not support this idea. In one study, 86 children aged 10 to 12 years read and wrote text messages in conventional English and in textese, and then completed tests of spelling and reading (Kemp & Bushnell, 2011). Children took significantly longer and made more mistakes when they read messages written in textese than in conventional English. Moreover, they were no faster at writing messages in textese than in conventional English, regardless of the texting method they used or their experience. However, those children who had greater speed and accuracy in reading textese also demonstrated better literacy skills. A similar study of 227 Australian children found that the students who sent more text messages had better general spelling ability than those who sent fewer (Bushnell, Kemp, & Martin, 2011).

These findings add to the growing evidence for a positive correlation between texting proficiency and traditional literacy skills, including spell-ing. But why? The best guess for now is that the child's brain needs to perform a mental word analysis to decide how best to abbreviate the word. This very act requires neural circuits to remember the word's correct spell-ing in order to convert it to textese.

## Developing Spelling Skills

Recent research studies suggest that children move through five stages as they develop their spelling skills (Bear, Invernizzi, Templeton, & Johnston, 2008). Figure 3.4 illustrates these five phases and some of their characteristics. Essentially, brain networks are not only mapping sounds to letters, but also looking for patterns to remember that will help the child decode and encode unfamiliar words in the future.

**Figure 3.4** Research seems to indicate that when learning to spell, children go through five stages. The first two stages deal with sound, both emerging sounds that resemble words and the recognition of short vowels and consonants. The next two stages deal with patterns, including diphthongs, syllables, and homophones as well as affixes. In the final stage, the child recognizes how prefixes and suffixes alter not only a word's meaning but its use in a sentence (Bear et al., 2008).

### Five Stages of Spelling Development

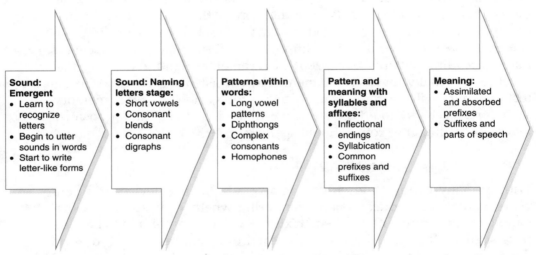

---

### How Do I Teach Spelling?

- Effective spelling instruction focuses on helping children go from sound to letter, which strongly reinforces their reading—going from letter to sound. Spelling instruction is more than memorizing word lists. It should follow a logical sequence that starts with phonemic awareness, demonstrates which letters represent which sounds, and introduces the notion that the same sound can have different spellings (Shaywitz, 2003).
- Studies show that effective primary-grade teachers combine three methods for teaching spelling (Schlagel, 2007): (1) memorization, whereby students memorize how specific words are spelled; (2) generalization, whereby students are taught directly the skills and rules for spelling unfamiliar words; and (3) developmental, whereby students extend their understanding of spelling rules through word study activities, such as word sorting.
- *Moving away from invented spelling.* Techniques, such as using sound boxes (also known as Elkonin boxes) drawn on paper, can help the child enunciate the word slowly and recognize other sounds that need to be represented by letters. For example, if the child spells *dog* as *dg,* you

draw a box for the first sound, /d/ = *duh,* and the child enters the letter *d* and puts a marker or coin on it. By stretching out the pronunciation of the word, the child hears the /ô/ = *auh* sound. Now draw another box, enter the letter *o,* and ask the child to push a marker into it. This continues until the last phoneme, /g/ = *guh,* is represented by the letter *g.* The process can be repeated until the child is confident in hearing the middle vowel sound (Figure 3.5).

**Figure 3.5**    This sound (Elkonin) box technique requires the student to move a marker (or coin) into the box several times while pronouncing the letter's sound. It helps the child detect the middle vowel sounds and thus represent them in spelling (Sipe, 2001).

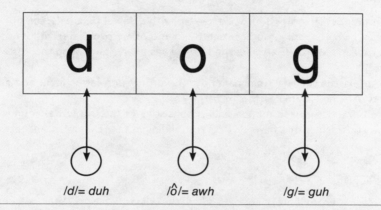

/d/= duh        /ô̂/= awh        /g/= guh

- Another technique for correcting spelling is the Have-a-Go Chart (Bolton & Snowball, 1993). Students use this chart (Figure 3.6) when they need your assistance with words they have misspelled. The student writes the misspelled word in the first column. Use the sound box (Figure 3.5) to stretch the word and ask the student to listen for phonemes. After sounding out the word several times, the student writes the word again in the Have-a-Go column. If incorrect, you can write the word correctly. The student then writes the correct word in the third column. Now encourage the student to recall the correct spelling mentally and to write it again in the fourth column to enhance retention of the correct spelling in long-term memory.

**Figure 3.6**    Students write the misspelled word in the first column. The teacher might use the sound box (Figure 3.5) to stretch the word and ask the student to listen for phonemes. The student writes the word again in the Have-a-Go column. If incorrect, the teacher either writes the word or refers the student to a dictionary. The student then writes the correct word in the third column and copies it again in the fourth column to enhance retention in long-term memory (Bolton & Snowball, 1993).

### Have-a-Go Chart

| Misspelled Word | Have-a-Go | Correct Spelling | Copied Spelling |
|---|---|---|---|
| Bots | Boats | | Boats |
| Clen | Cleen | Clean | Clean |

*(Continued)*

(Continued)

- As spelling progresses, introduce children to spelling strategies they can use to help spell new words. Later, tell them about words, like *colonel* and *could,* that do not match the spelling rules they were taught.
- A study conducted by Ahmed and Lombardino (2000) analyzed the spelling of 100 kindergarten children for letter omission and substitution, as well as letter voicing and devoicing. Based on their spelling scores, the children were identified as low, middle, or high in spelling acquisition. The researchers suggested that teachers consider the following strategies, based on the students' spelling acquisition levels:

*Low-level spellers:*

- Teach that a monosyllabic word must be spelled with a vowel (Example: *cat,* not *ct*).
- Show children how to distinguish between the name of a vowel letter and its sound in closed monosyllabic words (Example: The letter *a* has a different sound than its name in the word *cat*).
- Help children master spelling consonants that have only one letter form and a corresponding letter name (Examples: *b, d, m, p, t*).
- Have children practice closed monosyllables consisting of the five vowel sounds (*a, e, i, o, u*) and the consonants that have one corresponding letter (Examples: *bat, met, sit, not,* and *put*).

*Mid-level spellers:*

- Teach the vowel-lengthening rule by adding the silent letter *e* after a consonant (Examples: in *lake* and in *time*).
- Help children learn to spell consonants that do not have a corresponding letter name (Examples: *ch-* as in *child* and *sh-* as in *shop*).
- Teach how to spell consonant blends (Examples: *dr-* as in *drink, tr-* as in *trap, -mp* as in *damp, -ng* as in *wing,* and *-nk* as in *think*).

*High-level spellers:*

- Have children practice the spelling of frequently occurring vowel digraphs (Examples: *-ai* as in *sail, -ee* as in *bee, -oa* as in *coat*).
- Then practice the floss rule—double a word's final *-f -l,* or *-s* if it follows a short vowel (Examples: *buff, fill,* and *toss*).
- Help children understand the meaning of the suffixes *-ed* and *-ing,* and practice their spellings.

In the past, writing was often delayed until children could spell every word correctly. Such an approach inhibited the flow of thoughts necessary for children to become literate. Accepting invented spelling allowed children to engage in meaningful writing more than they ever expected. Furthermore, the processes used by teachers to correct spelling develop phonemic awareness and reading. The key to corrective spelling lies with the interventions that teachers *purposefully* use to guide children's writing from invented to conventional spellings. If left alone to grapple with the bizarre nature of English orthography, children will grow frustrated with spelling. But with appropriate teacher interventions, children can overcome the orthography maze and eventually learn the rules, patterns, and exceptions that control spelling in English.

## How Teaching Writing Can Affect Spelling and Reading

Over the past several decades, hundreds of research studies have looked at the associations between writing practices and students' reading performance. Some studies had better research designs than others. Until recently, it was a time-consuming task to sift through these studies, decide which were well designed, and then ferret out their findings. Fortunately, in 2010, the Carnegie Corporation of New York tackled this issue and published a report of a **meta-analysis** that selected nearly 100 such studies that met rigid research criteria to determine which effects were consistent and significant (Graham & Hebert, 2010). Most of the selected studies covered Grades 4 through 12, but others covered Grades 1 through 3.

The researchers used a statistical measure called *effect size* to measure the strength of the writing intervention used. A positive effect size means that the writing strategy used had a positive effect on the students' reading performance. In general, an effect size of 0.20 to 0.49 indicates a mild effect, 0.50 to 0.79 a moderate effect, and 0.80 (or larger) a strong effect.

Three major findings emerged from this extensive meta-analysis. Students' reading performance improves significantly when teachers

- ask students to write about the text they just read;
- teach students to be better writers; and
- increase the amount of time that students write.

Several other strategies, which were subsets of the major findings, also produced reasonable effect sizes. Table 3.1 summarizes the effect sizes of the three major findings and their subcategories. The meta-analysis reveals that practices such as summary writing, note-taking, answering questions, and extended response all have a positive impact on students' reading competence. These results imply that, for older students, teaching reading and writing together helps students develop more literacy skills and knowledge. These results can also guide teachers at all grade levels as they design age-appropriate writing strategies for their students.

## Fluency Instruction

**Fluency** is the ability to read a text orally with speed, accuracy, and proper expression. It represents the reader's ability to shift from concentrating on the decoding process and focusing more on the content of the text. Case studies report that fluency is one component that is often neglected in the classroom. Children who lack fluency read slowly and laboriously, often making it difficult for them to remember what has been read (recall the limited capacity of working memory) and to relate the ideas expressed in the text to their own experiences. Frequent practice in reading is one of the main contributors to developing fluency.

Fluency bridges the gap between word recognition and comprehension. Because fluent readers do not need to spend much time decoding words, they can focus their attention on the meaning of the text. With practice, word recognition and comprehension occur almost simultaneously. Of course, a student will usually not read all text with the same ease. Fluency depends on the reader's familiarity with the words, and

Table 3.1    Effect Sizes of Studies of the Impact of Writing Strategies on Reading

| Strategy | Effect Size |
|---|---|
| Major Finding: Ask students to write about the text they just read. For example, use guided journal writing to analyze a situation in the text, or complete an analytic essay about the material. | |
| • Using norm-referenced tests for evaluation | 0.40 |
| • Using researcher-designed tests for evaluation | 0.51 |
| Subcategories: | |
| • Respond to a text by writing personal reactions, and analyzing and interpreting the text. | 0.77 |
| • Write summaries of the text, including identifying the main information, and deleting trivial and redundant information. | 0.52 |
|    o All grades | |
|    o Elementary grades | 0.79 |
|    o Middle/high school grades | 0.33 |
| • Ask students to write notes about the text, including structured notes using a flow chart or creating a concept map of important concepts contained in the text. | 0.47 |
| • Ask students to answer questions in writing about the text, such as two inferences, one detail, and one main idea, or generate their own questions about the text and answer them. | 0.27 |
| Major Finding: Teach students to be better writers, such as teaching how to combine simple sentences in more complex ones, and how to write a persuasive text. | |
| • Using norm-referenced tests for evaluation | 0.18 |
| • Using researcher-designed tests for evaluation | 0.27 |
| Subcategories: | |
| • Teach spelling and sentence construction to improve reading fluency. | 0.79 |
| • Teach spelling rules to improve word reading skills. | 0.68 |
| Major Finding: Increase the amount of time students write. For example, have two writers pen pal and exchange writings about topics of interest (exchange can be between younger and older students), or ask for a daily writing sample about a topic of the students' choice. | 0.30 |

SOURCE: Graham and Hebert (2010).

with the amount of practice reading the text. The fluency of even skilled readers will slow down when encountering unfamiliar vocabulary or topics. To read with expression, readers must be able to divide sentences into meaningful chunks that include phrases and clauses. As comprehension speed increases, readers develop a sense of knowing when to pause appropriately at the ends of sentences, and when to change tone and emphasis.

## Fluency and Automaticity

Although the terms are often used interchangeably, it should be noted that fluency is not the same as automaticity. **Automaticity** is the fast and effortless word recognition that comes after a great deal of reading practice. It does not refer to reading with expression. Thus, automaticity is necessary, but not sufficient, for fluency. Two approaches, each of which has several variations, have been used to teach fluency:

- *Guided repeated oral reading.* This approach encourages students to read passages aloud several times and receive systematic and explicit guidance and feedback from the teacher.
- *Independent silent reading.* This approach encourages students to read silently on their own, inside and outside the classroom, with minimal guidance and feedback.

Researchers have investigated these two main approaches and have found the following (NIFL, 2001):

- Monitored *repeated oral reading* improves reading fluency and overall reading achievement. Students who read passages aloud and receive guidance from their teachers become better readers because this process improves word recognition, speed, accuracy, and fluency. It also improves reading comprehension, but to a lesser extent. This approach even helps struggling readers at the higher elementary grade levels.

- *Round-robin reading*—where students take turns reading parts of a text aloud, but not repeatedly—in itself does not increase fluency. This may be because students usually read a small amount of text and only once. Furthermore, the children are likely to pay attention only when it is their turn to read.

- Children become good readers when they gain an increased sensitivity for how the printed word relates to how it is pronounced. This ability requires the child to pay attention to letter strings and the phoneme sequences in those strings. Children who have attained this ability can read pronounceable nonwords, and the pronunciation errors that they make in reading are plausible. When this occurs, the child's brain is apparently doing some form of phonological recoding—that is, recoding the spellings so they can be pronounced. Opportunities for this recoding occur when children read aloud to a parent or teacher. Feedback from these attempts build up the child's recognition of the written (orthographic) form of unfamiliar words. Several research studies conclude that reading aloud promotes the acquisition of printed word representations in the child's mental lexicon and builds meaning (Biemiller & Boote, 2006). Not surprisingly, other studies have found that students' oral reading fluency in first, second, and third grades is a reliable predictor of how well they score on high-stakes tests of reading comprehension at the end of third grade (Wanzek et al., 2010).

- Many studies indicate that good readers read the most and poor readers read the least. The suggestion here is that the more children read, the better their fluency, vocabulary, and comprehension. However, these findings do not indicate cause and effect. It is possible that the more children read, the better their fluency. But it may just be that better readers simply choose to read more.

- The popular belief that fluency was a direct result of proficiency in word recognition is not supported by recent research. Although word recognition is a necessary skill, fluency is now seen as a separate component that can be developed through instruction. Informal reading inventories (IRIs), running records, and miscue analysis are appropriate measures for identifying problems that students are having with word recognition, but are not suitable measures of fluency. Simpler measures, such as calculating words read correctly per minute, are more appropriate for monitoring fluency.

- Research evidence remains inconclusive on whether instructional time spent on *independent silent reading* with minimal guidance and feedback improves fluency and overall reading achievement in young readers. There are hundreds of studies showing that the best readers read the most and the poorest readers read the least. But these studies yield correlations, and a correlation does not mean causation. It could just be that better readers simply decide to read more. Some studies have found no correlation between silent reading and improved fluency, including in the primary grades (e.g., Prior et al., 2011; Reutzel, Fawson, & Smith, 2010), or improved comprehension (e.g., Hale et al., 2010).

- Given that instructional time is limited, there may be better ways to spend reading time in the classroom than silent reading. Nonetheless, you should encourage students to read more outside of school rather than devote instruction time to independent reading. Students could also read on their own in class during independent work time when, for example, they have finished one activity and are waiting for another one to begin. Independent reading does build a reader's vocabulary. Some researchers estimate that young readers who engage in independent reading for just 10 minutes a day read over 600,000 more words each year than students who do no independent reading. Increasing the reading time to 20 minutes a day raises the words read to over 2 million a year (Hart & Risley, 2003).

## How Do I Teach Fluency?

- Have students read aloud and provide effective guidance and feedback to improve their fluency. Students need instruction in fluency (a) when their word recognition errors exceed 10 percent when reading a text they have not practiced, (b) when they cannot read orally with expression, or (c) when their comprehension is poor after reading a text orally.
- Combine reading instruction with opportunities for your students to read books at their independent level of reading ability. One technique is to use *literature circles* where small groups of students discuss a piece of literature in depth. The group is formed by the choice of the book rather than by ability. Literature circles allow students to discuss, on their own, events, characters, and their own personal experiences related to the story. This process helps students engage in reflection and critical thinking as well as construct

meaning in their interactions with other students. For more information on literature circles, see the "Resources" section.

- Read aloud daily to your students. By your being a good model of fluent reading, students learn how a reader's voice can help text make sense. Then have the students reread the text, perhaps up to four times to improve fluency. Students can practice reading aloud in several ways. The methods are listed in Figure 3.7 in the order of increasing student independence and of decreasing teacher involvement (Carbo, 2003).

- *Shared reading.* This is an interactive reading activity in which students join in the reading of a large book as guided by the teacher. After placing the book on an easel so it can be easily seen, the teacher uses a pointer to guide the reading, pointing to the words as they are read. The teacher may wish to read the text first, asking students to predict a word or phrase or summarize what is happening. Later, the teacher and students take turns reading, and choral reading may also occur. The goal is to work toward phrase fluency rather than reading the text word by word.

- *Student-adult reading or neurological impress.* In this one-on-one method, the adult provides a model of fluent reading by reading the text first. The student then reads the text, and the adult provides encouragement and assistance as needed. The student rereads the passage three or four times until fluency is attained. In a variation of this method, called neurological impress, the teacher reads a passage softly into the student's dominant ear as they both use their fingers to follow along in the text.

- *Tape/digital-assisted reading.* An audiotape or digital recording of a fluent reader is used for this strategy. The reader should read at a speed of about 80 to 100 words per minute to ensure that the students can follow the words and gain meaning. At first, the students read the passage to themselves. Then they listen to the recording and follow along, pointing to the words in their books as the reader says them. Next, the students read aloud along with the recording several times until they can read the text independently.

- *Choral (unison) reading.* Students read along as a group with an adult reader, either from a big book or from their own copy. Choose a text that is short and aimed at the independent reading ability of most students. Begin reading and invite students to join in as they

**Figure 3.7** This diagram illustrates the range of teacher and student involvement for various models of teaching reading.

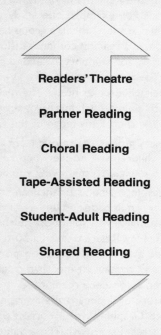

More Student Independence
Less Teacher Involvement

**Readers' Theatre**

**Partner Reading**

**Choral Reading**

**Tape-Assisted Reading**

**Student-Adult Reading**

**Shared Reading**

Less Student Independence
More Teacher Involvement

SOURCE: Adapted from Carbo (2003).

*(Continued)*

(Continued)

recognize the words you are reading. After three or four readings, the children should be able to read the text independently.

- *Partner or paired reading.* This technique pairs a more fluent reader with a less fluent reader. The more fluent student reads first, providing a model of fluency. Then the less fluent student reads aloud while the stronger partner provides assistance with word recognition and feedback. Another format is to pair readers of similar fluency to reread parts of a story to each other.
- *Readers' theatre.* In this activity, students rehearse (but do not memorize) and then perform a play in front of their classmates. They read from scripts that have been taken from books rich in dialogue. A narrator may be used to give any necessary background information, and the students read lines as characters in the play. This novel approach provides an enjoyable opportunity for rereading text, practicing fluency, and promoting cooperation among the students in the class. Numerous studies show the effectiveness of readers' theatre. For example, one study of nearly 200 fifth-grade students found that the students in a readers' theatre group had significantly higher achievement scores in word recognition and reading comprehension (Trainin & Andrzejczak, 2006). Readers' theatre is appropriate for students in second grade through high school.
- Consider having other adults, such as parents and other family members, read to the class and to their children at home. The more models of fluent reading the children hear, the better. Such an approach increases the children's vocabulary, their familiarity with written language, and their knowledge of the world.
  - o In primary grades, read aloud from a big book while pointing to each word as you read it. The children will notice when you are raising or lowering your voice, and you may need to explain to them why you are reading a sentence in a certain tone.
- Fluency develops when students can read a text repeatedly with a high degree of success; that is, they can decode and understand about 95 percent of the words. If the text is more difficult, students will spend so much effort and time on decoding that they will not develop fluency. Restrict text to 50 to 200 words, depending on the age of the reader, and include a variety of nonfiction, poetry, and stories to maintain interest.
- Because they contain rhyme, rhythm, and meaning, poems are an easy and enjoyable way for children to practice reading.
- One measure of fluency is the average number of words the student can read correctly in a minute. Graphing words correct per minute (WCPM) throughout the year can show a student's reading growth. These values can be compared to published norms to determine whether students are making suitable progress in their reading fluency. After making the WCPM calculation, compare the result to average oral reading frequency norms. Some local school districts have set their own norms to help teachers assess their students' progress in fluency. Table 3.2 lists oral reading frequency norms compiled by Hasbrouck and Tindal (2006). Figure 3.8 suggests a sample graph for Grade 2 that you could use to show a student's progress in WCPM throughout the school year.

Table 3.2   Average Reading Rates for Students in Grades 1 to 8

| Grade Level | Words Correct per Minute by End of Year (50th Percentile and Above) |
|---|---|
| 1 | 53–111 |
| 2 | 89–142 |

| Grade Level | Words Correct per Minute by End of Year (50th Percentile and Above) |
|---|---|
| 3 | 107–162 |
| 4 | 123–180 |
| 5 | 139–194 |
| 6 | 150–204 |
| 7 | 150–202 |
| 8 | 151–199 |

SOURCE: Adapted from Hasbrouck and Tindal, 2006

**Figure 3.8**   This is a sample graph of a student's WCPM scores throughout the school year. It is an easy way to show progress in developing reading fluency. In this example, the student's progress was monitored monthly, but less frequent assessments are also appropriate.

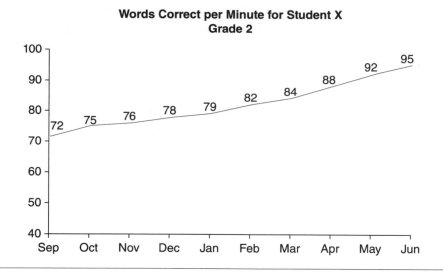

**Words Correct per Minute for Student X**
**Grade 2**

## Answer to Test Question #4

**Question:** Research studies have concluded that neither the phonological approach nor the whole-language approach is more effective in teaching most children how to read.

**Answer:** *False.* Numerous research studies have found that mastering the alphabetic principle does not come naturally to most children, and that instructional techniques that explicitly teach this principle through phonological awareness are more effective with most children than those that do not.

**QUESTIONS FOR DISCUSSION/REFLECTION**

- *What are the basic characteristics of the various approaches to reading instruction?*
- *What strategies are effective for teaching phonemic awareness, phonics, spelling, fluency, vocabulary, and comprehension?*
- *What strategies are effective for teaching reading to students who have limited English proficiency?*

## What's Coming?

Now that we have explored strategies for teaching phonological awareness, writing, spelling, and fluency, we turn our attention to text comprehension. Surprisingly, it is possible for beginning and intermediate readers to read aloud with confidence and fluency, yet not have much of a clue about *what* they are reading. Sometimes, teachers assume that a fluent reader is also a comprehending reader. But that is not always the case. In the next chapter, we take a look at strategies designed to increase vocabulary and to help students understand what they read.

# 4

# Teaching Reading for Comprehension

*The more that you read, the more things you will know. The more that you learn, the more places you'll go.*

—Dr. Seuss, *I Can Read With My Eyes Shut!*

## RESEARCH FINDINGS ON READING ✿ INSTRUCTION—COMPREHENSION

The ultimate goal of reading is for children to become sufficiently fluent to understand what they read. This understanding includes literal comprehension as well as more sophisticated reflective understandings, such as "Why am I reading this?" and "What is the author's point?" Reading comprehension depends heavily on spoken language comprehension. As children master the skill of word identification, their reading comprehension improves dramatically. Reading comprehension is a complex cognitive process that relies on several components to be successful. To develop reading comprehension skills, children need to

- develop their vocabulary and linguistic knowledge; and
- thoughtfully interact with the text to derive meaning.

Let us take a look at each of these areas and review the relevant research.

## Vocabulary and Linguistic Knowledge Instruction

*Vocabulary* refers to the words we know that allow us to communicate effectively. Words that we use in our speech or that we recognize when listening comprise our *oral* vocabulary. Words we recognize or use in print comprise our *reading* vocabulary. Oral vocabulary becomes the basis for comprehension in reading. A child with a good grasp of the alphabetic principle can encounter an unfamiliar printed word and decode the word into speech. If the word is in the mental lexicon, the child will be able to understand it. However, if the word is not in the lexicon, the child will have to determine its meaning by other methods. Consequently, the larger the child's oral vocabulary, the more easily the child will comprehend text. As children learn, pronounce, and use more words in their speech and reading, their linguistic knowledge develops. They get more confident in their understanding of letter-sound combinations, more adept at recognizing syntactic and semantic differences, and more aware of the various classes of words (e.g., adjectives, nouns, and verbs) used in a sentence.

---

### What Are Decodable Texts?

Some confusion exists about what constitutes a decodable text. Why does this confusion exist?

First, the word *decodable* is used differently by researchers and by educators and policy makers. In research studies, *decodability* is a measure of the regularity of word pronunciation as decoded by the reader's phonological module. It does not refer specifically to phonics instruction. To educators and policy makers, however, decodable text contains a certain number of words that students are expected to be able to pronounce (i.e., decode) as a result of phonics lessons already taught.

Second, the documents issued by educators and policy makers offer many different definitions of a decodable text. In general, the documents state that a decodable text should be composed of words that use the letter-to-sound correspondences that have already been taught, but there is no universal agreement on what the percentage of such words should be. Several states have mandated a minimum decodability for their beginning reading texts. For example, California requires at least 75 percent decodability, while Texas sets the minimum at 80 percent (Mesmer, 2006).

---

The scientific research on vocabulary instruction reveals that some vocabulary must be taught directly but that most vocabulary is learned indirectly. The research also has shown the following:

• Children learn the meanings of most words indirectly, through everyday experiences with oral and written language. These experiences include conversations with other people, listening to adults read to them, and reading on their own. They learn vocabulary words directly when they are explicitly taught individual words and word-learning strategies.

• Some vocabulary should be taught directly. Direct instruction is particularly effective for teaching difficult words representing complex concepts that are not part of the children's everyday experiences.

• Repeated exposure to vocabulary in many contexts aids word learning and linguistic knowledge. The more children see, hear, and read specific words, the better they learn them and their various meanings.

• Vocabulary acquisition can be affected by several factors. In the last major broad review of the research literature on vocabulary, Swanborn and de Glopper (1999) found that factors such as ability, age, and text density have an impact on the chances that students will learn new words in context. Table 4.1 shows the factors and their influence on vocabulary acquisition. Low-ability students have only an 8 percent chance of learning new words in context, but that number climbs to 19 percent for high-ability students. Not surprisingly, students in Grade 11 have a 33 percent chance of learning new words while fourth graders have only an 8 percent chance. Text density measures the number of new words per given number of words. The lower the text density (1 new word in 150), the greater the chances of learning a new word (30 percent). The chances drop to only 7 percent when the text density reaches to 1 new word in 10.

**Table 4.1** Factors Influencing Chances of Learning New Words in Context

| Factor | | Chances of Learning New Word |
|---|---|---|
| *Ability:* | Low | 8 percent |
| | Medium | 12 percent |
| | High | 19 percent |
| *Age:* | Grade 4 | 8 percent |
| | Grade 11 | 33 percent |
| *Text Density:* | | |
| | 1 new word in 10 words | 7 percent |
| | 1 new word in 74 words | 14 percent |
| | 1 new word in 150 words | 30 percent |

SOURCE: Swanborn and de Glopper (1999).

• Linguistic knowledge includes one's ability to (1) hear, distinguish, and categorize the sounds of speech (phonology); (2) understand the rules that constrain how words are put together in phrases and sentences (syntax); and (3) understand the meaning of individual words and sentences and the relationships between them (semantics).

## How Do I Teach Vocabulary?

***Selecting Vocabulary.*** Selecting which vocabulary words to teach separately is an important instructional decision. To help in this selection process, consider the following:

- Be sure to teach those terms that are central to the unit of study. These should be terms that are so important that students who do not understand them will have difficulty comprehending the text. Avoid selecting words that will have little value to students after they complete the unit test.
- Remember the capacity limits of working memory and keep the number of new words per lesson to no more than five for elementary students and up to seven for secondary school students. This will give you more time to teach each word in depth, resulting in greater student comprehension.
- Choose other new words with care. Although a chapter may have 10 to 15 new words, only 3 or 4 may address critical components of the chapter. Avoid selecting words in the text just because they are italicized or in boldface print, or words that the student will never encounter again.
- Include words that will be used continually throughout the text or unit of study. Having a deep understanding of these words will allow students to build on them as they develop new information over the long term.

***Other Guidelines.*** Here are some other guidelines for teaching vocabulary.

- You can promote indirect learning of vocabulary by doing each of the following:
  - Reading aloud to your students, regardless of the grade level or subject that you teach. Students of all ages will learn vocabulary better if you read text containing difficult words. Discuss the text before, during, and after you read to help students attach meaning to unfamiliar words by connecting them to past knowledge and experiences. Then ask the students to use the newly learned words in their own sentences.
  - Encouraging students to read extensively on their own.
- You will not have time to teach directly all the words that students might not know in a text. In fact, it is better not to try to teach all the unknown words so that students can develop their own word-learning strategies. Word-learning strategies include using the following resources:
  - *Dictionaries and other reference aids.* Students need to learn how to use dictionaries, thesauruses, and glossaries to deepen and broaden their knowledge of words. You can show them how to find an unknown word in the classroom or online dictionary and note that there may be several different definitions for the word. Read the definitions one at a time and have the class discuss which one is more likely to fit the context of the story. For example, in the sentence "The workers went into the mine," the children may confuse *mine* with the possessive word form. After you finish reading the various definitions from the dictionary, the students can eliminate the inappropriate definitions and settle on "a hole made in the earth to find coal or minerals."
  - *Information about word parts to figure out the meanings of words in text.* Word parts include affixes (prefixes and suffixes), base words, and word roots. Students learn that certain affixes change the meaning of words in a specific way. For example, the prefix *dis-* usually means the negative or reverse of the root word's meaning (*disrespect* means showing no respect). Base words are words from which many other words can be formed. The base word *complete* can form the words *completely, incomplete,*

*incompleteness, completion,* and *completing.* Word roots are the words from other languages (mainly Latin and Greek) that are the origin of many English words.

- o *Context clues to determine the meaning of words.* Context clues are hints about the meaning of an unknown word that are provided by the words, phrases, and sentences that surround the word. The clues may be descriptions, examples, definitions, or restatements. However, not all context clues are helpful, because they give little information about a word's meaning. Descriptive words that are used in a literary or obscure way are particularly difficult to comprehend through context clues. For example, in the sentence "She gave a strained response," *strained* could have a number of meanings in this context, such as *squeaky, hoarse, noisy, difficult, tense,* and so on.
- o *Associating an image with a word.* Imagery is a powerful memory device. Whenever students can associate an image (or other symbolic representation) with a new word, they are more likely to remember the word and its meaning. What we are doing here is strengthening the connections between the brain's visual recognition and language processing systems.

- With early readers, you will probably be able to teach about 10 new words per week. Focus your teaching time on the following types of words:

  - o *Important words.* Directly teach those new words that are important for comprehending a concept or the text. Give the students some word-learning strategies to figure out the meanings of other words in the text.
  - o *Useful words.* Teach directly words that students are likely to encounter and use repeatedly. For example, it is more useful for students to learn the word *biology* than *bionic,* and the word *journey* is more useful than *excursion.*
  - o *Difficult words.* Provide instruction for words that are particularly difficult for the students. Especially challenging are words that are spelled or pronounced the same but have different meanings, depending on the context. Here are but a few examples of words that are spelled the same but have different meanings in a sentence:

    The bandage was *wound* around the *wound.*

    When shot at, the *dove dove* into the bushes.

    She did not *object* to the *object.*

    They were too *close* to the door to *close* it.

Problems also arise with words that are spelled and pronounced the same, but have different meanings, such as *store* (a place to buy things) and *store* (to put away), *land* (a piece of ground) and *land* (to bring down an airplane), and *arms* (limbs) and *arms* (weaponry).

- When selecting reading texts, it is important to know the level of word knowledge that students will have for those texts. Students know the vocabulary words in their mental lexicon in varying degrees that researchers divide into the following three levels:

  - o An *unknown* word is completely unfamiliar, and its meaning is unknown.
  - o An *acquainted* word is somewhat familiar, and the student has some idea of its basic meaning.
  - o An *established* word is very familiar, and the student can immediately recognize its meaning and use the word correctly.

Assess the child's level of familiarity with the words in a specific text according to these three categories. If the assessment indicates few or no unknown words, consider selecting a more difficult text to challenge the child and to build vocabulary.

## How Do I Teach Linguistic Knowledge?

Linguistic knowledge refers to one's understanding phonology, syntax, and grammar. It is a critical element in learning to read. Here are some ways to assess a student's linguistic knowledge (SEDL, 2001):

- *Phonology.* To assess phonological skill, play the "same or different" game by generating pairs of words that either are identical or differ in some subtle way. Say them aloud and ask if they are the same or different. Most children should not miss hearing the different ones. Sometimes children can hear the differences between similar-sounding words, such as *glow* and *grow,* but have difficulty articulating that difference in their own speech. Difficulty with articulation does not mean difficulty with perception. When a child mispronounces a word, say the mispronounced word back to the child as a question. The child with normal phonologic skills will repeat the statement, trying to make you understand the meanings.

- *Syntax.* The rules of English prohibit the haphazard arrangement of words in a sentence. Poor syntax can make meaning ambiguous (see Chapter 2). One way to assess syntactic skill is to give the children sentences with a key word missing. Ask them to supply the word that would correctly fill the blank. Remember that a child's answer may not make sense, yet still be syntactically correct. Develop syntactic skills by helping children build more complex sentences. For example, after showing a short video, ask students to describe something they saw or heard ("I saw a tree" or "I heard a bird"). Then ask them to build their sentences ("I saw a tree and heard the bird singing").

- *Semantics.* Semantics describes meaning. One way to assess semantics is to create sentences and stories that have logical inconsistencies and see if the children can detect them ("Mary went to the store because she enjoys staying home"). Instructional activities that develop semantics include asking children to substitute words (synonyms) that would have the same meaning in context, and suggesting that they use context to guess the meaning of unknown words.

### Text Comprehension

As we mentioned earlier, just because readers are able to sound out words does not guarantee that they will comprehend what they read. Many reading teachers have witnessed group reading sessions where students could sound out a story with great effort but really had little understanding of what had been read. Children who are first learning to sound out words are using substantial mental effort, so fewer cerebral resources remain for the cognitive operations needed to comprehend the words being read aloud. It is critical for children to develop fluency in word recognition. When they are fluent, word recognition requires far less mental effort, freeing up the child's cognitive capacity for understanding what is read. Thus, explicit instruction in word recognition to the point of fluency is a vital component for text comprehension.

Tan and Nicholson (1997) conducted a study that showed the importance of word-recognition instruction to the point of fluency. Struggling primary-level readers who were taught new words with instruction that emphasized word recognition to the point of fluency (i.e., they practiced reading the individual words until they could recognize them automatically) answered more comprehension questions correctly than did students who experienced instruction emphasizing individual word meanings (i.e., instruction involving mostly student-teacher discussions about word meanings). Having a student-teacher discussion about the reading passage topic, prior to actually reading it, improves comprehension, even in poor readers. Prior knowledge of the passage topic was found in one study to significantly increase fluency and reduce reading errors in poor readers (Priebe, Keenan, & Miller, 2012). Possessing prior knowledge of the reading topic could be stimulating neural networks and visual processing sites, thus making word recognition less challenging.

Text comprehension occurs when readers derive meaning as a result of intentionally interacting with the text. Such comprehension is enhanced when readers actively relate the ideas represented in print to their own knowledge and experiences and can construct mental representations in their memory. Hence, good readers are both purposeful and active. Purposeful means they may read to find out how to use a computer, read a magazine for entertainment, read a classic novel for enjoyment, read a guidebook to gather information about a tourist spot, or read a textbook needed for a course. Good readers are active in that they get the most out of their reading by using their experiences and knowledge about the world, their understanding of vocabulary and language structure, and their knowledge of reading strategies. When problems with reading occur, they know how to solve them.

The scientific research on text comprehension reveals the following:

- Comprehension is a complex interactive process that begins with identifying words by using knowledge outside the text, accessing word meaning in context, recognizing grammatical structures, drawing inferences, and self-monitoring to ensure that the text is making sense. When confronted with several meanings for a word in a sentence, the brain needs to select the one that makes sense in context. How this happens is the subject of much research. One possible mechanism, called the *structure-building framework* (Gernsbacher, Robertson, Palladino, & Werner, 2004), suggests that readers construct meaning by activating mental representations of concepts that are relevant to the text and blocking those that are irrelevant. Figure 4.1 illustrates the cognitive mechanism, using the example of a reader encountering the sentence "The man planted a tree on the bank." *Bank* has two common meanings, but only one fits the context of this sentence. The mental lexicon may activate both at first, but skilled readers quickly suppress the irrelevant meaning. Less skilled readers, however, spend more time considering alternative meanings and may not make the correct selection in the end. Many English words have dozens of meanings, depending on their context. Thus, developing the ability to quickly block irrelevant meanings becomes a necessity for reading fluency and comprehension. (This process is similar to the syntactic blocking described in Chapter 1, whereby syntactic rules are blocked for the formation of irregular verbs.)
- Text comprehension is improved by direct, explicit instruction that helps readers use specific strategies to make sense of the passage. These strategies represent the purposeful steps that enable readers to reason strategically whenever they encounter barriers to understanding what they are reading. Comprehension strategies include self-monitoring, graphic and semantic organizers, answering questions, generating questions, recognizing story structure, and summarizing.

*(Continued)*

(Continued)

- Teaching comprehension strategies in the context of specific academic areas can be effective at all grade levels. Cooperative learning is a particularly useful technique for helping students to understand content-area texts (see Chapter 7).

**Figure 4.1**    This diagram illustrates how the brain deals with multiple meanings of a word. Spoken language experience activates the relevant meaning while blocking the irrelevant meaning.

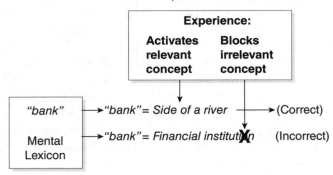

## How Do I Teach for Text Comprehension?

Text comprehension occurs when the brain's frontal lobe is able to derive meaning by processing the visual and auditory input that result from reading with the reader's prior knowledge. Teachers should emphasize text comprehension as early as the primary grades, rather than waiting until children have mastered reading basics. The basics of decoding can be learned in a few years, but reading to learn subject matter does not occur automatically and requires constructing meaning at all grade levels.

**Start Teaching Comprehension Strategies Early.** At what grade level can teachers begin to include instruction in comprehension strategies? Tradition curricula have favored honing word-recognition skills in the primary grades while developing comprehension skills in the later grades. Research studies suggest, however, that instruction aimed at improving comprehension (i.e., instruction beyond word-recognition) does make a significant impact on literacy during the primary years (NRP, 2000; Stahl, 2004). Student reading achievement in the primary grades improved when decoding and word recognition were taught systematically with comprehension strategies. This approach was particularly effective in raising reading achievement for children in high-poverty schools (Taylor, Pearson, Clark, & Walpole, 2000).

The instructional approaches that have received the strongest support from scientific research are the following (NIFL, 2001; Stahl, 2004):

- *Comprehension monitoring.* This is a self-monitoring strategy to help students recognize when they understand what they are reading and when they do not. They also learn appropriate strategies for resolving problems in comprehension. Metacognition (thinking about our own thinking) is an effective means of monitoring comprehension. Before reading, simply ask your students to clarify their purpose for reading this text and preview the text with them. As part of the preview, ask the students what they already know about the content of the selection. During reading, they should monitor their understanding and adjust their reading speed to match the difficulty of the text. Students can use several different forms of monitoring, such as

- o identifying where the difficulty occurs ("I don't understand the third paragraph on page 10");
- o identifying what the difficulty is ("I don't know what the author means when he says...");
- o restating the difficult passage in their own words ("Oh, so the author means...");
- o looking back through the text ("The author talked about...in the previous chapter. Maybe I should reread that chapter to find out what he is talking about now"); or
- o looking ahead in the text for information that might help resolve the difficulty ("Oh, the next section seems to have some information that may help me here").

After reading, they should summarize in their own words what they understood from the passage. Their summaries can be addressed to the teacher or shared with other students in cooperative learning groups.

- *Using graphic and semantic organizers.* Graphic organizers are effective visual tools for illustrating the interrelationships among concepts in a text. Known by many different names (e.g., *frames, clusters, webs, text maps, visual organizers*), they provide cues about connections between and among ideas that can help students better understand difficult concepts. Semantic organizers look a little like a spider web. They have lines connecting a main idea to a variety of related ideas and events. Both of these types of organizers help students read to learn subject matter in all content areas because they capitalize on the brain's innate aptitude for remembering patterns. Figure 4.2 illustrates examples of a spider map and a semantic map that can be used to enhance reading comprehension. Chapter 7 contains more on different types of graphic organizers. Moreover, the Internet has numerous sites with many different types of organizers for use at all grade levels. See the "Resources" section of the book for information on these sites.

**Figure 4.2** Visual organizers come in many forms. Here are examples of a spider map of types of mammals (left) and a semantic map for a simple classification of living things.

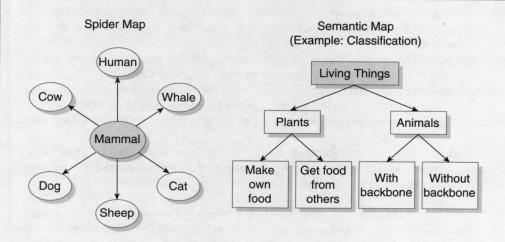

*(Continued)*

(Continued)

- *Answering questions.* Research and case studies show that teachers' questions strongly support and advance how much students learn from reading (e.g., Argus, 2012). The questions are effective because they

  - give students a purpose for reading;
  - focus the students' attention on what they are to learn;
  - help students to interact with what they read;
  - encourage students to monitor their comprehension; and
  - help students relate what they are learning to what they already know. The instruction helps readers learn to answer questions that require an understanding that is

    - *text explicit*—stated explicitly in a single sentence;
    - *text implicit*—implied by information presented in two or more sentences; or
    - *scriptal*—not found at all in the text, but part of the reader's prior knowledge or experience.

- *Generating questions.* Teaching students to ask their own questions helps them become aware of whether they understand what they are reading. By generating their own questions, students focus on the purpose of the reading, improve their active mental processing, and learn to integrate information from different segments of the text.
- *Recognizing story structure.* Story structure describes how the events and content of a story are organized into a plot. Teaching about story structure helps students learn to identify categories of content, such as initiating events, goals, setting, internal reactions, and outcomes. How this content is organized into a plot can often be revealed through story maps. Story maps are a type of graphic organizer that illustrates the sequence of events in a simple story. They can be powerful aids for understanding and remembering stories (see Figure 6.2).
- *Summarizing.* When summarizing, students synthesize and integrate the most important information and concepts in the text. To do this successfully, students must identify the main ideas, connect them to each other, eliminate unnecessary information, and remember what they read.
- *Mental imagery.* Readers (especially young readers) who form mental pictures, or images, during reading understand and remember what they read better than readers who do not visualize. Urge readers to form visual images of what they are reading, such as picturing a character, event, or setting described in the text. This will not be easy because children today are exposed to technology that provides many images for them. Consequently, they have little practice at imaging and need to be given clear directions on how to do it.
- *Paraphrasing.* This strategy aids in comprehension by having students first hear the text read aloud, then reading it quietly themselves and taking notes, rewriting it in their own words, and discussing their paraphrased text with their classmates. Paraphrasing is effective because it involves reading, writing, speaking, and listening, all of which lead to a deeper understanding and greater memory of the text (Hagaman, Casey, & Reid, 2012).

Another particularly effective strategy for developing comprehension focuses on reading and other activities related to a central theme. Because the varied classroom activities center on this theme, students can more easily comprehend their related readings (NIFL, 2001).

- *Concept-oriented reading instruction (CORI).* The teaching framework for CORI includes four phases: (1) observe and personalize, (2) search and retrieve, (3) comprehend and integrate, and (4) communicate to others. Here is an example of how CORI was implemented in one school. First, the teachers identified a conceptual theme for instructional units to be taught for 16–18 weeks in the fall and spring. The themes selected by third-grade teachers were the adaptations and habitats of birds and insects for the fall. In the spring, the third-grade units were weather, seasons, and climate. Fifth-grade units in the fall were life cycles of plants and animals, and the spring units emphasized earth science, including the solar system and geological cycles.

At the beginning of each unit, students performed observation and hands-on activities both outside and inside the classroom. Third and fifth graders participated in such activities as collecting and observing crickets, constructing spider webs, dissecting owl pellets, and building weather stations. Within each activity, students personalized their learning by composing their own questions as the basis for observing, reading, and writing. Student questions included a structural focus, such as "How many types of feathers does a bird have?" Then conceptual questions, such as "Why does that bird have such a long beak?" evolved as students attempted to explain the phenomena they had observed. These questions generated opportunities for self-directed learning. Students chose their own subtopics, found particular books, selected peers for interest-based activities, and constructed their goals for communicating to others.

The second phase of the CORI framework consisted of searching and retrieving information related to the students' questions. Students were taught how to use the library, find books, locate information within expository texts, and use a diversity of community resources. In addition, direct strategy instruction was provided to help students integrate information across sources including texts, illustrations, references, and human experts. Along with informational texts, woven through the instruction were stories, folklore, novels, and poetry. Most of the teachers began the units with a narrative related to the theme that students read at the same time they were conducting science observations. Following observation and the formation of conceptual questions, teachers moved to the informational texts. As students concluded their in-depth study of multiple informational texts, teachers introduced novels, novelettes, and poetry related to the conceptual theme of the unit.

The last phase of the CORI framework is communicating to others. Having gained expertise in a particular topic, students were motivated to speak, write, discuss, and display their understanding to other students and adults. In both third- and fifth-grade classrooms, students made posters, wrote classroom books, and composed extended displays of their knowledge. One class made a videotape of its weather unit, providing a lesson on weather prediction and an explanation for the rest of the school.

## How Effective Is CORI?

Several studies have looked at the effectiveness of CORI in the classroom. One study of Grade 5 students that included both low and high achievers in reading found that both groups benefitted from CORI when compared to similar student groups in traditional instruction (Guthrie et al., 2009). Figure 4.3 shows the pre- and posttest results of these groups. Although all students benefited from instruction in topics such as comprehension skills, fluency, concept usage, decoding, and inferencing, the students in the CORI groups did better.

⚙ *Transactional strategies.* Transactional strategies combine some of the preceding strategies with whole-language instruction to improve reading comprehension. They begin with the teacher explaining to students how they can

- make predictions about upcoming contents;
- relate the text to prior knowledge;
- ask questions about the information;
- seek clarification when the meaning is not clear;
- visualize the meaning; and
- summarize along the way.

*(Continued)*

(Continued)

**Figure 4.3** This chart shows the significant gain in reading scores of low achievers in traditional instruction (TI) and in Concept-Oriented Reading Instruction (CORI).

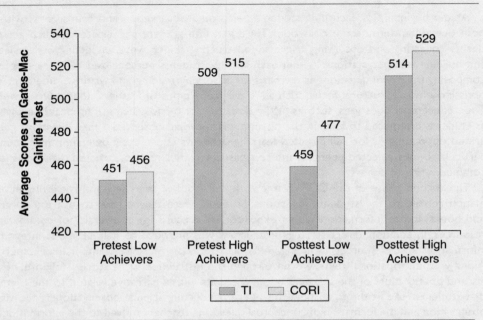

Students learn to use these strategies, especially in small reading groups that focus on high-quality literature. As students have trouble decoding a word, the teacher helps them use fix-up strategies they have learned, such as sounding out the word, rereading it, looking it up, and even skipping the word. Skipping the word is acceptable because main ideas are often expressed in several different ways in the text. This approach empowers students to read more challenging material by suggesting that they should not avoid reading texts that contain some unfamiliar words. For transactional strategies to be successful, teachers need to thoroughly understand the components of skilled reading and how to teach the related strategies. Professional development programs devoted to this topic can be very effective for content-area teachers (Concannon-Gibney & McCarthy, 2012).

Transactional and other strategies can even be used in the primary grades. A survey of studies that look at strategies for teaching comprehension in the primary grades (e.g., Alvermann & Mallozzi, 2010; Duke & Block, 2012; Pearson & Duke, 2002; Scull, 2010) show they are effective when teachers

- use explicit instruction, modeling, and discussion as a means of teaching comprehension strategies, focusing particularly on visualizing, questioning, predicting, clarifying, and making associations between the text and the students' experiences. Anytime you can link new learning to past experiences, retention increases significantly;
- emphasize not only the nature of the strategy but also when and how to apply it in actual reading;
- model the use of the strategies by thinking aloud in the presence of students about their own use of comprehension strategies;
- encourage students to discuss their comprehension of texts as well as the strategies they are using to achieve that comprehension. When students talk about what they are learning, they are more likely to remember it; and

- teach students to attend to their own reading processes, to the context in which they are reading, and to the text.

For older students, on the menu of the strategies best suited to promoting understanding of the text being read (Ness, 2009) are

- *thinking aloud*, where students talk about character development, identifying with a character, and imagining how a character might feel;
- *comprehension monitoring*, where students learn how to become aware of their own understanding of what they are reading and to develop procedures to deal with any comprehension problems that arise;
- *constructing images*, where students use graphic and semantic organizers to represent visually the meanings and relationships of the ideas in the text;
- *summarizing*, where students identify and write about the most important ideas, especially when the text contains multiple meanings;
- *predicting*, where students activate their prior knowledge to make a prediction about the outcome of the story;
- *questioning*, where students look for different points of view and question their validity, and ask the who, what, where, why, when, and how questions;
- *clarifying*, where students clear up any questionable areas and, where possible, relate the text to their personal experience;
- *analyzing story grammar*, where students relate one text to another; and
- *analyzing text structure*, where students look for specific text features, such as point of view, tone, or mood.

## Developing Critical Reading Strategies in Older Students

Students read thousands of pages of text as they progress through secondary school. They often need to make judgments about what they are reading. These judgments are based largely on the prior knowledge, beliefs, and values that students bring to the reading process. The brain's frontal lobe is thought to be the place where critical thinking occurs. Here, past experiences are mingled with the reading to construct meaning and to acquire new knowledge. Critical readers assess the reliability and validity of the text, and ask questions about themselves, the writer, and the writing. They read beyond the obvious meanings to the assumptions, strategies, and arguments behind them. How does the writer reason with readers and manipulate them? Reading critically helps learners separate nonfiction from fiction, creativity from fantasy, and fact from opinion, and is thus a valuable lifelong skill. Regrettably, not enough time is devoted to teaching students how to become critical readers.

If teachers want students to develop critical reading strategies, they should create a classroom climate that fosters inquiry by encouraging students to question, to make predictions, and to support their value judgments. Students employ higher-order thinking skills to evaluate evidence, draw conclusions, make inferences, and defend their line of thinking. This process is made somewhat easier when students write notes and mark up the text to stimulate their thinking, such as when they

- underline key words, phrases, and sentences;
- write comments or questions in the margin;

- number related points in sequence;
- bracket important sections of the text;
- connect ideas with lines or arrows; or
- make note of anything important, questionable, or interesting.

Critical reading strategies include the following:

- *Previewing.* This strategy allows students to get an overview of the content and organization of the reading by skimming the headnotes, captions, summaries, and other introductory material.
- *Contextualizing.* As students read, what they comprehend is colored by their own experiences and by living in a particular time and place. But some of the texts they read were written in a radically different place and time. To read critically, they need to put the text in its biographical, cultural, and historical contexts to recognize the differences between their own contemporary values and those represented in the text.
- *Questioning to Understand and Remember.* Students write down questions that come to mind as they read the material for the first time. The questions should focus on main ideas, not details, and should be expressed in their own words. This activity also helps in retention of new learning.
- *Challenges to the Students' Beliefs and Values.* Students put a mark next to sections that challenge their attitudes, beliefs, and values. They make notes in the margin about how they feel or about what particularly challenged them. Then they review their notes and look for any patterns.
- *Evaluating an Argument.* Writers make assertions that they want the reader to accept as true. Critical readers do not accept anything at face value but evaluate the claim and support for each argument. Students assess the reasoning process as well as its truthfulness. The support should be appropriate to the claim, and the statements should be consistent with each other.
- *Outlining and Summarizing.* Students use an outline to reveal the basic structure of the text, its main ideas, subtopics, and supporting details. This requires a close analysis of each paragraph and a listing of the main ideas. In summarizing, however, the students write a synopsis in their own words of what they have read. Thus, students experience creative synthesis by putting ideas together in a condensed and new form.
- *Comparing and Contrasting Related Readings.* Different authors discuss the same issues in different ways. Comparing and contrasting the arguments of various authors on a particular issue helps to better understand the approach each author used.

### Questions That Promote Critical Reading

Critical reading can be prompted by specific questions that relate to the reader, the author, and the writing. Students can use the following questions to sharpen their critical reading skills (Duncan, 2004; Olson, Larsen, Bolton, & Verhelst, 2007):

*About the reader*

- What do I know about this topic?
- What are my beliefs and values about this topic?
- Why am I reading this material?

*About the writer*

- What is the writer's background?
- How might that background affect the writer's approach to the topic as well as the selection and interpretation of the evidence presented?
- What are the writer's value assumptions about this topic?

*Writer's arguments, evidence, and conclusions*

- What is the basis for the writer's argument?
- What evidence does the writer present to support the argument?
- What is the writer's conclusion?

*Writer's use of evidence to support the conclusion*

- Are there any logical fallacies?
- What evidence does the writer use to support the conclusion(s)?
- Are the writer's sources credible?
- If the writer uses research studies:
- Is the research timely?

   o Is the sample group representative of the target population?
   o Who conducted the research and what was its purpose?
   o Has the research been replicated?
   o Do the graphic illustrations represent the data in a truthful manner?
   o What is the source of the data in the illustration?
   o Do the physical dimensions of the graphic illustration accurately portray numerical relationships?
   o Are the statistical findings and the writer's conclusion focused on the same topic?

*Reader's reaction to the reading*

- Do I accept the writer's evidence as reliable and as a valid support of the conclusion?
- How does the conclusion relate to what I already know about this topic?
- How has the writer's argument changed my views on this topic?

Teaching students to read, write, and think critically takes time and may represent a shift from what happens in many secondary school language arts classes. Teachers feel pressed for time and face the ever-increasing demands of high-stakes testing. Nonetheless, critical reading strategies can make reading much more productive and satisfying and thus help the students handle difficult material well and with confidence.

## Students Who Are English Language Learners

Children for whom English is a new language continue to enter schools across the country in ever-increasing numbers, posing unique challenges to teachers of reading. These challenges have been intensified by recent state and federal policy initiatives mandating that all students demonstrate adequate yearly progress. Thus, schools with large English language learner (ELL) populations are under pressure to help these students succeed. One of the more vexing problems is whether it is better to promote literacy in these children's native or second language. The research evidence suggests that initial reading instruction in a child's home language (e.g., Spanish) contributes positively to that child's ability to attain literacy in both languages, and also to the prevention of reading difficulties (Rolstad, Mahoney, & Glass, 2005; Slavin & Cheung, 2005).

At first sight, this result may seem counterintuitive. How can improving reading skills in the ELLs' native language help them read in their second language? Several possible explanations exist, but the most likely one is the powerful concept of transfer, whereby skills in one content area transfer to another. Research studies have suggested that literacy as well as other skills and knowledge transfer across languages. Thus, if a student learns something in one language, such as decoding or comprehension strategies, then the student can learn it in another language. Phonological awareness might transfer across languages, but does not appear to be helpful if the ELL's native language has a very different writing system, such as Russian, Arabic, or Chinese (Bialystok, McBride-Chang, & Luk, 2005).

It is generally counterproductive to hasten young non-English-speaking children into reading in English without adequate preparation. Reading in any language requires a solid mental lexicon of spoken vocabulary. Thus, learning to *speak* English becomes the child's first priority, because it provides the foundation for hearing and reflecting on the structure of spoken words and then to learning the alphabetic principle as it applies to the sounds of English. Likewise, learning to read for meaning depends on comprehending the language of the text being read.

### *Reminder About Orthography*

You may recall from Chapter 2 that written English has a deep orthography; that is, its 44+ phonemes can be represented by many different letter combinations. This makes it difficult for ELLs whose native language, such as Spanish or Italian, has a shallow orthography. They are accustomed to very consistent rules of spelling with few exceptions. Thus their pronunciation of a word they have never seen in their native language is almost always accurate. In English, however, they are faced with inconsistent rules and a large number of exceptions. This is an important matter to keep in mind when working with ELL students and assessing their progress.

The report of the National Literacy Panel on Language-Minority Children and Youth (August & Shanahan, 2006) suggested that if children come to school with no proficiency in English but speaking a language for which there are instructional guides, materials, and locally proficient teachers, then these children should be taught how to read in their native language while acquiring oral, and eventually reading, proficiency in the English language. Those non-English-speaking children with a native language for which there are no materials should focus on developing their oral proficiency in English. Formal reading instruction should be postponed until the child can speak English with an adequate level of proficiency.

One format for providing this type of instruction is paired bilingual instruction whereby ELL students are taught to read in their native language and in English at different times of the day. This can be expanded to two-way bilingual instruction in which ELL and native English speakers learn to read in both languages (Calderón & Minaya-Rowe, 2003). In an analysis of 17 research studies, Slavin and Cheung (2003) found that most studies showed significant positive effects of the bilingual approach, especially the two-way format, on the students' reading performance. Most of these studies evaluated the Success for All program, which is a comprehensive reading program emphasizing systematic phonics, cooperative learning, tutoring for struggling students, and family support programs. Evaluations of both the English and Spanish versions of the Success for All program have consistently found them to improve English and Spanish reading performance in beginning readers. Two other programs that have been successful with helping ELL students learn to read in their native language and then in English are the Spanish version of Reading Recovery (Escamilla, 1994) and the small-group version of Direct Instruction (Gunn, Biglan, Smolkowski, & Ary, 2000).

## Cooperative Learning Strategies With ELL Students

As children with limited English proficiency begin to acquire English, cooperative learning seems particularly appropriate and effective for bilingual education. First of all, cooperative learning should improve the reading performance of students in their native language. In an analysis of nearly 100 studies, Slavin (1995) showed that student achievement in a variety of settings using cooperative learning methods increased significantly those of the control groups.

---

### Answer to Test Question #5

**Question:** Non-English-speaking children can be taught to read English even if their spoken English vocabulary is weak.

**Answer:** *False.* During reading, the brain relies heavily on a person's spoken vocabulary to decode words. With only a small number of English words in the mental lexicon, learning to read in English becomes very frustrating. Bilingual programs that build a child's native reading skills while also enhancing English language skills have shown success in helping the child learn to read English.

---

Research on second-language learning has found that students need to engage in a great deal of oral interaction, jointly solving problems and determining meaning, if they are to achieve a high level of proficiency in the new language. Because cooperative learning provides many opportunities for students to work together to share understandings, it is likely to be an especially beneficial strategy for students making the transition to reading in English.

One form of cooperative learning has been particularly successful with bilingual students. Known as Bilingual Cooperative Integrated Reading and Composition (BCIRC), this method assigns students to four-member heterogeneous learning teams. After their lesson, the students work in teams on cooperative learning activities including identification of main story elements, vocabulary, summarization, reading comprehension strategies, partner reading, and creative writing using a process writing approach. In a major study (Calderón, Hertz-Lazarowitz, & Slavin, 1998) of 222 students with limited English proficiency in Grades 2 and 3, teachers used the BCIRC model, first working with students in their native language and then helping them to make the transition to English. As part of BCIRC, the teachers used a total of 15 different strategies before, during, and after reading. Most of the activities were completed in a five-day cycle. They were the following:

1. *Building background and vocabulary.* Teachers select vocabulary that might be particularly difficult, strange, or important. They write the words on chart paper and develop semantic maps with the students. The maps are displayed on a wall and are used later during reading, discussion, and writing activities.

2. *Making predictions.* Teachers model how to make and confirm predictions. Students then work in their teams with the title and illustrations of a story and predict the elements of that story.

3. *Reading a selection.* Students track as the teacher reads aloud the first part of a story. During the second part, the students are encouraged to read in a whisper with the teacher.

4. *Partner reading and silent reading.* For partner reading, the students sit in pairs and take turns reading alternate paragraphs aloud. They assist each other in pronouncing and decoding the meaning of words. Then each student reads the assigned text silently.

5. *Treasure hunting: Story comprehension.* After partner reading, pairs discuss the answers to questions about key elements of a narrative, such as characters, setting, problems, and problem solutions. Working together, students help each other to understand the questions, to look up the answers, to look for clues to support their answers, to make inferences, and to reach consensus.

6. *Mapping the story.* After the treasure hunts are done, each team reviews a variety of graphic organizers and chooses one to map the story. This visual aid helps to organize the story elements. After discussing story elements, such as character names, the setting, the main idea, major events of the story, and problems the characters encountered, the team members represent these creatively in the story map. They can use the maps later to provide visual clues for retelling the story and for story-related writing later in the cycle.

7. *Retelling the story.* Students use the maps to retell the stories to the partners within their teams and evaluate their partners' verbal

summaries. Afterward, the students discuss with their partners what they liked about the story.

8. *Story-related writing.* In this part of the lesson cycle, students engage in a variety of writing activities that are related to the selection they have been reading all week. For the students who are acquiring English, the teacher models the writing process extensively each time. Then, with a partner or in teams of four, students write in various genres. During this time, the students help each other to develop story lines and characters, to sequence events, and to give each other feedback. They are also learning to engage in a process of drafting, revising, rewriting, editing, and publishing.

9. *Saying words aloud and spelling.* Words from the story become the word bank to be used throughout the week. Students say the words aloud to ultimately master their meaning, pronunciation, and spelling. This activity includes 10 to 12 words from the story that students must be able to read fluently, spell, and use correctly in meaningful sentences.

10. *Checking the partner.* When students complete the activities listed above, their partners initial a student assessment form indicating that they have completed and achieved the task. The teacher gives the student teams the daily expectations about the number of activities to be completed. However, the teams can proceed at their own rate and complete the activities earlier if they wish, creating additional time for writing and for independent reading of other books on the same theme. Because the scores of individual students also become the team's score, the partners have a vested interest in making sure all students correctly finish their work.

11. *Making meaningful sentences.* The students carefully select five or more words from the story. They discuss their meanings and use these words to write meaningful sentences that denote the definitions and give a clear picture of the word's meaning.

12. *Taking tests.* After three class periods, the teacher gives the students a comprehension test on the story. It includes asking them to write meaningful sentences for each vocabulary word and to read the word list aloud to the teacher. Students are not permitted to help one another on these tests because the test scores and evaluations of the story-related writing are the major components of students' weekly team scores. These weekly tests provide teachers a progressive view of the students' listening, speaking, reading, and writing performance.

13. *Direct instruction in reading comprehension.* Throughout the lesson cycle, the teacher provides direct instruction in reading comprehension skills such as identifying main ideas, drawing conclusions, and comparing and contrasting. The students practice these skills in their teams and take quizzes on them individually (without the help of their teammates) to contribute to their team scores.

14. *Writing workshops.* These workshops consist of a series of mini-lessons on the writing process. First, the teacher gives step-by-step

explanations and ideas for completing a writing assignment. Then the students work closely with their peers and with the teacher through the phases of prewriting, writing, revising, and editing.

15. *Independent reading.* The teacher asks students to read a book of their choice for at least 20 minutes each evening. Parents are encouraged to discuss the reading with their children and to initial forms indicating that the children have read for the minimum time. The students earn points for their team if they submit a completed form each week. Additional points can be earned by completing a book report every two weeks.

The students who were part of the BCIRC program in the second and third grades performed significantly better on tests of Spanish and English reading than comparison students. Second graders taught primarily in Spanish scored significantly higher on a Spanish writing scale and somewhat higher on the reading scale than comparison students. Third-grade students who had been in the program for two years were more likely than the comparison group to meet the criteria necessary for exiting the bilingual program in language and reading. Although there have been no subsequent controlled studies on BCIRC, numerous schools with high proportions of ELLs continue to use the program. Their anecdotal evaluations show it remains an effective method.

## Monitoring Reading Progress

Just as with native English-speaking students, the ELLs' progress in reading will vary from student to student because of a number of factors. These include age, level of reading proficiency in their native language, size of their English mental lexicon, and developmental problems that may affect their ability to read. Consequently, these students' progress in reading should be monitored periodically. Studies reveal that measures of phonological processing, knowledge of letters, and word and text reading were valid for determining which ELLs may need additional support in reading (Geva & Yaghoub-Zadeh 2006). Further, those ELL students who received early intervention in the primary grades learned to read at rates comparable to native English speakers (Lesaux & Siegel, 2003). Assessing the ELL students' progress can be challenging, but most studies show this is necessary to ensure the student is on the right path for English language and reading acquisition (Durán, 2008; Sousa, 2011b).

My purpose in this chapter was to present the latest research on the effectiveness of strategies that educators use for teaching reading. In the past few decades, methods for teaching reading have become highly politicized. Given the wide variation in the cognitive abilities of children and their environments as well as the complexities involved in learning to read, it is clear that no one approach will be successful for all children. Some preschool children will have had such rich exposure to spoken language and print that they are already mastering the alphabetic principle and are prepared for enriched reading experiences as early as kindergarten. Others can be so language deprived that instruction will need to focus mainly on developing phonemic awareness. And, of course, there are all the possible variations in between.

Faced with this heterogeneous mix, teachers of reading still need sound guidance, not rhetoric, regarding research-based methods for teaching beginning reading. It seems clear that the latest review of scientific research on reading leads us to the following three conclusions. For *most* children,

- mastering the alphabetic principle is essential to learning how to read successfully;
- instructional techniques that explicitly teach this principle are more effective than those that do not; and
- the reading teacher remains the most critical component of any reading program.

These conclusions are even more important when applied to children who are at risk for having difficulty learning to read. This is not to deny that literature-based activities that supplement phonics instruction can help to ensure the application of the alphabetic principle to enriched readings. Such activities can make reading meaningful and enjoyable.

When children receive instruction in phonemic awareness and the alphabetic principle and learn to apply that knowledge to decoding words, they are likely to succeed at learning to read. But once they fall behind, they almost never catch up. A longitudinal study of more than 17,000 students in the Chicago Public Schools showed that only 45 percent of third-grade students who were reading below grade level graduated high school in 5 years (Lesnick, Goerge, Smithgall, & Gwynne, 2010). However, 60 percent of third-grade students who read at grade-level and 80 percent who read above grade level graduated high school. Consequently, the sooner that parents and teachers can recognize children with reading problems, the better.

---

**QUESTIONS FOR DISCUSSION/REFLECTION**

- *How do I teach vocabulary and linguistic knowledge?*
- *What strategies help students read with comprehension?*
- *How can I develop critical reading skills in older students?*
- *What considerations are important when teaching reading to English language learners (ELLs)?*

---

## What's Coming?

We now know that many reading difficulties can be overcome with early diagnosis and systematic intervention. Just how to go about determining whether a child has a reading problem is the topic of the next chapter.

# 5

# Recognizing Reading Problems

*To learn to read is to light a fire; every syllable that is spelled out is a spark.*

—Victor Hugo (1802–1885), *Les Misérables*

## THE READING GAP ⚙

### Recent NAEP Assessments

About one student in three has reading problems. The 2011 and 2012 reports from the National Assessment of Educational Progress on reading described the reading achievement of students in the fourth and eighth grades. They included comparisons between NAEP reading performance of students in 2012 and the performance of their counterparts in previous assessments. Reading performance is reported in two ways: (1) average scale scores and (2) achievement levels. The average scale score reflects the overall reading performance of a particular group, using a scale of 0 to 500 to provide information about student performance for all three grades. Achievement levels describe what students should know and be able to do at each of three levels, *Basic, Proficient,* and *Advanced.*

### National Scale Scores

Figure 5.1 shows the average reading scale scores for the two grades tested during 2012.

Despite the efforts of the No Child Left Behind Act and other initiatives, you can see that little progress has been made in improving the average reading scale scores over the past decade. The fourth-grade average score increased slightly from 2003 to 2007, but has not changed since. The eighth-grade scores showed a slight increase over this time period but dropped in 2012.

### Achievement Levels for Fourth Grade

NAEP (2011) gives the following specific definitions of the Basic, Proficient, and Advanced achievement levels in reading for Grade 4:

- *Basic:* Fourth-grade students at the Basic level should demonstrate an understanding of the overall meaning of what they read. When reading text appropriate for fourth graders, they should be able to make obvious connections between the text and their own experiences and extend the ideas in the text by making simple inferences.

- *Proficient:* Fourth-grade students at the Proficient level should be able to demonstrate an overall understanding of the text, providing inferential as well as literal information. When reading text appropriate to fourth grade, they should be able to extend the ideas in the text by making inferences, drawing conclusions, and making connections to their own experiences. The connection between the text and what the student infers should be clear.

- *Advanced:* Fourth-grade students at the Advanced level should be able to generalize about topics in the reading selection and demonstrate an

**Figure 5.1**   This chart shows the average NAEP reading scale scores for Grades 4 and 8 from 2003 to 2011 (NAEP, 2011, 2012).

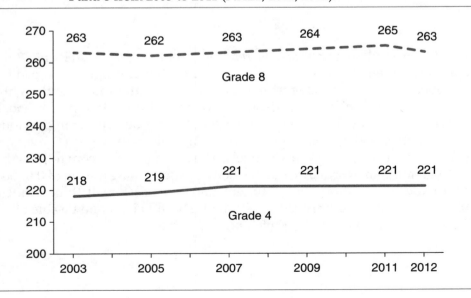

awareness of how authors compose and use literary devices. When reading text appropriate to fourth grade, they should be able to judge text critically and, in general, to give thorough answers that indicate careful thought.

The fourth-grade results by reading achievement level are displayed in Table 5.1. They show that one-third of these students continue to perform below Basic achievement levels. Unfortunately, the percentages in the At Proficient and Advanced achievement levels have not changed. The report also noted that although females scored slightly higher than males, the difference was not significant (NAEP, 2011).

Clearly, little progress is being made toward significantly increasing the number of elementary students who become Proficient readers, despite the large amounts of resources and time devoted to teaching reading. If school districts are to meet the expectations and deadlines regarding reading that are set forth in federal and state regulations as well as in the Common Core State Standards, educators must reexamine how and when they are identifying students with reading problems, and what steps they are taking to help these at-risk students.

Table 5.1   Percentage of Fourth-Grade Students by Reading Achievement Level

| NAEP 2003 to 2011 | | | | |
|---|---|---|---|---|
| Year | Below Basic | At Basic | At Proficient | At Advanced |
| 2011 | 33 | 33 | 26 | 8 |
| 2009 | 33 | 34 | 25 | 8 |
| 2007 | 33 | 34 | 25 | 8 |
| 2005 | 36 | 33 | 23 | 8 |
| 2003 | 37 | 32 | 23 | 8 |

SOURCE: NAEP (2011).

## Achievement for Black and Hispanic Students

Of continuing concern is the consistently low achievement levels for Black (Figure 5.2) and Hispanic (Figure 5.3) students over the last decade when compared to White students. There were no significant changes in fourth-grade average scores for Black and Hispanic students from 2009 to 2011, although the 2011 scores were slightly higher for eighth-grade students than in 2009. In 2011, Hispanic students scored slightly higher on average than Black students. This persistent poor performance of minority students in reading cannot be explained solely by specific cognizant impairments, such as dyslexia. After all, the White student population also includes children with reading problems, yet their average scores remain higher. Furthermore, there is little scientific evidence that Black and Hispanic children are at a substantially greater risk for developmental dyslexia than these testing results would suggest. The size of the reading gap and the number of students involved suggests that this problem has

**Figure 5.2**   Since 2003, Black students in Grades 4 and 8 consistently scored below White students. Grade 8 Black students have made some gains in recent years, but the scores of Grade 4 Black students have changed little (NAEP, 2011).

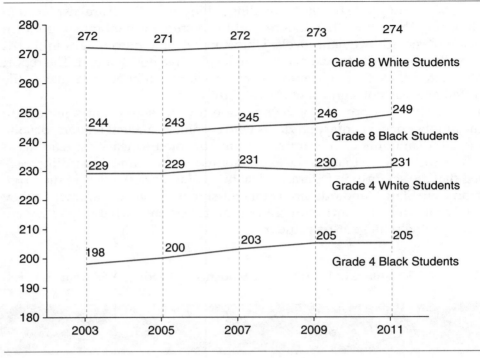

**Figure 5.3**   Since 2003, Hispanic students in Grades 4 and 8 consistently scored below White students. The scores of Grade 8 Hispanic students have shown some improvement in recent years, but those of Grade 4 Hispanic students have changed little (NAEP, 2011).

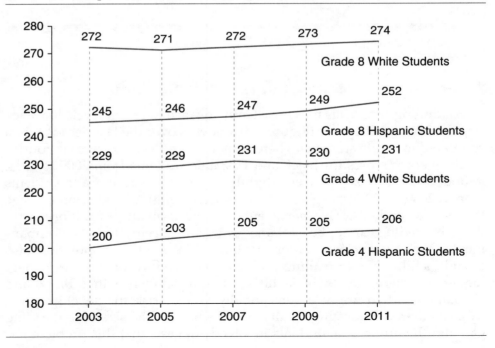

roots in at least three separate but related areas: inadequate reading instruction, social and cultural conditions, and physical causes.

## INADEQUATE READING INSTRUCTION ✿

Some children have reading problems because they did not get adequate instruction in the skills needed for decoding, such as concepts about the nature of print, recognizing letters, and the alphabetic principle. They may not have had ample opportunities for systematic and focused practice in decoding real words. As a result, they failed to develop a rich mental lexicon, which is essential for promoting fluency and comprehension. To successfully understand a language, children need to develop a rich vocabulary and an appreciation for semantics, and combine that understanding with what they know about the real world. They also need to have a good understanding of the mechanics of language (syntax), and they need to be attuned to the phonology of the language so that they do not confuse similar-sounding words, such as *chair* and *cheer*.

None of these areas can be described as social, cultural, or physical problems that lead to reading difficulties. These deficits are intrinsic not to the child, but to the classroom and to the school system that has not provided the appropriate instructional environment. Schools situated in high-poverty areas are often competing for limited materials and resources. Conscientious but inadequately trained teachers may be using outdated programs and methodologies. This unfortunate combination can be the cause of some children's reading difficulties. Children in this situation do not have dyslexia. Their problem is that they were simply never taught the skills needed to learn how to read. To be successful in teaching all children, teachers should become extremely knowledgeable about effective strategies as well as diagnostic in their approach to reading instruction.

Just as we do not expect beginning readers to acquire the alphabetic principle on their own, we cannot expect prospective teachers to independently acquire the knowledge and skills they will need to recognize and implement research-based strategies. They need to be exposed to the latest research on how the brain learns and, specifically, how it learns to read. This information should be presented in their college courses as well as during continuing in-service professional development programs to keep their knowledge base up to date. We will discuss teacher preparation further in Chapter 8.

## SOCIAL AND CULTURAL ✿
## CAUSES OF READING PROBLEMS

A large number of Black and Hispanic children performing below White children in reading display no signs of specific learning impairments. Clearly, other factors are at work. Multiple studies have identified social conditions that have an impact on the achievement of children in inner-city schools. Limited teacher training, large class sizes, the absence of literature in the home, and poor parental support for schools have all been cited as causes for lack of student progress. Although these conditions cannot be ignored, schools need to focus more on the direct connections between what we are learning about how the brain learns to read and the *linguistic* barriers interfering with that learning.

Some researchers believe that these children are performing poorly on reading tests because their home language differs substantially from the language used in reading instruction (Labov, 2003). Others noted that Black children were being immersed in a language dialect that has become known as African American Vernacular English (AAVE). Residential desegregation has increased the impact of AAVE, as has the rapidly escalating popularity of hip-hop and rap music. Meanwhile, as Spanish-speaking populations increase, children are faced with learning to read English in school while speaking Spanish at home and in their communities.

Consequently, some of the causes of poor performance by Black and Hispanic children can be attributed to impediments resulting from linguistic differences. That is, their native dialect or language is different in significant ways from what is being taught in school. They come to school with a mental lexicon whose word representations often do not match what they are trying to decode on the printed page. Learning to read involves determining which words *are* present in their mental lexicon, what they represent, and whether they can be comprehended in context. This is not a physiological deficit; it is a social and cultural problem. For these children, we should be looking not at what is wrong with them but at how we can alter instruction to make them more successful in learning to read. Such alterations can be made when teachers of reading are properly trained to recognize when a child's reading problems are the result of linguistic clashes and not a pathology. Furthermore, that training should also help teachers understand how they can use some of the linguistic attributes of AAVE and Spanish to help children pronounce, decode, and understand standard English.

## ✿ PHYSICAL CAUSES OF READING PROBLEMS

As noted earlier, nature long ago crafted sophisticated neural networks in the brain to process spoken language. But decoding written text is a wholly artificial creation that calls upon neural regions designed for other tasks. Because there is no single neural region for reading, numerous brain areas must be recruited to perform the task of decoding artificial symbols into sound. Reading is so complex that any small problem along the way can slow or interrupt the process. It is small wonder that children have more problems with reading than with any other skill we ask them to learn. Difficulties result essentially from either environmental or physical factors, or some combination of both. Environmental factors include limited exposure to language in the preschool years, resulting in little phoneme sensitivity, letter knowledge, print awareness, vocabulary, and reading comprehension. Physical factors include speech, hearing, and visual impairments and substandard intellectual capabilities. Any combination of environmental and physical factors makes the diagnosis and treatment more difficult.

Recent research into the causes and nature of reading problems has revealed more about the neural processes involved in reading. Recall from

Chapter 2 that successful reading involves two basic processes— (1) coordination between the language and visual recognition processing systems that leads to (2) decoding and comprehension—that are generated by three neural systems. Figure 5.4 is a simplified illustration of how these three systems interact. Decoding written text into sounds that represent words results when the visual recognition and auditory processing systems see and sound out the words in the reader's head. The frontal lobe interprets the meaning conveyed by those word form representations.

Problems with any one or more of these systems can cause reading difficulties. In some children, the problems occur during early brain development and affect their ability to process the sounds of language and, eventually, to decode written text. This developmental deficit appears to be the most common cause of reading difficulties, and usually results in a lifelong struggle with reading. Less common are problems with reading caused by organic impairments in hearing and vision that can occur at any time in a person's life.

Most research studies on reading have focused primarily on developmental reading problems that scientists refer to as *developmental dyslexia.* (There are several other types of dyslexia, such as trauma dyslexia, which is caused by trauma during childhood affecting the brain's reading areas.) In developmental dyslexia, the child experiences unexpected difficulty in learning to read despite adequate intelligence, environment, and normal senses. It is a spectrum disorder, varying from mild to severe, that has a genetic component. Estimates of the percentage of U.S. schoolchildren with dyslexia vary widely, from 5 to 15 percent. This range seems high, but that may be because there is not full agreement on the threshold used to define the impairment. But neuroscience is helping with this dilemma. Neuroimaging studies have established that there are significant differences in the way normal and dyslexic brains respond to specific spoken

Figure 5.4    Successful reading requires the coordination of three systems: (1) Visual recognition and (2) auditory processing to decode the words, and (3) frontal lobe processing to determine meaning.

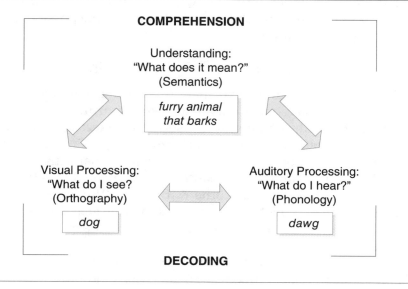

and written language tasks. Furthermore, there is adequate research evidence that these differences may lessen with appropriate instructional interventions.

Scientists have long been searching for the causes of reading problems. This has not been an easy task because of the large number of sensory, motor, and cognitive systems that are involved in reading. Struggling readers may have impairments in any one or more of these systems, but not all struggling readers have dyslexia. Deficits in auditory processing, low IQ, the complexity of English orthography, or a poor educational environment can also explain reading problems in some children.

## Linguistic Causes

Several potential linguistic causes of reading problems and developmental dyslexia have emerged from recent research studies, including phonological deficits, differences in auditory and visual processing speeds, the varying sizes of brain structures, memory deficits, genetics, and brain lesions. It is possible that several of these causes are related to each other and can coexist in the same individual.

### Phonological Deficits

The ability to sound out words in one's head plays an important role in reading familiar words and sounding out new ones. Phonological information is used by the working memory to integrate and comprehend words in phrases and sentences. Numerous studies continue to show that phonological operations are impaired in many dyslexics (e.g., Vellutino, Fletcher, Snowling, & Scanlon, 2004), but not all (van Ermingen-Marbach, Grande, Pape-Neumann, Sass, & Heim, 2013). But the exact causes of the impairment were not clear. Because many people with dyslexia have average or above-average intelligence, researchers suspected that the phonological processing deficits appeared only when the brain was trying to decode writing. Exactly why that happens is not fully known. However, studies of the differences in auditory and visual processing speeds as well as functional magnetic resonance imaging (fMRI) scans of the brain during reading are shedding new light on the possible causes of the phonological impairments.

### Differences in Auditory and Visual Processing Speeds

One of the more intriguing explanations of some reading difficulties, including dyslexia, has come from research studies using magnetoencephalography (MEG), a technique for measuring the electric signals emitted during brain activation as a result of mental processing. These studies noted abnormal auditory activation but normal visual activation during reading (Helenius, Salmelin, Richardson, Leinonen, & Lyytinen, 2002; Renvall & Hari, 2002; Schulte-Körne & Bruder, 2010; Tallal et al., 1996; Temple et al., 2003). Sometimes referred to as *temporal processing impairment*, the differences in the processing speeds could explain some of the symptoms common to dyslexia.

The explanation goes like this: When reading silently, our eyes scan the words on the page (visual processing), and we sound out those words in our head. This sounding out represents the auditory processing necessary for us to decode and interpret what we are reading. To read successfully, the visual and auditory processing systems have to work together—that is, be in synchrony.

When a child begins to learn to read, it is essential that the letter (grapheme) the child sees corresponds to what the child hears (phoneme) internally. In Figure 5.5, the child with normal auditory processing (left) is looking at the letter *d*, and the auditory processing system is simultaneously sounding out /*d*/ or *duh*. As the eye moves to *o*, the phoneme /*ô*/ or *awh* will sound out, and then *g* produces the phoneme /*g*/ or *guh*. Later, when this child is asked to write *dog*, the /*d*/ phoneme will recall the letter *d*, and so on.

However, if the auditory processing system is impaired and lags behind the visual processing system, then the child's eye is already scanning to the letter *g* while the phoneme /*d*/ or *duh* is still being processed in the auditory system. As a result, the child's brain incorrectly associates the letter *g* with the phoneme sound of /*d*/ or *duh*. Now, when we ask the child to write the word *dog*, the child hears the first phoneme /*d*/ or *duh* but incorrectly recalls the letter *g*, perhaps eventually writing the word *god*.

If this notion is correct, then finding a way to bring the auditory and visual processing systems in closer synchrony should help to remedy the problem. That is exactly what several researchers tried. They developed a computer program, known as Fast ForWord, designed to help poor readers slow down visual processing to allow the auditory processing sufficient

Figure 5.5    In normal auditory processing (left), the phoneme that the child hears correctly matches the letter that the eyes see—in this case, the sound *duh* corresponds to the letter *d*. If the auditory processing system is delayed, however, the child's eyes are already on the letter *g* while the *duh* phoneme is still sounding in the child's head. The brain errs in matching *duh* with *g*.

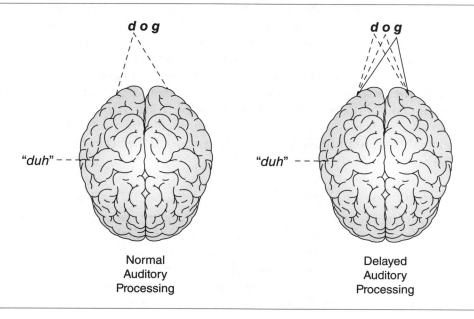

Normal Auditory Processing        Delayed Auditory Processing

time to recognize the sound of the initial phoneme. Using this program with children who had reading problems produced surprisingly successful results. The program and process are discussed in greater detail in Chapter 6. Recent studies suggest that temporal processing impairment may lessen as children with reading problems, including dyslexia, mature into adults (Vandermosten et al., 2011).

### Structural Differences in the Brain

Some MRI studies have found that the brains of people diagnosed with dyslexia are structurally different from nondyslexic brains. In one study, the researchers noted that the dyslexic brains of 16 men had less gray matter (surface of the cerebrum) in the left temporal lobe, frontal lobe, and cerebellum than the brains of 14 nondyslexic subjects (Brown et al., 2001; Steinbrink et al., 2008). Having less gray matter (and thus fewer neurons) in the left temporal lobe (where Wernicke's area is located [see Chapter 1]) and in the frontal lobe (where comprehension occurs) could contribute to the deficits associated with dyslexia.

Many brain imaging studies in recent years are yielding similar results regarding how the brain activity in people with dyslexia differs from that in typical readers. One common finding is the reduced level of activity in the left temporal lobe where the visual word form area (see Chapter 2) is located (e.g., McCrory, Mechelli, Frith, & Price, 2005), as well as reduced connectivity to other language processing areas (van der Mark et al., 2011). This could be the result of a lesser amount of white matter in this region compared to the amount in typical readers, as some studies have reported (e.g., Rimrodt, Peterson, Denckla, Kaufmann, & Cutting, 2010). Another abnormality frequently found in dyslexia relates to the left frontal cortex where Broca's area, one of the brain's language processing regions (see Chapter 1), is located. This area is frequently overactive when people with dyslexia attempt to read or carry out various phonological tasks (Georgiewa et al., 2002; Grande, Meffert, Huber, Amunts, & Heim, 2011). It may be that this hyperactivity in Broca's area is an attempt to compensate for the insufficient activation in the brain's decoding sites.

A third anomaly common to people with dyslexia deals with the visual recognition system. Apparently, they are not able to recall the letters that comprise a word simultaneously, which explains their slow reading time. To compensate, they often activate regions in the right hemisphere, hoping to access the word's phonology—an inefficient and often unproductive endeavor (Zoccolotti et al., 2005). In sum, as the research evidence accumulates, it seems clear that most children with developmental dyslexia have visual analysis and phonological decoding areas of the brain that are insufficiently active and dysfunctional.

### Phonologic Memory Deficits

Skilled reading requires an ability to retain verbal bits of information (phonemes) in working memory. Studies have shown distinct deficits in this phonologic memory among poor readers. The deficits more commonly involve serial tasks, such as holding a string of phonemes to make a word and a sequence of words to generate a sentence (Carretti, Borella, Cornoldi, & De Beni, 2009; Howes, Bigler, Burlingame, & Lawson, 2003). In addition, some studies suggest that the memory deficits could result from difficulties with cognitive processing in the frontal lobe (Wang & Gathercole, 2013). However, for some children, this may be a symptom of a developmental delay that could correct itself as they mature.

### Genetics and Gender

Studies of genetic composition have long shown strong associations between dyslexia and genetic mutations in twins and families (Pennington, 1990), and recent investigations have actually identified some half-dozen of the specific genes involved (e.g., Benítez-Burraco, 2010; Kaminen et al., 2003). Preliminary studies seem to indicate that the genetic mutations disrupt the migration of neurons in the fetal brain as they attempt to travel to areas of the cortex to their final position. Instead, they accumulate in disorganized tangles, often around the visual word form area (Meng et al., 2005; Paracchini et al., 2005). These tangles prevent this brain region from carrying out its normal functions of recognizing and decoding written text. As a result, the brain is forced to construct alternate and less efficient pathways. Thus, dyslexia is a lifelong condition and not just a "phase."

Nationwide, three to four times more boys are identified with reading problems than girls. Although this was once thought to be the result of genetic deficits, the true reason may be because boys are overidentified (often due to their rambunctious behavior) and girls are underidentified (if they sit quietly in class and obey the rules). Studies show that many girls are affected as well but are not getting help (Shaywitz, 2003).

Another reason that boys are overidentified as poor readers may be that teachers confound competence in early reading and writing skills. They may assume that poor writing skills also mean poor reading skills. But studies show that boys are almost as skilled as girls in reading, but do, in fact, display significantly poorer writing skills (Berninger, Nielsen, Abbott, Wijsman, & Raskind, 2008). By assessing reading and writing skills separately, fewer boys may be identified as poor readers.

### Lesions in the Word Form Area

Researchers using **positron emission tomography (PET)** scans have noticed that people with developmental dyslexia have lesions in the left occipitotemporal area of the brain. You may recall from Chapter 2 that this area is identified as the visual word form area most used by skilled readers to decode written text. Another discovery in these studies was that the amount of blood flowing to this brain region predicted the severity of the dyslexia (Rumsey et al., 1999). Regardless of the cause, a lesion and reduced blood flow would likely hamper the ability of this patch of neurons to decode written text. In this case, the individual may display a condition known as *alexia*, which is difficulty in identifying a string of letters, although speech production and comprehension remain intact. However, demonstrating its impressive plasticity, other studies show that when a lesion occurs in the brain's visual word form area during childhood, an area exactly symmetrical to the VWFA, located in the right hemisphere, can take over the functions, albeit not as efficiently (Cohen et al., 2004).

## Nonlinguistic Causes

Some people, who are otherwise unimpaired, have extreme difficulties in reading because of deficits in auditory and visual perception not related to linguistic systems. This revelation was somewhat of a surprise because conventional wisdom held that impairments in reading (and also in oral language) were restricted to problems with linguistic processing. The following are some possible nonlinguistic causes found in the research literature.

### *Perception of Sequential Sounds*

The inability to detect and discriminate sounds presented in rapid succession seems to be a common impairment in individuals with reading and language disorders. These individuals also have difficulty in indicating the order of two sounds presented in rapid succession. This particular deficit is related to auditory processing of sound waves in general and is not related directly to distinguishing phonemes as part of phonological processing. Hearing words accurately when reading or from a stream of rapid conversation is critical to comprehension (Wright, Bowen, & Zecker, 2000).

### *Sound-Frequency Discrimination*

Some individuals with reading disorders are impaired in their ability to hear differences in sound frequency. This auditory defect can affect the ability to discriminate tone and pitch in speech. At first glance, this may seem like only an oral language–related impairment. However, it also affects reading proficiency because reading involves sounding out words in the auditory processing system (Wright et al., 2000). A longitudinal study showed that children who had problems with pitch discrimination as newborns had more difficulties than typical children when learning to read. This was especially evident for children in the study with a family history of dyslexia (Leppänen et al., 2010).

### *Detection of Target Sounds in Noise*

The inability to detect tones within noise is another nonlinguistic impairment that seems to affect learning to read. These students have difficulty hearing the differences between tones and noise. This makes reading very challenging because the child's language processing system cannot distinguish phonemic tones from all the incoming auditory information (Chait et al., 2007; Wright et al., 2000). When added to the findings in the two deficits mentioned above, this evidence suggests that auditory functions play a much greater role in reading disorders than previously thought. It also suggests that the evaluation of children who are having reading difficulties should include a thorough assessment of their auditory processing skills.

### *Visual Magnocellular-Deficit Hypothesis*

The interpretation of some research studies has led to a hypothesis about the functions of the visual processing system. This proposes that certain forms of reading disorders are caused by a deficit in the visual processing system, which leads to poor detection of coherent visual motion and poor discrimination of the speed of visual motion. This part of the visual system involves large neurons and so is referred to as the *magnocellular* system. Impairment in this system may cause letters on a page to bundle and overlap, or appear to move—common complaints from some struggling readers and dyslexics. Current studies continue to show a strong correlation between deficits in the visual magnocellular system and developmental dyslexia (e.g., Laycock, Crewther, & Crewther, 2012). This correlation is also found in Chinese dyslexics, lending further credence to the notion that deficits in detecting visual motion and outlines affect one's ability to read different orthographic symbols (e.g., Wang, Bi, Gao, & Wydell, 2010).

## *Motor Coordination and the Cerebellum*

Several imaging studies show that many people with dyslexia have processing deficits in the cerebellum of the brain (Baillieux et al., 2009; Nicolson, Fawcett, & Dean, 2001). Another study determined that nearly 75 percent of the subjects with dyslexia had smaller lobes on the right side of the cerebellum compared to nondyslexic participants (Eckert et al., 2003). The cerebellum is located at the rear of the brain just below the occipital lobe (Figure 5.6). It is mainly responsible for coordinating learned motor skills. Deficiencies in this part of the brain could result, according to researchers, in problems with reading, writing, and spelling. Problems in reading may result if cerebellar deficits delay the time when an infant sits up and walks, and begins babbling and talking. Less motor skill coordination can mean less articulation and fluency in speech. This, in turn, leads to less sensitivity to onset, rime, and the phonemic structure of language.

Handwriting, of course, is a motor skill that requires the precise coordination and timing of different muscle groups. Lack of coordination of these muscles due to a cerebellar deficit would create difficulties in writing, a characteristic that many dyslexics display. Problems with spelling would arise from poor phonological awareness, trouble with word recognition, and difficulties in automating spelling rule skills. It remains to be seen whether these problems will lessen or worsen as children become more accustomed to composing text on keyboards, and as more schools abandon instruction in cursive writing.

The possibility of deficits in visual and auditory perception and memory as well as in motor coordination on various reading tasks accounts for the wide range of individual differences observed among those with reading disorders. Analyzing these differences leads to a better understanding of the multidimensional nature of reading disorders and possible treatment.

**Figure 5.6**   The cerebellum is located at the rear of the brain and is responsible for coordinating learned motor skills.

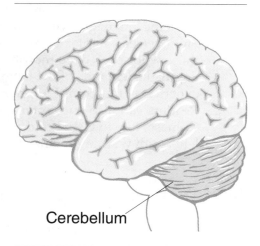

Cerebellum

*Attention Deficit/Hyperactivity Disorder*

Attention deficit/hyperactivity disorder (ADHD) is a developmental disorder characterized by difficulty in focusing and sustaining attention. Children with ADHD are often assumed to also have developmental reading problems. But that is not necessarily the case. ADHD and developmental dyslexia are separate disorders, although some brain regions may be affected by both. Estimating the exact percentage of ADHD children who also have dyslexia is difficult because of the inconsistency of criteria used for diagnosis. The accepted range at the time of this printing is between 15 and 40 percent (Kibby et al., 2009).

---

**Answer to Test Question #6**

**Question:** Most children with attention deficit/hyperactivity disorder (ADHD) are also dyslexic.

**Answer:** *False.* ADHD and developmental dyslexia are separate disorders. Less than one-half of ADHD children also have dyslexia.

---

*Is Dyslexia Present in Readers of Other Languages?*

Dyslexia appears in all languages, including those that are read from right to left, such as Hebrew and Arabic. People with dyslexia who speak highly phonetic languages with shallow orthography, such as Spanish, Italian, and Finnish (see Chapter 2), are usually identified with the disorder later than those who speak deep morphological languages such as English, where the linguistic demands of the language are more challenging. English speakers experience the complex phonetic structure early on in their schooling. Readers can also encounter difficulties in logographic languages, such as Chinese, due to visual confusion of the more than 3,000 characters or problems with working memory and recall (Siok, Spinks, Jin, & Tan, 2009).

## ✿ DETECTING READING PROBLEMS

In recent years, researchers have made significant progress using fMRI scans to understand how novice, skilled, and dyslexic brains read. Yet, despite these advancements, fMRI scans are not a practical tool at present for diagnosing dyslexia in a single individual. That is because the results of fMRI studies are usually reported for groups rather than for individuals. Researchers have found some variations in the activated areas of the brain among individuals within both the dyslexic and control groups. More research is needed to clarify these differences before fMRI or any other imaging techniques can be used for diagnostic purposes. Until that time, however, researchers can use the information gained from imaging studies to develop other kinds of diagnostic tests that more closely align with our new understanding of dyslexia.

For the moment, critical observation of a child's progress in learning to speak, and eventually in learning to read, remains our most effective tool for spotting potential problems. Most difficulties associated with reading do not go away with time. Therefore, the earlier that parents and teachers can detect reading problems in children, the better. The problems often begin to reveal themselves first in spoken language and later while learning to read.

## Spoken Language Difficulties

We discussed in previous chapters that learning to read is closely connected to fluency in spoken language. Both speaking and reading rely on the proper functioning of the phonologic areas of the brain where sounds are combined to form words and words are broken down into their basic sounds. Consequently, difficulties that children have with spoken language are often clues to potential reading problems. Parents and teachers should remember that it is normal for all children to make occasional language errors while speaking. But frequent language errors, stemming from any one or a combination of the following conditions, could indicate that a child may run into trouble when beginning to learn to read.

Some of the spoken language difficulties may involve any one or more of the following (Dehaene, 2009; IDA, 2003; NAEYC, 1998; Shaywitz, 2003):

- *Delay in speaking.* Children generally say their first words at about 12 months of age and follow with phrases when between 18 and 24 months old. Because learning to read is closely linked to a child's phonologic skills in spoken language, delays in speaking may be an early indication of potential reading problems, especially in a family that has a history of dyslexia.

- *Difficulties with pronunciation.* Children should have little difficulty pronouncing words correctly by 5 or 6 years of age. Difficulties in pronouncing words (sometimes referred to as "baby talk") may be an indication of future reading problems. Such trouble pronouncing long or complicated words could signal a snag in the parts of the brain that generate spoken language, causing a mix-up in the processing of the phonemes. Mispronunciations often involve mixing syllables within words (*aminal* for animal) and leaving off the beginning syllables (*luminum* for aluminum).

- *Difficulty in learning the letters of the alphabet.* Learning the names of the letters of the alphabet is an important, though not essential, step in learning to read. Marked difficulties in learning the letters could indicate a potential reading problem.

- *Recalling incorrect phonemes.* A child looks at a picture of a donkey and recalls the word *doggie*, a word similar in sound but not in meaning. This recall of incorrect phonemes may cause a child to talk about a word without actually recalling it. The child may get frustrated because of the inability to say the word. As these children get older, they may resort more to vague words in order to mask their difficulties in

*(Continued)*

(Continued)

retrieving specific words. They use general words like *things* and *stuff*, making their conversations hard to follow. It is important to remember that the problem here is not with their thinking, but with their ability to use expressive language—that is, to recall a word on command.

- *Insensitivity to rhyme.* Part of a young child's enjoyment of spoken language is playing with rhyme. Hearing and repeating rhyming sounds demonstrates how words can be separated into smaller segments of sound, and that different words may share the same sound. Children with good rhyming skills are showing their readiness for learning to read. Those with little sensitivity to rhyme, on the other hand, may have reading problems because they are unable to detect the consonant sound that changes the meaning of closely rhyming words.

- *Genetics.* We mentioned earlier that heredity is a key factor in dyslexia. Looking at the family tree for signs of dyslexia in close relatives is a clue because about 25 to 50 percent of the children born to a dyslexic parent will also be dyslexic. Whether the child actually displays dyslexia depends somewhat on that child's environment. This revelation came from studies of identical twins. Because they share the same genes, if one twin has dyslexia, so should the other. But in reality, in 30 to 35 percent of the cases, one twin is dyslexic while the other is not (Fisher & DeFries, 2002). Apparently, even though these children had a genetic predisposition for dyslexia, differences in the home and school environments played important roles in determining how successful these children would be at learning to read.

## Looking for Early Indicators of Reading Problems

Until the time that brain imaging becomes a standard diagnostic tool, researchers will continue to look for ways to accurately identify students with reading problems as early as possible. Multiple research studies have sought to find indicators of reading problems that are more valid than solely the professional judgment of the evaluating team. The obvious problem here is that the application of professional judgment is only as good as the training and competence of the team members. This approach can often lead to considerable variability in identification from one school district to another, and even from state to state. Using more objective measures would reduce this variability. Research studies have found that letter fluency is a useful measure in kindergarten, while response to instruction can be a valuable measure in second grade.

### Letter Fluency Tasks as Kindergarten Indicators

The earlier that children who are at risk for reading problems can be identified, the better. Trying to carry out such identification procedures in kindergarten is difficult because of the broad range of background experience these children bring to the classroom. Nonetheless, studies involving kindergarten children do seem to indicate that letter-name fluency and nonsense word fluency can be valid indicators of early reading skills, such as **oral reading fluency (ORF)**.

One study (Speece & Mills, 2003) tested 39 kindergartners in the spring in several language skill areas, including receptive vocabulary, phonological awareness, letter-name knowledge, letter-sound knowledge, letter-name fluency, and nonsense word fluency. These same children were again tested one year later in first grade in similar skills, plus ORF. Nonsense word fluency and letter-word fluency, respectively, were the highest predictors of ORF. In fact, the fluency measures were more accurate at predicting ORF than national normed measures of reading and phonological awareness, which identified only 33 percent of the poor readers in this study. Subsequent studies have found similar results (e.g., Burke, Hagan-Burke, Kwok, & Parker, 2009).

### Using Response to Intervention

Another technique for avoiding the misidentification or nonidentification of students with reading problems is to place increased emphasis on measures of school performance, especially in the primary grades. The response-to-intervention (RTI) model identifies students based on low achievement, application of certain criteria for exclusion, and their response to varying degrees of interventions. The goal is to screen all students to identify those who, despite a strong general education program in the regular classroom, are still failing. In Tier 1, they receive careful monitoring and special assistance as needed. Students who do not make adequate progress in Tier 1 move to Tier 2 where they receive targeted evidence-based interventions, usually from a team of educators. If more assistance is needed, the student moves to Tier 3, which involves more frequent and intensive interventions by a multidisciplinary team. Some schools and districts also have a fourth tier, while in others students in Tier 3 are identified as being in need of special education services. All students in an RTI model can move between tiers according to their rate of progress.

**Models for RTI Identification.** A survey of the research literature reveals several models that exist for using the RTI process to identify students at risk for reading difficulties. Three of the most common models proposed by researchers include the direct route models, the progress-monitoring models, and the risk index models. Here is a brief description of each:

- *Direct route models:* Students who are identified by screening measures as being at risk for reading difficulties are placed immediately into Tier 2 intervention. Screening is often done through the results of one reading skills measure (e.g., word identification) (Jenkins, Hudson, & Johnson, 2007). The problem with this model is that it may mistakenly identify students as being at risk.

- *Progress-monitoring models:* Students who are initially identified as at risk for reading difficulties are monitored for a number of weeks to see if their performance improves. This model helps to prevent students who were identified at the beginning of the school year as at risk when, in fact, their reading performance may have decreased simply due to the summer break. These students often respond positively to the first few weeks of reading instruction and will no longer be considered at risk. Progress-monitoring models have resulted in high levels of accuracy in studies examining their use, especially for students in the first grade (Compton, Fuchs, Fuchs, & Bryant, 2006). Although this model has a higher predictive value, it also postpones interventions during the monitoring phase.

- *Risk index models:* Identifying students at risk with this model involves looking at all variables collected on a student, including assessment results and other related factors, such as when the student is an English language learner, and the education level of the student's parents. The probability for risk is reported as a percentage of students who have similar profiles and who later performed poorly on some measure of reading skills. Thus, the higher the risk index, the greater the likelihood that the student may encounter difficulties when learning to read. Because risk index models take into account the impact of numerous variables, they tend to be more accurate than screening processes that rely on only a single measure (Johnson, Jenkins, Petscher, & Catts, 2009).

**Screening Measures.** Some screening measures have a higher predictive value of future reading ability than others. A comprehensive review of research studies found the following screening tools effective for Grades 1 to 3:

- Grade 1: Word identification fluency (WIF), letter knowledge, and phonological awareness are the common measures. Studies show that WIF is one of the strongest predictors of reading ability at this grade level (e.g., Compton et al., 2006).
- Grades 2 and 3: ORF and WIF are the measures regularly used. Although there are fewer studies of screening measures for these grades, both of these tools are strong predictors, especially for second-grade students.

Studies that tested this approach provided children in primary grades with incremental periods of instruction, usually through RTI, and moved them out when they made adequate progress. One study used data from nearly 400 linguistically diverse students to examine the usefulness of RTI measures in Grades 1 and 2 for predicting reading difficulties at the start of Grade 3 (Beach & O'Connor, 2013). Reading skills measured in first grade included oral reading fluency, phoneme segmentation fluency, and nonsense word fluency. Measures in second grade included tests of word identification, word attack, and word and passage comprehension. Students at both grade levels who met the intervention criteria were placed in small groups of two to three students and received support as needed for 25 to 30 minutes, four times per week. The instruction focused on letter-sound correspondence, sight word identification, decoding, and reading of sentences and decodable books. Some of the second-grade students needed practice in word study with multisyllabic words, vocabulary, and comprehension activities. They also received support in reading and rereading books at the students' current reading level, as well as opportunities for short spelling and sentence writing. English language learners were also included in these groups and received the same instruction.

The students were assessed at the beginning of third grade using tests of written spelling, ORF, picture vocabulary, word attack, WIF, and passage comprehension. The results showed that measures of first-grade WIF and second-grade ORF had correctly identified nearly 89 percent of students with reading difficulties (including English language learners), compared to 86 percent for average readers. Other measures, such as passage comprehension, also contributed to the identification, but to a lesser degree. This multifaceted identification process ensured that students with reading difficulties were monitored and given extra support in third grade, as needed. The study reaffirms the value in using multiple measures in the early primary grades to identify children at risk for reading difficulties.

Predictive Power of the Measures. One critical element of identifying children at risk for future reading difficulties is deciding which screening measures to use. As we mentioned earlier, many measures are commercially available, but not all have the same degree of predictive power. If an RTI model is to be effective, the screening procedures need to include measures that accurately identify all students at risk for reading problems (true positives), while reducing the number of students who are incorrectly identified (false positives). Practitioners who perform such screening should use care in selecting these measures. Some studies have evaluated the predictive power of the more commonly used measures for assessing the students' level of reading skills (e.g., Petscher, Kim, & Foorman, 2011).

Remember that all children make errors in spoken language and while reading. But the number of errors should decrease with time, and there should be clear evidence of growth in vocabulary and reading comprehension. Determining whether a child has consistent problems with reading requires careful and long-term observation of the child's fluency in speaking and reading. Most children display obvious improvements in their speaking and reading skills over time. Researchers, clinicians, and educators who study dyslexia and who work with poor readers look for certain clues that will show whether a child's reading ability is progressing normally.

The checklists that follow contain indications of reading problems commonly found in struggling readers, including those diagnosed with dyslexia. The indications have been gathered from several sources (e.g., Birsh, 2005; Brady & Moats, 1997; Clark-Edmands, 2000; IDA, 2003; Munro & Dalheim, 2008; NAEYC, 1998; Shaywitz, 2003; Stinson, 2003) and are separated into grade-level groupings. **The lists are not intended to be used for final diagnosis. Diagnosis of dyslexia or any other learning disorder can be made only by experienced clinicians.** However, the lists will help you to assess the degree of difficulty a child may be having in learning to read and to determine whether additional testing and consultations are required.

Use the following checklist to determine whether a child may be displaying problems. Circle the appropriate response to the right of each indicator. Those indicators marked "often" should be discussed among parents, teachers, and specialists in speech and language pathologies.

*Preschool*

| Indicator<br><br>(Inconsistent with the child's age or cognitive abilities)<br><br>After the skills have been taught, the child . . . | Rating | | |
|---|---|---|---|
| has difficulty pronouncing words | Rarely | Sometimes | Often |
| has difficulty with rhymes | Rarely | Sometimes | Often |
| is unable to recall the correct word | Rarely | Sometimes | Often |
| has difficulty in learning/remembering the names of letters | Rarely | Sometimes | Often |
| has difficulty following multistep directions or routines | Rarely | Sometimes | Often |
| has difficulty telling/retelling a story in correct sequence | Rarely | Sometimes | Often |
| has trouble learning common nursery rhymes | Rarely | Sometimes | Often |
| has difficulty separating sounds in words | Rarely | Sometimes | Often |
| has difficulty blending sounds to make words | Rarely | Sometimes | Often |
| has difficulty listening to and discussing storybooks | Rarely | Sometimes | Often |

*Kindergarten and First Grade*

| Indicator<br><br>(Inconsistent with the child's age or cognitive abilities)<br><br>After the skills have been taught, the child . . . | Rating | | |
|---|---|---|---|
| has difficulty recognizing that words can be separated into their basic sounds, such as *shoe* can be broken down into /sh/ and /oo/ | Rarely | Sometimes | Often |
| has difficulty recognizing that words can be separated, such as *horseshoe* into *horse* and *shoe* | Rarely | Sometimes | Often |
| has trouble sounding out individual words in isolation | Rarely | Sometimes | Often |
| has difficulty using descriptive language | Rarely | Sometimes | Often |
| says that reading is difficult | Rarely | Sometimes | Often |
| has difficulty connecting letters to their sounds | Rarely | Sometimes | Often |
| says a word that is very different from its text, such as saying *house* when reading *giant* | Rarely | Sometimes | Often |

| Indicator<br><br>(Inconsistent with the child's age or cognitive abilities)<br><br>After the skills have been taught, the child . . . | Rating | | |
|---|---|---|---|
| has difficulty pronouncing the beginning sounds in words | Rarely | Sometimes | Often |
| has difficulty spelling high-frequency short words | Rarely | Sometimes | Often |
| has difficulty reading orally with fluency | Rarely | Sometimes | Often |
| has difficulty using context to identify new words | Rarely | Sometimes | Often |
| has difficulty learning new vocabulary | Rarely | Sometimes | Often |
| has difficulty following simple directions, such as "Take out your notebook" | Rarely | Sometimes | Often |
| has difficulty retelling a story | Rarely | Sometimes | Often |
| has difficulty comprehending what was read | Rarely | Sometimes | Often |

*Second to Fourth Grade*

| Indicator<br><br>(Inconsistent with the child's age or cognitive abilities)<br><br>After the skills have been taught, the child . . . | Rating | | |
|---|---|---|---|
| makes letter reversals, as *b* for *d* and *q* for *p* | Rarely | Sometimes | Often |
| makes letter inversions, as *n* for *u* and *w* for *m* | Rarely | Sometimes | Often |
| makes word reversals, as *pot* for *top* | Rarely | Sometimes | Often |
| confuses small words, as *and* for *said* and *goes* for *does* | Rarely | Sometimes | Often |
| has difficulty pronouncing long, unfamiliar words | Rarely | Sometimes | Often |
| confuses words that sound alike, as *left* for *felt* or *ocean* for *motion* | Rarely | Sometimes | Often |
| relies on guessing and context to decode new words rather than sounding them out | Rarely | Sometimes | Often |
| omits parts of words when sounding them out, as *enjble* for *enjoyable* | Rarely | Sometimes | Often |
| has difficulty breaking multisyllabic words into their component syllables | Rarely | Sometimes | Often |
| avoids reading aloud | Rarely | Sometimes | Often |

*(Continued)*

(Continued)

| Indicator<br><br>(Inconsistent with the child's age or cognitive abilities)<br><br>After the skills have been taught, the child . . . | Rating | | |
|---|---|---|---|
| pauses and hesitates during speech, and uses lots of *ums* | Rarely | Sometimes | Often |
| has difficulty responding orally when questioned | Rarely | Sometimes | Often |
| relies heavily on memorizing instead of comprehending | Rarely | Sometimes | Often |
| has difficulty remembering facts | Rarely | Sometimes | Often |
| transposes number sequences | Rarely | Sometimes | Often |
| confuses arithmetic signs | Rarely | Sometimes | Often |
| has difficulty finishing written tests on time | Rarely | Sometimes | Often |
| has difficulty planning and organizing time and tasks | Rarely | Sometimes | Often |
| has difficulty representing the complete sound of a word when spelling | Rarely | Sometimes | Often |

*Fifth to Eighth Grade*

| Indicator<br><br>(Inconsistent with the child's age or cognitive abilities)<br><br>After the skills have been taught, the child . . . | Rating | | |
|---|---|---|---|
| reverses letter sequences, as *soiled* for *solid* | Rarely | Sometimes | Often |
| has difficulty identifying and learning prefixes, suffixes, and root words | Rarely | Sometimes | Often |
| spells the same word differently on the same page | Rarely | Sometimes | Often |
| reads aloud slowly, laboriously, and without inflection | Rarely | Sometimes | Often |
| performs disproportionately poorly on multiple-choice tests | Rarely | Sometimes | Often |
| avoids reading aloud | Rarely | Sometimes | Often |
| relies on guessing and context to decode new words rather than sounding them out individually | Rarely | Sometimes | Often |
| avoids writing | Rarely | Sometimes | Often |

| Indicator<br>(Inconsistent with the child's age or cognitive abilities)<br>After the skills have been taught, the child . . . | Rating | | |
|---|---|---|---|
| has difficulty with word problems in mathematics | Rarely | Sometimes | Often |
| has difficulty with comprehension when reading | Rarely | Sometimes | Often |
| has difficulty remembering facts (rote memory) | Rarely | Sometimes | Often |
| has difficulty responding orally when questioned | Rarely | Sometimes | Often |
| has difficulty with nonliteral language, such as idioms, jokes, slang, and proverbs | Rarely | Sometimes | Often |
| avoids reading for pleasure | Rarely | Sometimes | Often |
| has difficulty planning and organizing time, materials, and tasks | Rarely | Sometimes | Often |
| has difficulty learning a foreign language | Rarely | Sometimes | Often |
| writes with difficulty with illegible handwriting | Rarely | Sometimes | Often |

These lists can be useful tools in assessing whether a child (or an adult) displays the symptoms common to those diagnosed with reading problems, including dyslexia. The symptoms must be persistent and not the occasional error. Persistence over a prolonged period of time is the key to determining the likelihood of dyslexia or any other physical condition that is interfering with the child's ability to read.

It is not unusual for struggling readers and dyslexic students to be depressed by their reading failures and self-conscious about their difficulties in the classroom. They often find the classroom a very stressful environment and are likely to exhibit behavior problems if they do not receive the special consideration that they need. Because dyslexia is a spectrum disorder ranging from mild to severe, children who are only mildly affected may exhibit one or a few of the problems mentioned in the checklists.

## Remember the Strengths of Struggling Readers

Remember that struggling readers frequently have strengths in other areas, such as higher-order cognitive thinking that can help them manage or overcome their difficulties with reading. Many students with dyslexia are able to go on to higher education and be successful. But their reading deficits do not go away. One study looked at more than 100 college students with and without dyslexia and compared their reading ability (Kirby, Silvestri, Allingham, Parrila, & La Fave, 2008). Not surprisingly, the students with dyslexia reported that they continued to experience reading difficulties, especially in word reading, despite their average mental ability. They scored lower than the students without dyslexia on tests of selecting the main idea and on test-taking strategies. Students with dyslexia also reported using more study aids and time management strategies, and they were more likely to use a deep approach to learning than students without dyslexia. But the differences between the two groups were weaker in other reading measures, suggesting that those with dyslexia were able to compensate for their persistent word reading difficulties and become sufficiently competent readers to survive successfully in a university.

Growing scientific evidence continues to support the notion that most dyslexia is caused by deficits in phonological processing. It is important to recognize that dyslexia does not reflect an overall impairment in language, intelligence, or thinking skills. Many smart people are dyslexic. Rather, for most people it reflects an overall problem with the ability of a specific brain system, referred to earlier as the *visual word form area,* to put together the sounds of language to form words and to break words down into their basic sounds. This focus allows research to more closely examine the nature of these deficits and to explore methods for remediation. Other research evidence suggests that dyslexia may have multiple causes that require different forms of intervention. No doubt, some individuals display dyslexic symptoms because of visual and auditory problems not directly associated with phonological processing, but their numbers are small.

Famous people with dyslexia include:

Hans Christian Andersen (Author)

Winston Churchill (Statesman)

Tom Cruise (Actor)

Leonardo da Vinci (Painter)

Walt Disney (Producer)

Albert Einstein (Physicist)

Jay Leno (Comedian)

Auguste Rodin (Sculptor)

Steven Spielberg (Director)

W. B. Yeats (Poet)

Because reading does not come naturally to the human brain, children learning to read have to put much effort into associating their spoken language with the alphabet and with word recognition. To do this successfully, phonemic awareness is essential. In light of recent research, educators should have second thoughts about reading programs that delay phonemic awareness or that treat it as an ancillary skill to be learned in context with general reading.

Educators should also become more aware of the scientific research into dyslexia and be able to recognize when students are having persistent reading problems. Early identification of struggling readers leads to early intervention. Researchers agree that a systematic, intensive, and comprehensive approach to early intervention can significantly reduce the number of students reading below the Basic level of proficiency.

## A Note About "Cures" for Dyslexia

From time to time we read about a newly discovered scientific "cure" for dyslexia. Remember that dyslexia is mainly the result of persistent difficulties with phonological processing. It is a language-based disorder. Any treatments that focus on other causes should be viewed with caution. For example, one claim from Britain was that dyslexia was caused by an underdeveloped cerebellum—the part of the brain responsible for motor coordination. Treatment involves stimulating the cerebellum by repeated physical activities and balancing exercises. According to the proponents, dyslexic students using this intervention showed improvement in reading and writing.

Another claim is that dyslexia is caused mainly by vision problems. One "cure" involves "vision therapy" including eye exercises, while another suggests that colored lenses are the answer. Here, too, proponents claim that dyslexic children have improved their reading skills.

None of the above claims is supported or explained by current scientific knowledge or research. The scientific community is generally skeptical of any claims of curing developmental dyslexia. It is a lifelong spectral disorder that can be overcome best through early and appropriate interventions that are systematic, sequential, and focused on developing phonological awareness.

## Answer to Test Question #7

**Question:** Dyslexic students often have problems in other cognitive areas.

**Answer:** *False.* Dyslexic students have had to construct extensive neural pathways and enhance specific neural regions when struggling to read. As a result, they often have strong capabilities in problem solving, reasoning, critical thinking, and concept formation.

## QUESTIONS FOR DISCUSSION/REFLECTION

- *What are the most common causes of reading problems?*
- *What have brain imaging scans revealed about struggling and dyslexic readers?*
- *What are some methods for detecting reading problems?*

## What's Coming?

After recognizing that certain students are having reading problems, the next step is to select interventions that have been shown to be successful in helping struggling readers. All teachers are teachers of reading, and thus should have the training to strengthen the reading skills of students at every grade level. How to teach students with difficulties in reading is the focus of the next chapter.

# 6

# Overcoming Reading Problems

*Reading is a basic tool in the living of a good life.*

—Joseph Addison (1672–1719)

Many teachers work hard every day trying to help students with reading problems overcome their difficulties. Just how successful are these teachers? Are they using the evidence-based practices required by federal regulations, especially in special education classes designed to help students with reading difficulties? We observed in Chapter 5 that the NAEP reading scores of fourth-grade students have not significantly improved in the last decade (Figure 5.1). Clearly, we need to do better.

The key to helping children overcome reading problems is early diagnosis. Chapter 5 dealt with the various clues that can alert parents and teachers to potential difficulties in learning to read. When there is sufficient evidence that a child is at risk for developing reading problems, quick and early intervention is essential. Several reading programs that are based on the more recent research have proven successful with struggling readers. The programs adhere to the notion that for children to become literate, they must break the reading code. Children with dyslexia may use different neural pathways and may have to work harder, but they still must master the skills of decoding printed text into recognizable sounds.

## ✿ SOME CONSIDERATIONS FOR TEACHING STUDENTS WITH READING PROBLEMS

The regular classroom teacher typically works the most with struggling readers and helps them learn to read. When teachers suspect that a student has reading problems, it is generally useful to assess that student's skill level. Commercially available tests include the Lindamood Auditory Conceptualization Test, the Phonological Awareness Test, and the Gray Oral Reading Test. These and other tests assess specific skills, ranging from phonemic awareness to processing speed as well as auditory and verbal comprehension. Results from these assessments help teachers to design the instructional strategies and interventions that are most likely to succeed with a particular student. The following points might make the instructional process somewhat easier and more successful (DITT, 2001; Wawryk-Epp, Harrison, & Prentice, 2004).

### General Considerations

- Make your classroom expectations clear in age-appropriate language.
- Ensure that classroom procedures are orderly, structured, and predictable.
- Remember that many struggling readers *can* learn to read. They just need different kinds of instructional strategies and intense practice.
- Be constructive and positive. Labeling the child rather than the behavior can be disabling. Avoid labels and sarcasm that undermine the instructional environment and adversely affect the child's self-concept and performance.
- Recognize that struggling readers may take up to three times longer to complete work and will tire quickly.
- Avoid appeals to "try harder." Scanning studies show that the brains of struggling readers are already expending extra effort while decoding print, and these appeals will not improve performance. What is needed is slower speed with clearer comprehension.
- Determine and then complement these children's abilities, and teach through their strengths. Plan lessons so the students experience a sense of accomplishment rather than failure.
- Use formative assessments frequently to measure students' progress and level of skill acquisition.

### In the Elementary Classroom

- Get a complete explanation of the child's history of problems encountered when learning to read.
- Select scientifically researched reading strategies and use a multi-sensory approach.
- Recognize the frustration that these students feel as they struggle to read.
- Show concern and understanding.
- Recognize that performance may be well below the child's potential.
- Remember that this child learns in different ways, but can learn.

- Realize that the child may have behavioral and self-esteem problems.
- Develop good student-teacher rapport.
- Maintain contact with the child's parents and give them periodic progress reports. Make suggestions of what they can do with the child at home to complement your classroom strategies.
- Ensure that other classmates understand the nature of dyslexia so that the child is not bullied or mocked.
- Assign a buddy to help the struggling reader in the class and school.
- Encourage the child to point out talents and strengths.

## In the Secondary Classroom

- Get a complete explanation of the student's history of reading problems.
- Use a multisensory approach in classroom instruction.
- Recognize the compounded frustrations of an adolescent with dyslexia.
- Remember that students with dyslexia learn in different ways, but they *can* learn.
- Realize that these teenagers may have problems with their self-esteem.
- Recognize that these students may also have behavior or truancy problems.
- Realize that these students often have a significant gap between their performance and their potential.
- Show concern and understanding.
- Use diagrams and graphic organizers when teaching. Advanced organizers that contain important notes about the lesson are also very helpful and can help prevent failure.
- Develop good student-teacher rapport.
- Maintain contact with the student's parents and give them periodic progress reports. Make suggestions of what they can do with the student at home to complement your classroom strategies.
- Ensure that these students' legal rights are adhered to when taking tests.
- Children with mild dyslexia often develop coping strategies in elementary school. Be aware that these strategies may be inadequate for the complex and multifaceted secondary curriculum.
- Ensure that any remedial materials are relevant to the maturity and not the academic level of the student.
- Be aware that struggling readers can have great difficulty reading an unseen text aloud in class. Asking them to do this can adversely affect their self-esteem.

## BASIC INGREDIENTS OF EARLY INTERVENTION PROGRAMS

The National Reading Panel (NRP, 2000) and the National Early Literacy Panel (NELP, 2008) have strongly recommended that beginning reading programs focus on systematic and explicit instruction in helping children master the alphabetic principle, especially for children at risk for reading difficulties. Dozens of reading programs flood the market every year. Deciding which program can best meet the needs of struggling readers is now easier thanks to our greater understanding of how the brain learns to read. Based on this understanding, a reading program is likely to be successful in helping children with reading difficulties if it includes explicit instruction in phonological awareness and the alphabetic principle, as well as word identification skills that lead to accurate, fluent reading and comprehension. Multiple research studies demonstrate the success of this approach, especially for English language learners and children from low-income urban areas (e.g., Menzies, Mahdavi, & Lewis, 2008; O'Connor, Bocian, Beebe-Frankenberger, & Linklater, 2010; Yurick, Cartledge, Kourea, & Keyes, 2012).

## Response to Intervention

When the Individuals with Disabilities Education Act (IDEA) was reauthorized in 2004, it included an assistance model known as response to intervention (RTI). This model is a three-tier approach to the early identification and support for students with learning and behavior needs. RTI's Tier 1 starts with high-quality, scientifically based instruction in the general education classrooms. Ongoing screen and assessment provide information about each student's rate of learning and level of achievement, both as an individual and in comparison with the peer group.

Students who do not make adequate progress in Tier 1 move on to Tier 2 where they get increasingly intensive instruction, depending on their needs and rates of progress. This instruction is in small groups and is in addition to the general curriculum. Students who continue to have difficulties and show little progress in achievement are considered for Tier 3. Instruction at this level is intensive and individualized to target the student's specific deficits. If the student's level of achievement is still not adequate, then that student is referred for a comprehensive evaluation and eligibility for special education services.

There are a number of successful variations of the RTI model that schools are using to assist students with reading difficulties (e.g., Jenkins, Schiller, Blackorby, Thayer, & Tilly, 2013). Research studies show that, when appropriately implemented, RTI is an effective approach for helping students improve their reading skills (e.g., Callender, 2007; Vaughn, Wanzek, Linan-Thompson, & Murray, 2007; Vellutino, Scanlon, Zhang, & Schatschneider, 2008).

## How Do I Develop Phonemic Awareness in Struggling Readers?

Training in phonemic awareness needs to be more intense for children with reading disabilities. Reading programs are filled with activities for separating words into phonemes, synthesizing phonemes into words, and deleting and substituting phonemes. Research studies (e.g., Harn, Linan-Thompson, & Roberts, 2008; Menzies et al., 2008) suggest that the development of phonemic awareness is more likely to be successful if it contains three important components. First, there should be a monitoring system that assesses the students' progress and the rate at which they acquire reading skills. Too often, student assessments in the primary grades are random and too widely spaced in time. As a result, students who are not making adequate progress can be overlooked, while others may not receive instruction appropriate to their advanced skill level.

Second, instruction is intense by placing students in small groups. Having a low student-teacher ratio allows teachers to individualize and differentiate instruction, approaches that have been shown to be effective in numerous studies. Third, instruction is explicitly aimed at improving phonemic awareness and the understanding of the alphabetic principle. For example, one instructional component can focus on phonemic awareness, another on decoding and fluency, and a third one on guided reading techniques.

Teachers are likely to be successful in developing phonemic awareness with struggling readers if they consider these general principles when planning instruction (Chard & Osborn, 1998; Phillips & Torgesen, 2006):

- *Continuous sounds before stop sounds.* Start with continuous sounds such as /s/, /m/, and /f/ that are easier to pronounce. As students become more successful with these sounds, move to the stop sounds of /b/, /k/, and /p/.
- *Modeling.* Be sure to model carefully and accurately each activity when it is first introduced.
- *Easy to complex tasks.* Move from easier tasks, such as rhyming, to more complex tasks, such as blending and segmenting. Monitor progress along the way.
- *Larger to smaller units.* Move from the larger units of words and onset-rimes to the smaller units of individual phonemes.
- *Additional strategies.* Use additional strategies to help struggling readers, such as concrete objects (e.g., bingo chips or blocks), to represent sounds.

We have already discussed how early awareness of phonemes is a strong indicator of later reading success. Further, the research on interventions clearly demonstrates the benefits of explicitly teaching phonemic awareness skills. No students benefit more from this instruction than those already burdened with reading problems. The development of phonemic awareness occurs over several years. It is the last step in a developmental continuum that begins with the brain's earliest awareness of rhyme. Figure 6.1 illustrates the continuum from rhyming to full phoneme manipulation (Ehri & Roberts, 2006).

### General Guidelines

The five steps in Figure 6.1, from recognizing and generating rhymes to blending and segmenting phonemes, can occur during the preschool years in the appropriate environment. If the parent sings rhyming songs and reads to the child from rhyming books, the child's brain begins to recognize the sounds that comprise beginning language. However, many children begin school with a very weak phonological base. As we mentioned earlier, teachers must then assess where students lie on the

Figure 6.1     The development of phonemic awareness is a continuum that begins with recognizing and generating rhymes and ends with the successful manipulation of individual phonemes.

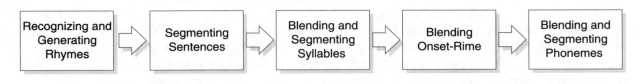

phonological continuum and select appropriate strategies to move them toward phonemic awareness. Teachers should consider the following guidelines when selecting strategies to help students recognize and successfully manipulate phonemes (Edelen-Smith, 1998; Ehri & Roberts, 2006; McGee & Ukrainetz, 2009).

- *Be specific.* Identify the specific phonemic awareness task and select the activities that are developmentally appropriate and that keep the students engaged in the task. Select words, phrases, and sentences from curricular materials to make this meaningful. Look for ways to make activities enjoyable so students see them as fun and not as monotonous drills. Use chants, poetry, rhymes, and songs to stimulate the students' curiosity about language structure and to develop their awareness of phoneme manipulation.

- *Avoid letter names.* Use the phonemic sounds of the alphabet when doing activities, and avoid letter names. Letters that sound as they are named only confuse the learner. Keep in mind that one sound may be represented by two or more letters. Target specific sounds and practice beforehand so students can hear them clearly.

- *Treat continuant and stop sounds differently.* Continuant sounds are easier to manipulate and hear than the stop sounds. When introducing each type, treat them differently so students become aware of their differences. Exaggerate continuant sounds by holding on to them: *sssssssing* and *rrrrrrun.* Use rapid repetition with the stop consonants: /K/-/K/-/K/-/K/-/K/-/K/-athy.

- *Emphasize how sounds vary with their position in a word.* Generally, the initial position in the word is the easiest sound. The final position is the next easiest, and the middle position is the most difficult. Use lots of examples to make this clear, such as *mop, pin,* and *better.*

- *Be aware of the sequence for introducing combined sounds.* When introducing the combined sounds, a consonant-vowel pattern should come first, then a vowel-consonant pattern, and finally a consonant-vowel-consonant pattern. For example: first *tie,* then *add,* and finally *bed.*

### Simple Phonemic Awareness

Young students are usually unaware that words are made of sounds that can be produced in isolation. This leaves it up to the teacher to find ways to emphasize the concept of speech sounds through *systematic* and *direct* instruction. A multimodality approach facilitates the processing and retention of sounds. This approach can include techniques such as illustrating, tracing, and chanting of sounds so that the students' brain processes sounds in different ways. This is particularly effective with children who have dyslexia as they usually have difficulty recognizing and processing phonemes. For students with phonological difficulties, the teacher may call their attention to how their mouth forms various sounds, or ask them to place their hand in front of their mouth when making voiced sounds.

An effective reading program should include activities that help children manipulate phonemes. Here are some ways to do this (Daly, Chafouleas, & Skinner, 2005; Edelen-Smith, 1998):

- *Recognizing isolated sounds.* Associate certain speech sounds with an animal or action that is familiar to the students. For example, the buzzing sound of a bee or snoring in sleep is zzzzzzzz-, the hissing of a snake, sssssss-, the sound of asking for quiet, shhhhhhhh-, or the sound of a motor scooter or motorboat, pppppppp-. Alliteration also helps with this task. Talking about Peter Piper picking a peck of peppers affords the valuable combination of sound recognition, storytelling, and literary context. It also provides self-correcting cues for initial-sound isolation and for sound-to-word matching.
- *Counting words, syllables, and phonemes.* It is easier for a child's brain to perceive words and syllables than individual phonemes. Thus word and syllable counting is a valuable exercise for sound recognition that can lead later to more accurate identification of phonemes. Start with a sentence from the curriculum and say it aloud. Do not write it out because the students should focus on listening. Ask the students to count the number of words they think are in the sentence. They can use markers or tokens to indicate the word number. Then show or write the sentence and have the students compare the number of words to their own count. Syllable counting can be done in many ways. Students can count syllables in the same way they identified the word count. Also, they can march around the room while saying the syllables, or they can clap hands, tap pencils, or do any other overt activity that indicates counting.
- *Synthesizing sounds.* Sound synthesis is an essential yet easily performed skill for phonemic awareness. Start with using the initial sound and then saying the remainder of the word. For example, the teacher says, "It starts with *b* and ends with *-and*; put it together, and it says *band*." The students take turns using the same phrasing to make up their own words. Variations include limiting the context to objects in the classroom or in the school, or to a particular story that the class has recently read.

Guessing games can also be productive and fun activities for playing with sounds. One game involves hiding an object in a bag or some other place and then giving clues to its name sound-by-sound or syllable-by-syllable. When a student guesses the word correctly, you reveal the object. Songs can also be used. Blending the music with the sounds of words increases the chances that the phonemes will be remembered.

- *Matching sounds to words.* This activity asks the learner to identify the initial sound of a word, an important skill for sound segmentation. Show the student a picture of a kite and ask, "Is this a *dddd-ite*, or a *llll-ite*, or a *kkkk-ite?*" You could also ask, "Is there a *k* in *kite?*" or "Which sound does *kite* start with?" This allows the students to try three onsets with three rimes and to mix and match until they get it correct. Consonants make a good beginning because they are easier to emphasize and prolong during pronunciation. Have students try other words in threes. Be sure to use the phoneme sound, not the letter name, when referring to a letter.

- *Identifying the position of sounds.* Segmenting whole words into their components is an important part of phonemic awareness. This ability is enhanced when learners recognize that sounds occur in different positions in words: initial, medial, and final. Edelen-Smith (1998) suggests explaining that words have beginning, middle, and end sounds just like a train has a beginning (engine), a middle (passenger car), and an end (caboose). Slowly articulate a consonant-vowel-consonant (CVC) word at this time, such as *c-a-t,* and point to the appropriate train part as you sound out each phoneme. Then have the students sound out other CVC words from a list or recent story, pointing to each train part as they say the parts of the word.

- *Segmenting sounds.* One of the more difficult phonemic tasks for children is to separately pronounce each sound of a spoken word in order. This process is called sound segmentation. Developing this skill should start with isolating the initial phonemes. The previous activities—matching sounds to words and identifying the position of sounds—help the learner identify and recognize initial phonemes. Visual cues can also play an important part in segmenting sounds. Select words that are familiar to the students (or have the students select the words) so that they can use contextual clues for meaning. After sufficient practice, eliminate the cards so that students can perform the sound-segmenting task without visual cues.

- *Associating sounds with letters.* For the reading process to be successful, the brain must associate the sounds that it has heard during the prereading years of spoken language with the written letters that represent them. This is particularly difficult for students with disabilities that hamper the learning of reading. Consequently, extensive practice is essential. Nearly all of the activities mentioned above—especially those involving visual cues—can be modified to include associations between sounds and letters. As the students master individual sounds, their corresponding letter names can then be introduced. A type of bingo game can also be used to practice sound-with-letter association. Each student gets a card with letters placed into a bingo grid. Draw a letter from a container and call out the phoneme. Students place tokens on the letter that corresponds to the phoneme. The student who first gets "phoneme bingo" names the letters aloud. Teachers can devise all types of variations to this bingo game to maintain the practice while keeping the task interesting and fun.

## Compound Phonemic Awareness

In compound phonemic awareness, the learner must hold one sound in memory while matching it to a second sound. For example, "Do *dog* and *deer* begin with the same sound?" The two activities that develop compound phonemic awareness involve matching one word to a second word and the deleting of sounds in a word.

- *Matching one word to another word.* Byrne (1991) has suggested three games to develop phonemic word matching skills. The words and pictures used in each of these games should relate to themes and readings done in the classroom. One involves making a set of dominoes that have two objects pictured on each tile. The students have to join the tiles showing objects that share the same beginning or ending sounds.

A second game uses picture cards that are placed face down in a pile. Each student draws a card from the pile and places it face up. Students continue to draw cards and place them in the face-up pile. The first student to match the beginning or ending sound of a drawn card with the top card on the face-up pile says the match aloud and collects the pile.

The third game is a variation of bingo. Each bingo card contains pictures, which the students mark when their picture has the same beginning or ending sound as the word said by the caller (student or teacher).

- *Deleting sounds.* Deleting sounds from words and manipulating phonemes within words are more difficult tasks for the young brain to accomplish. Studies show that most children must attain the mental age of 7 years before this task can be accomplished adequately (Cole & Mengler, 1994). Furthermore, segmentation skills and letter names must be mastered before sound deletion tasks can be successfully learned.

Three tasks seem to be particularly important to mastering this skill: deleting parts of a compound word, identifying a missing sound, and deleting a single sound from a word.

1. *Deleting parts of a compound word.* To illustrate deleting parts of a compound word, point to a picture or an object that is a compound word and demonstrate how each word can be said with one part missing. For example, "This is a classroom. I can say *class* without the *room.* And this is a farmhouse [or greenhouse]. I can say *farm* [*green*] without *house.* Now you try it. This is a playground." Use other common examples, such as *lighthouse, airplane, grandmother, seashore, sandbox, toothpaste,* and *nightlight.*

2. *Identifying the missing sound.* In this task, focus on deleting the initial and final sounds instead of the medial sounds, which is the first step to master for the young brain. Take word pairs, such as *ate-late,* and ask, "What's missing in *ate* that you hear in *late?*" Other examples are *ask-mask, able-table,* and *right-bright.* After a few trials, have the students make up their own word pairs, preferably from lesson material.

3. *Deleting a single sound from a word.* This task should begin with segmentation practice. First, separate the sound for deletion. For example, separate *g* from *glove.* "Glove. It starts with *g* and ends with *love.* Take the first sound away, and it says *love.*" Use words for which a sound deletion results in another real word. Other examples are *spot-pot, train-rain, scare-care,* and *snap-nap.* After practicing this skill, say a word aloud and ask students to say the word with the initial sound missing: "Say *mother* without the *m.*" Visual clues can help those who have difficulty saying a word with the deleted sound.

## Onset and Rime

The young brain's awareness of onsets, rimes, and syllables develops before an awareness of phonemes. **Onsets** are the initial consonants that change the meaning of a word; **rimes** are the vowel-consonant combinations that stay constant in a series. For example, in *bend, lend,* and *send,* the onsets are *b, l,* and *s;* the rime is *-end.* Note that the first step in Figure 6.1 is recognizing and generating rhymes. Rhyme generation can be used as an instructional strategy to develop explicit phonemic awareness skills by providing students with practice in manipulating the onset and the rime.

**Rhyme Generation.** Rhyme generation is a sequence of steps that starts by introducing the notion of rhyme generation to students. The teacher presents the concept of "rhyme" and asks students to define it and give examples. In the next step, the teacher presents rhymes in context, such as in a poem or song, and then asks students to identify the rhymes. Now the teacher demonstrates how to manipulate the onset and the rime. Using visual tools such as color codes on chart paper or word ladder graphics, the teacher shows how to generate new rhymes from previous words. First list the initial consonants and demonstrate how to manipulate the onset to create a new rhyme. For example, the word *bet* may be changed to *pet* by selecting a new onset.

In the next step, the teacher displays selected sentences from the original song or poem on sentence strips. Students show what they have learned by creating their own sentence that generates a new rhyme for the song or poem's context. Finally, the teacher encourages the students to do rhyme generation with their names. They use their own names to generate rhymes on a word ladder as well as those of their classmates. Teachers can use literature, word families, and direct instruction as strategies that focus on word play designed to enhance onset and rime recognition (Edelen-Smith, 1998; Ehri & Roberts, 2006; Joseph, 2007). Here are some examples of those strategies.

- *Literature.* Books with rhyming patterns (like many books by Dr. Seuss) are easily recalled through repeated exposure. Almost any literary source that plays with word sounds is valuable. Books that particularly develop awareness of sound patterns associated with onset and rime are those using alliteration (the repetition of an initial consonant across several words, e.g., *Peter Piper picked a peck of peppers*) and assonance (the repetition of vowel sounds within words, e.g., *The rain in Spain stays mainly on the plain*).
- *Word families charts.* Using words from a story or book, construct a chart that places a different beginning letter in front of a rime. For example, start with the rime *-at* and add *f, h, b,* and *s* to form *fat, hat, bat,* and *sat.* Have the students make up a story line whenever the word changes (e.g., *The fat cat chased a hat*). Encourage the students to make their own charts with different rimes and to keep them for future reference.
- *Direct instruction.* Students who have difficulties distinguishing the sounds among rhyming words need more direct instruction. Model rhyming pairs (e.g., *sun-fun* and *hand-band*) using flash cards so students match what they see with what they hear. Be sure they repeat each rhyming pair several times to reinforce auditory input. Another activity includes three cards, only two of which have rhyming words. Ask students to pick out and say the two that rhyme, or the one that doesn't. Later, change the rhyming words to two rhyming pictures out of three (e.g., a nose, a rose, and a horse).

## Successful Early Intervention Programs: Some Surprises

Numerous programs claiming to be effective intervention programs for struggling readers are available. Although controlled studies are needed to determine whether a program is truly effective, schools often purchase programs based on the strength of their marketing. Researchers supported by the U.S. Department of Education issued a report in 2009 that examined several hundred studies that looked at commercial programs and instructional approaches that focus on helping struggling readers (Slavin, Lake, Davis, & Madden, 2009). After screening these studies for controls, duration of study, and valid measures of effectiveness, 96 studies, involving a total of more than 14,000 children, were included. Table 6.1 shows those programs that were rated as having strong evidence of effectiveness based on the results of their studies. All the programs in Table 6.1 had large effect sizes—a statistical measure of the strength of an intervention.

**Table 6.1** Programs for Struggling Readers With Strong Evidence of Effectiveness

| Program | Brief Description |
|---|---|
| *Success for All* | Offers school staff training and materials to improve strategies relating to reading, and also provides tutoring to struggling children, mostly in the first grade. Classroom interventions use a structured, fast-paced approach with a strong emphasis on cooperative learning, phonics, metacognitive skills, and frequent assessments. In second grade and beyond, students are placed in four-member teams. The program also emphasizes parent involvement and interventions for behavior and other non-academic problems. |
| *Direct Instruction/ Corrective Reading* | Corrective Reading promotes reading accuracy (decoding), fluency, and comprehension skills of students in third grade or higher who are reading below their grade level. The program has 10 levels: four that focus on decoding skills and six levels that focus on comprehension skills. It can be implemented in small groups of four to five students or in a whole-class format. Corrective Reading is intended to be taught in 45-minute lessons, four to five times a week. |
| *Peer Assisted Learning Strategies (PALS)* | Students work in pairs, taking turns as learner and teacher, to learn literary skills such as blending sounds, phonemic awareness, phonics, reading of passages, and telling stories. Students use simple error-correction techniques with teacher guidance. |
| *Reading Recovery* | Provides extensive training, observation, and feedback to certified teachers. Program includes 30-minute lessons to the lowest 20 to 30 percent of first graders until they are reading at the level of average first graders in their school. Teachers usually work with four students one-half of each school day and teach a regular first-grade class the other half. Sessions involve (a) rereading of a familiar book, (b) independent reading of a text at the student's level, (c) teaching of letter knowledge, (d) composing and writing a sentence, (e) reconstructing a cut-up sentence, and (f) introducing a new book. The books are leveled readers with predictable text. Over the years, the program has added more of an emphasis on phonics and decoding skills. |

*(Continued)*

Table 6.1     (Continued)

| Program | Brief Description |
| --- | --- |
| *Targeted Reading Intervention (TRI)* | This is a one-to-one tutoring model designed for isolated rural schools. Classroom teachers work individually with struggling readers in kindergarten or first grade for 15 minutes a day. They receive professional development both for tutoring and for reading instruction in an summer institute followed by weekly Web conferencing from a university-based consultant to follow up on training, discuss individual children, and resolve problems. |
| *Quick Reads (Small-group tutorials)* | QuickReads texts are written for a specific grade, so 98 percent of the words in a text fit the grade-level curriculum. The texts are at a length that a grade-level reader should be able to read—when reading fluently—in one minute. They can be read throughout the day. It is a fluency and comprehension program that uses grade-level-appropriate concepts in science and social science texts. |

SOURCE: Slavin et al. (2009).

It is interesting to note that none of the dozen or so programs for struggling readers that rely essentially on computer-assisted instruction (CAI) had sufficient evidence of effectiveness to be on this list. A few CAI programs did show modest achievement gains, but they were too low compared to the programs cited in the table. Given all the focus these days on using technology in the classroom, the low effect size scores for CAI are particularly intriguing. It may be that the students involved with the computer instruction do not get enough teacher input, guidance, and supervision while they are working their way through the program. As a result, the CAI programs may not provide the intensity of instruction that we know struggling readers need to develop phonological awareness and to master the alphabetic principle.

The authors of this extensive review stress that the findings

- support the current RTI model that focuses on giving struggling readers high-quality instruction to start, and following that up with intensive instruction for those few students who continue to have reading difficulties despite the high quality of instruction (e.g., Gersten et al., 2009);
- show that one-on-one rather than small-group instruction works best for students with the most serious difficulties;
- support the idea that high-quality interventions over several years are required if we are to expect progress to endure, instead of the expectation that brief, intensive tutoring will put struggling readers back on track permanently; and
- are consistent with those of previous reviews of reading programs that found that programs offering extensive professional development to teachers had more positive effects than those providing technology, alternative curricula, or other interventions that essentially do not change daily instructional practices.

# PROGRAMS FOR OLDER STUDENTS ⚙

Educators cannot assume that strategies that are effective for students in the primary and intermediate grades will be equally effective with struggling adolescent readers, although some are. Older students may have already had numerous interventions addressing phonological awareness but few interventions to improve comprehension of text. Furthermore, older struggling readers may be better at hiding or compensating for their reading difficulties and thus require interventions that are more targeted and of longer duration.

Research studies assessing the skills of struggling adolescent readers reveal that their greatest needs are additional instructional support in fluency, vocabulary, and comprehension (Dennis, 2013). These studies further reveal considerable variability in the development of reading skills among this adolescent population (e.g., Brasseur-Hock, Hock, Kieffer, Biancarosa, & Deshler, 2011). The prominent high-stakes tests of today do not generally provide the information needed to make decisions about how to help *individual* students. Therefore, there is no one approach that will meet the needs of all struggling readers. Rather, it becomes necessary to use multiple measures of achievement to determine the strategies needed to address the individual variability in reading skills that exists among these students.

There are currently more than two-dozen commercial reading programs in the North American markets asserting that they can improve the reading skills of older struggling readers. Some have been subjected to controlled studies to measure their effectiveness, and some have not. (To find out more about research on specific programs, see the What Works Clearinghouse information in this book's "Resources" section.) Rather than recommend any specific commercial programs, I will suggest here some instructional strategies, approaches, and processes that are compatible with what we know about how the brain learns to read. Whether intentionally or inadvertently, the components of these suggested strategies are consistent with current research findings in educational neuroscience. Furthermore, when teachers add new instructional strategies—rather than self-contained programs—to their repertoire, they often see ways of using them when teaching other skills and different content areas. Finally, employing these strategies does not involve the significant expenditures required to purchase commercial programs.

## How Do I Develop Fluency and Comprehension in Older Struggling Readers?

Older struggling readers are able to develop strong reading capabilities when provided with effective instructional conditions. To be effective, reading programs must include activities that promote reading fluency. Shaywitz (2003) strongly supports the notion of short, intense daily practice sessions in reading in order to develop fluency. The children's practice continues over weeks and months as they reread passages until they attain high accuracy. Intense practice helps children build fluency because decoding becomes automatic, the same way that practice assists athletes and musicians with performing motor skills almost without thinking (Shaywitz calls this **overlearning**, the ability to perform something without attention or conscious thought).

Fluency comes through repetition of words and sentences. Such repetition increases the chances that words and common phrases will be stored in long-term memory, allowing for faster word recognition during subsequent encounters. The National Reading Panel (NRP, 2000) and subsequent studies (e.g., Strong, Wehby, Falk, & Lane, 2004) recommended reading programs that emphasize repeated oral reading accompanied by teacher feedback and guidance, a strategy referred to as *guided repeated oral reading*. The feedback is necessary because it gives children the opportunities to modify their pronunciation so that the stored representation of the word in their mental lexicon continues to approach its correct pronunciation and spelling. Whenever readers mispronounce words, it means that they do not have accurate mental representations of those words in their brains and will thus have difficulty storing or retrieving information related to them. Guided repeated oral reading is an especially effective technique for helping readers practice aloud unfamiliar vocabulary. Such practice builds accurate neural representations of the vocabulary and enhances comprehension. However, it is important to recognize that improvements in oral fluency do not necessarily correlate with improved comprehension. These are separate skills, and comprehension is a more complex cerebral process. Studies show that although oral fluency may improve in older students, comprehension may suffer, particularly as the text gets increasingly difficult (e.g., Paris, Carpenter, Paris, & Hamilton, 2004). This finding tells teachers that they should include instruction that targets comprehension skills while also working on fluency and advanced decoding strategies (Underwood & Pearson, 2004).

## What Strategies Teach Fluency and Comprehension to Struggling Readers?

Studies have shown that older students with reading problems are able to master the learning strategies that improve reading comprehension skills (e.g., Edmonds et al., 2009). For students with learning problems, learning to use questioning strategies is especially important because these students do not often spontaneously self-question or monitor their own reading comprehension.

Here are some strategies that researchers and teachers have found particularly effective.

### Questioning and Paraphrasing: Reciprocal Teaching

*Reciprocal teaching* is an approach that fosters student interaction with the text being read (Palincsar & Brown, 1984). In reciprocal teaching, students interact deeply with the text through the strategies of questioning, summarizing, clarifying, and predicting. Organized in the form of a discussion, the approach involves one leader (students and teacher take turns being the leader) who, after a portion of the text is read, first frames a question to which the group responds ("How . . . ?" or "Why . . . ?"). Second, participants share their own questions. Third, the leader summarizes the gist of the text ("The author is saying that . . . " or "The main idea here is . . . "), and participants comment or elaborate upon that summary. At any point in the discussion, either the leader or the participants may identify aspects of the text or discussion that need to be clarified ("I didn't understand . . . " or "I was confused when . . . "), and the group joins together to clarify the confusion. Finally, the leader indicates that it is time to move on and solicits predictions about what might come up next in the text ("I am wondering if . . . " or "I think that . . . ").

The value of paraphrasing, self-questioning, and finding the main idea are well-researched strategies. Students divide reading passages into smaller parts, such as sections, subsections, or paragraphs. After reading a segment, students are cued to use a self-questioning strategy to identify main ideas and details. The strategy requires a high level of attention to reading tasks because students must alternate their use of questioning and paraphrasing after reading each section, subsection, or paragraph.

Reciprocal teaching is an effective strategy because it requires the brain to integrate prior knowledge with new learning, to make inferences, to maintain focus, and to use auditory rehearsal to enhance retention of learning. Research studies support the value of reciprocal teaching from middle school to college. One study of 50 at-risk postsecondary students enrolled in a community college showed that the reciprocal teaching group performed significantly better than the comparison group on reading comprehension and strategy acquisition. There were no differences on perception of study skills. Poorer readers in the reciprocal teaching group outperformed poorer readers in the comparison group on both reading comprehension and strategy acquisition measures (Hart & Speece, 1998). Other studies report success using reciprocal teaching with college students who are struggling readers (e.g., Gruenbaum, 2012; Yang, 2010).

Another study involved more than 300 fifth-grade students, including those with typical and poor reading fluency skills (Schünemann, Spörer, & Brunstein, 2013). Those students who participated in reciprocal teaching had better reading comprehension than those in the control group. Furthermore, the improvement was sustained over an extended time period. See more about reciprocal teaching in Chapter 7.

## Questioning to Find the Main Idea

This self-questioning strategy focuses primarily on identifying and questioning the main idea or summary of a paragraph. Here's how it works. Students are first taught the concept of a main idea and how to do self-questioning. Students then practice, asking themselves questions aloud about each paragraph's main idea. They can use a cue card for assistance. Following the practice, the teacher provides immediate feedback. Eventually, following successful comprehension of these short paragraphs, students are presented with more lengthy passages, and the cue cards are removed. Continuing to give corrective feedback, the teacher finishes each lesson with a discussion of students' progress and of the strategy's usefulness. Studies show that students with learning disabilities who were trained in a self-questioning strategy performed significantly higher (i.e., demonstrated greater comprehension of what was read) than untrained students (Solis et al., 2012; Sousa, 2007).

### Story Mapping

One major challenge for older struggling readers is their difficulty in determining the relative importance of the material they are reading. They often cannot pick out main ideas from text or identify the information that leads to the main idea. Here is where story maps can help. Studies show story mapping to be an effective strategy with struggling readers (e.g., Edmonds et al., 2009), including those with emotional and behavioral problems (Vannest, Harrison, Temple-Harvey, Ramsey, & Parker, 2011).

In this strategy, students read a story, generate a map of its events and ideas, and then answer questions (Figure 6.2). To fill in the map, students have to identify the setting, characters, time, and place of the story; the problem, the goal, and the action that took place; and the outcome. The teacher models for students how to fill in the map, and then gives them many opportunities to practice the mapping technique for themselves and receive corrective feedback. The map is an effective visual tool that provides a framework for understanding, conceptualizing, and remembering important story events. The reading comprehension of students can improve significantly when the teacher gives direct instruction on the use of the strategy, expects frequent use of the strategy, and encourages students to use the strategy independently.

### Focusing on Comprehension

Students with reading disorders often have difficulty deriving meaning from what they read. If little or no meaning comes from reading, students lose motivation to read. Furthermore, meaning is essential for long-term retention of what they have read. Strategies designed to improve reading comprehension have been shown to improve students' interest in reading and their success.

**Figure 6.2**   These are just two examples of story maps. They help students discover the author's main ideas and to search out information to support them.

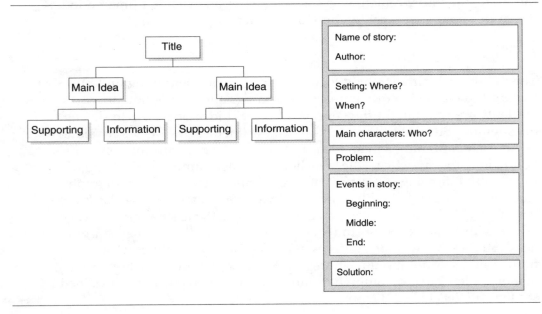

One such successful and brain-friendly strategy, suggested by Deshler, Ellis, and Lenz (1996), is a four-step process called by the acronym PASS (Preview, Ask, Summarize, and Synthesize). The teacher guides the students through the four steps, ensuring that they respond orally or in writing to the activities associated with each step. Grouping formats, such as cooperative learning, can be used to encourage active student participation and reduce anxiety over the correctness of each student's response.

1. Preview, Review, and Predict: This step helps the brain's frontal lobe search out some clues for determining the text's main ideas. Prediction engages the brain's creative networks and raises student interest.

   - Preview by reading the heading and one or two sentences.
   - Review what you already know about this topic.
   - Predict what you think the text or story will be about.

2. Ask and Answer Questions: If we expect the brain to remember what it has learned, the information must make sense and have meaning. These questions prompt the student to search long-term memory to find already-stored information that can help with sense and meaning.

   - Content-focused questions:
     o Who? What? Why? Where?
     o How does this relate to what I already know?

   - Monitoring questions:
     o Does this make sense?
     o Is my prediction correct?
     o How is this different from what I thought it was going to be about?

   - Problem-solving questions:
     o Is it important that it make sense?
     o Do I need to reread part of it?
     o Can I visualize the information?
     o Does it have too many unknown words?
     o Should I get help?

3. Summarize: By summarizing, the students are able to explain the text in their own words, thereby increasing the probability that it will make sense and have meaning.
   o Explain what the short passage you read was all about.

4. Synthesize: This step helps students decide in which memory networks they will store the newly learned information.

   - Explain how the short passage fits in with the whole passage.
   - Explain how what you learned fits in with what you knew.

If students have difficulty with any particular step, they can go back to the previous step to determine what information they need in order to proceed.

*Collaborative Strategic Reading*

Another excellent brain-friendly technique for helping students comprehend what they read and build vocabulary is called **collaborative strategic reading (CSR)**. It is particularly effective in classrooms where students have many different reading abilities and learning capabilities. The strategy is compatible with all types of reading programs.

CSR uses direct teaching and the collaborative power of cooperative learning groups to accomplish two phases designed to improve reading comprehension (Klingner, Vaughn, & Schumm, 1998). The first phase is a teacher-led component that takes students through four parts of a reading plan: Preview, Click and Clunk, Get the Gist, and Wrap-Up. The second phase involves using cooperative learning groups to provide an interactive environment where students can practice and perfect their reading comprehension skills. A variation of this strategy incorporates computer technology where appropriate.

## PHASE 1

### Teacher-Led Activities

- *Preview the reading.* Students know that previews in movies give some information about coming events. Use this as a motivational hook to the new reading. The learners preview the entire reading passage in order to get as much as they can about the passage in just a few minutes' time. The purpose here is to activate their prior knowledge about the topic and to give them an opportunity to predict what they will learn.

  Refer to student experiences about a movie, television program, or book that might contain information relevant to the new reading. Also, give clues to look for when previewing. For example, pictures, graphs, tables, or callout quotes provide information to help predict what students already know about the topic and what they will learn.

- *Click and clunk.* Students with reading problems often fail to monitor their understanding while they read. Clicks and clunks are devices to help students with this monitoring. Clicks are parts of the reading that make sense; clunks are parts or words that don't.

  Ask students to identify clunks as they go along. Then the class works with the teacher to develop strategies to clarify the clunks, such as

  - rereading the sentences while looking for key words that can help extract meaning from the context;
  - rereading previous and following sentences to get additional context clues;
  - looking for a prefix or suffix in the word that could help with meaning; and
  - breaking the word apart to see if smaller words are present that provide meaning.

- *Get the gist.* The goal of this phase is twofold. First, ask the readers to state in their own words the most important person, place, or thing in the passage. Second, get them to tell in as few words as possible (i.e., leaving out the details) the most important idea about that person, place, or thing. Because writing often improves memory, occasionally ask the students to write down their gists. Students can then read their gists aloud and invite comments from the group about ways to improve the gist. This process can be done so that all students benefit by enhancing their skills.

- *Wrap-up.* Wrap-up is a closure activity that allows students to review in their mind what has been learned to ensure that it makes sense and has meaning, thereby increasing the chances the brain will remember it. Focus students on the new learning by asking them to generate questions whose answers would show what they learned from the passage. They should also review key ideas.

  Start with questions that focus on the explicit material in the passage, such as who, what, where, and when. Afterward, move to questions that stimulate higher-order thinking, such as "What might have happened if . . . ?" and "What could be another way to solve this problem?" Writing down the response will help students sort out and remember the important ideas.

## PHASE 2

### Cooperative Learning Groups

This phase puts the students into cooperative learning groups to practice CSR in an interactive environment. Research on memory clearly shows that we are much more likely to remember information when we discuss, clarify, and review it with others. True cooperative learning groups are usually made up of about five students of mixed ability levels who learn and perform certain roles in the group to ensure completion of the learning task (Johnson & Johnson, 1989). The roles rotate among the group members so that every student gets the opportunity to be the leader and use the various skills needed to perform each task. Although there are many roles that students can perform, here are the most common (assuming five members per group):

- Leader. Leads the group through CSR by saying what to read next and what strategy to use.
- Clunk expert. Reminds the group what strategies to use when encountering a difficult word or phrase.
- Announcer. Calls on different group members to make certain that everyone participates and that only one person talks at a time.
- Encourager. Gives the group feedback on behaviors that are to be praised and those that need improvement.
- Reporter. Takes notes and reports to the whole class the main idea that the group has learned and shares a question that the group generated during its wrap-up.

Here are suggestions for using the cooperative learning groups with this strategy:

- *Cue sheets.* Giving all group members a cue sheet to guide them through the CSR provides a structure and focus for the group. The cue sheet should be specific for each role. For example, the leader's sheet contains statements that steer the group through each step of CSR (e.g., "Today's topic is . . . ," "Let's predict what we might learn from this," and "Let's think of some questions to see if we really understand what we learned") and also direct other group members to carry out their role (e.g., "Announcer, please call on others to share their ideas" and "Encourager, tell us what we did well and what we need to do better next time").

- *CSR learning logs.* Recording in logs helps students to keep track of what was learned. Students can keep separate logs for each subject. The log serves as a reminder for follow-up activities and can be used to document a student's progress as required by the individualized education plan.
- *Reading materials.* CSR was originally designed for expository text, but has also been used successfully with narrative text. For the strategy to be successful, select reading passages that are rich in clues, that have just one main idea per paragraph, and that provide a context to help students connect and associate details into larger ideas.

### Additional Strategies

**Reading Aloud.** Some of the models for teaching reading discussed in Chapter 3 that involve repeated oral reading are appropriate to use with older struggling readers. Paired (or partner) reading and readers' theatre are particularly effective classroom strategies. Reading aloud helps students of all ages gain confidence in their developing reading skills. This is especially important around the fourth grade where there is a large increase in vocabulary words with irregular pronunciations. Struggling readers need considerable practice with these words to develop fluency and avoid the well-known drop in reading performance that occurs in fourth grade. Two of the main sources of irregular pronunciation problems are

1. words that contain the same root but are pronounced differently— for example, *bough, cough, dough,* and *rough; have* and *gave;* or *bead* and *dead;* and

2. words where the same letters get different pronunciations, as in the following pairs: *electric-electricity, grade-gradual, nation-national, muscle-muscular,* and *sign-signature.*

These words must be learned and overlearned by repeated practice as part of the fluency exercises given in class.

**Question the Author.** Older struggling readers can be unenthusiastic about engaging with a text and processing information from it. Their motivation needs to be primed. This brain-friendly strategy is one way to do that. It encourages students to ask questions of the author and the text, such as "What is the author's message?" and "Does the author explain this clearly?" For the students, forming these questions raises their interest level, engages the problem-solving areas of their brain's frontal lobe, and helps them find sense and meaning in what they are reading. Doing so increases comprehension.

Using this strategy involves several steps (Beck, McKeown, Hamilton, & Kugan, 1997):

1. Select a passage from the text that both is interesting and can provoke a good conversation.

2. Decide on those points where you believe you need to stop in the text because you think the students need to obtain a greater understanding.

3. Create some questions for each of these stopping points. For example:
   - What is the author trying to say up to this point?
   - Why do you think the author used the following phrase . . . ?
   - Does what you have read so far make sense to you?

4. Show your students a short passage along with one or two questions that you have created ahead of time.

5. Model for your students how to think through the questions.

6. Ask the students to read and work through the questions that you prepared for their readings.

If appropriate, you can expand this activity by asking the students to summarize their ideas by completing the following phrase: "If I were the author, I would . . . " Ask some students to volunteer their responses, and engage the class in an appropriate discussion. Remember that your role is to facilitate the discussion, not lead it.

### Attention Therapy to Improve Comprehension

Successful reading requires sustained attention to the printed text. Researchers now recognize that attention is a complex process that requires the brain to focus, shift, sustain, and encode relevant stimuli while simultaneously impeding the processing of irrelevant stimuli (Posner, Rothbart, & Sheese, 2007). In reading, visual attention (the eyes scanning the page) must be sustained long enough for the visual processing system (in the rear of the brain) to perceive the text and send it to the visual word form area so that the cognitive processing system (frontal lobe) can eventually comprehend the text. Visual attention, therefore, is the catalyst that links perception to comprehension.

Students with attention deficits often have reading difficulties as well. Because visual attention is a learned skill, the research question here is this: Can giving students with reading difficulties attention therapy that improves visual attention practices lead to better reading comprehension? In a pivotal study (Solan, Shelley-Tremblay, Ficarra, Silverman, & Larson, 2003), 30 Grade 6 students with reading problems were split into two groups. One group received 12 one-hour sessions of individually monitored, computer-based attention therapy programs. The second group served as the control and was given no therapy during the 12-week period. The therapy program consisted of computer-based activities designed to improve perceptual accuracy, visual efficiency, visual search, visual scan, and visual span. Each session was followed with paper-and-pencil exercises for additional practice. The program also emphasized improving visual memory.

After completing the program, the mean reading comprehension scores improved significantly, from the 23rd to the 35th percentile, and a grade-equivalent increase from 4.1 to 5.2. Because this improvement is well over one standard deviation, it is unlikely that the results can be attributed to the practice that occurred as part of the program. This study is significant because it showed that (1) attention skills are malleable and measurable, (2) attention therapy improves attention duration, and (3) students who receive attention therapy score better on tests of reading comprehension than controls. Follow-up studies have revealed a common linkage between reading comprehension and visual attention (Solan, Shelley-Tremblay, Hansen, & Larson, 2007), and the positive impact of attention therapy on comprehension for struggling adolescent readers (Shelley-Tremblay, Langhinrichsen-Rohling, & Eyer, 2012).

Although the samples in these studies were small (from 30 to 42 students), the results were intriguing and consistent. If further studies continue to support these findings, then computer-based attention therapy programs may someday become another tool that teachers of remedial reading may consider in their efforts to improve their students' reading comprehension.

---

### Answer to Test Question #8

**Question:** Many poor readers have attention problems that schools are not equipped to handle.

**Answer:** *False.* Many poor readers expend a great deal of effort at first trying to decode text, but their struggle leads to frustration and eventually to inattentiveness.

---

## Tutoring in Reading for Fluency

Tutoring can be a significant enhancement to fluency in reading (Snow, Burns, & Griffin, 1998). Tutors can be volunteers, older students, or parents. Essentially, tutors provide individual guided practice and corrective feedback to a student while the student reads aloud from meaningful text at a suitable level of difficulty. To be effective, it is important that the tutors have a specific approach to the tutoring session. All tutors should be provided training in basic tutoring techniques and in the selection of appropriate materials. These materials should be closely related to the reading materials that the students are using in their classes.

Parker, Hasbrouck, and Denton (2002a) suggest three types of tutoring interventions: (1) repeated reading with a model, (2) oral reading with monitoring and feedback, and (3) error monitoring and reading practice.

### Repeated Reading With a Model

Simultaneous, repeated reading with a tutor is an effective method for improving the fluency of reluctant readers (e.g., Kuhn & Stahl, 2003; Ring, Barefoot, Avrit, Brown, & Black, 2013; Therrien, 2004). By carefully adjusting the timing and control of the repeated readings, the tutor helps the student foster independent reading skills. Here are the three steps to this approach:

- Step 1: Introduction
  - Start with a passage that will take 3 to 5 minutes for the student to read aloud.
  - Read the title.
  - Give a general description of the topic.
  - Ask if the student knows anything about the topic.
  - Give a reason or purpose for reading the topic.
  - Explain that the passage may be difficult, so you will read it together.

- Step 2: Simultaneous reading
  - Read the passage with the student, sitting slightly behind so as not to be a visual distraction.
  - Read slowly in a clear, soft voice as the student reads aloud at the same time.
  - Regulate your speed of reading to allow the student to keep up.
  - The student and you should move your fingers under the printed text as you read.
  - Listen carefully as to whether the student is following, reading with, or leading your reading of difficult words. Most students will initially follow the tutor. But with greater confidence, they will read more nearly with the tutor, and eventually will lead.
  - As the student comes closer to your reading speed, soften your voice. As the student leads more, soften your voice further and slow your pace slightly to allow the student to lead even more.

- Step 3: Simultaneous repeated readings
  - After a short break, begin rereading. From two to five readings will be beneficial, depending on the student's motivation and age.
  - With each rereading, maintain a smooth pace and encourage the student to read with you and to lead by softening your voice and slowing your pace slightly.

## Oral Reading With Monitoring and Feedback

Oral reading is one of the effective practices recommended by the National Reading Panel (NRP, 2000). This process uses a text that the student can read with 90 to 95 percent oral reading accuracy, and at a moderate level of difficulty. The tutor provides direct feedback on difficult words encountered in the text. The aim here is for the student to avoid long pauses while attempting to decode unfamiliar words and to build fluency and confidence in reading. Here are the two steps in this process:

- Step 1: Introduction
  - Ask the student to read the passage aloud as smoothly, quickly, and accurately as possible.
  - Reassure the student that, although you do not want to interrupt the reading, you will help with words that are unfamiliar or misread.

- Show the student how to use a finger or marker to pace the reading and to keep on track.
- Step 2: Providing feedback
  - Sit slightly behind the student so as not to be a visual distraction.
  - Immediately pronounce correctly any mispronounced word, and have the student quickly repeat it without breaking stride in reading.
  - Strive for minimal interruption, but immediately correct each error. If the student is making more than one error every 10 words or so, then the passage is too difficult.
  - Ask the student to use a finger or marker to pace the reading.
  - Take note of any pattern in the student's errors, such as any specific words that are missed with high frequency, missing specific letter or sound patterns, and violations of phonics rules. This is an advanced tutoring skill and should only be done by tutors who have a good knowledge of phonics and word structure.

### *Error Monitoring and Reading Practice*

This approach gives students the opportunity to practice difficult words not connected to text. Students practice reading word patterns, words, and sentences from flash cards. The flash card practice proceeds rapidly, without interruption, for 15 to 25 cards, or 3 to 5 minutes, depending on the student's age. If the student gets stuck on a word, wait only 1 to 3 seconds before saying it. Stick the more difficult words back in the deck toward the front so the student has more practice with them. Here are three different variations of this reading practice:

- Variation 1: Word patterns
  - Write the words to be practiced on index cards. The student can help make the cards, if appropriate.
  - Consider writing the word on both sides of the card to make it easier for you to see it.
  - Group flash cards with similar error patterns for later, focused practice.
- Variation 2: Word practice
  - As the student is reading a passage aloud, mark any word reading errors with a pencil check, or underline them on a separate copy.
  - Allow the reading to continue until the student has made 5 to 15 errors. Stop the reading at the end of a sentence or paragraph.
  - Prepare flash cards with selected missed words on them. Avoid the names of characters, places, or vocabulary specific to the story as well as unusual or rarely used words. Select words that are commonly used by the student and that reflect useful phonemic and structural patterns.
- Variation 3: Sentence practice (in context)
  - As the student is reading a passage aloud, mark on a separate copy any word reading errors with a pencil check or underline.

- o Allow the reading to continue until the student has made 5 to 15 errors. Stop the reading at the end of a sentence or paragraph.
- o Point out the student's first error and ask, "What is this word?" If the student cannot read it, identify the word.
- o Ask the student to read the entire sentence again until it can be done without hesitation or error. Continue this process with all the original errors.
- o When completed, have the student continue reading the passage until another 5 to 15 errors are made. Repeat the above steps.

## *Evaluating the Effectiveness of Tutoring*

Effective tutoring should enable the student to read meaningful, connected text at that student's instructional reading level. Reading performance can be evaluated by three indexes: oral reading accuracy (ORA), oral reading fluency (ORF), and comprehension as measured by answers to questions presented after the student has read a passage. These evaluations should be carried out periodically to provide feedback to the tutor.

**Oral Reading Accuracy.** Oral reading accuracy (ORA) is calculated by a simple formula in which the number of word errors (not counting repetitions or self-corrected errors) is subtracted from the total number of words read, and then dividing that result by the total number of words. The resulting decimal is multiplied by 100 to yield a percentage.

Have the student read a previously practiced passage without the tutor and calculate the student's ORA. For example, if the student reads a passage of 150 words and makes 15 errors while reading all the words, the calculation would be 150 minus 15, which is 135, divided by 150. The result is 0.9, which is then multiplied by 100 to yield 90 percent. The goal is for a 95 percent ORA. If the goal is not met, the student continues to practice on that passage with the tutor, attempting to reach the goal.

$$\frac{(\text{Total Number of Words Read}) - (\text{Number of Word Errors})}{(\text{Total Number of Words})} \times 100$$

= % Oral Reading Accuracy

**Oral Reading Fluency.** Because time is involved, ORF is also known as the student's *reading rate,* and is the same as the calculation of words correct per minute (WCPM) discussed in Chapter 3 (see Table 3.2).

For example, a third-grade student reads a passage of 150 words with 17 errors in one-and-a-half minutes. Subtracting the 17 errors from the 150 words yields a total of 133 words that were correctly read in 1.5 minutes. Dividing the 1.5 minutes into 133 words yields a WCPM of 89. Comparing the 89 to the average reading rates listed in Table 3.2 shows that this student is reading at the lower end of the range for third grade.

First calculate the ORF for an unpracticed reading and compare that to the ORF after the student has practiced with the passage. The change in ORF values will be a measure of the student's progress toward fluency. It is also helpful to compare the student's ORF with a chart of average reading rates for students in Grades 2 through 12 (see Table 3.2).

Both the ORA and the ORF can be charted on a bar or line graph to provide additional motivation for the student (see Figure 3.8). Having the students participate in creating the chart will also increase their sense of accomplishment.

## Tutoring in Reading for Comprehension

Poor readers often do not comprehend what they have read. This may occur because they failed to comprehend key words or sentences, or how the sentences related to each other, or simply because they did not maintain concentration or interest. It is also possible that the readers lack the background knowledge necessary to comprehend the text. Tutoring in reading comprehension starts with carefully selecting reading materials and with improving understanding and motivation. Here are some suggestions for how to accomplish this (Parker, Hasbrouck, & Denton, 2002b):

- Selecting reading passages or books
  - To select readable text, ask the student to read a 100-word segment of the selected text and calculate the student's ORA, as explained earlier. An ORA score of 80 or less means that the text is too frustrating for the reader. Scores of 85 to 90 percent are acceptable when the tutoring involves close monitoring and feedback from the tutor and multiple practices with the same text. An ORA score of 90 to 95 percent is considered best for closely monitored tutoring. A text with ORA scores of 95 percent and higher can be used with little tutor guidance and should be considered for independent reading practice by the student.
  - To select comprehensible text, ask the student to read a passage. Then ask three or four brief open-ended questions that cannot be answered by common knowledge alone. The questions should cover most of the content of the passage and should not rely on trivial details. For example, "Why did that happen?" "What did he mean when . . . ?" "What do you think will happen if . . . ?" If the student can answer two or three questions correctly, the text can be used in tutoring. On the other hand, if the student can answer none or just one question, the text is not appropriate for tutoring.

- Improving understanding
  - What did it say? Recognize that comprehension problems are often caused by problems with fluency. In their attempt to read smoothly and accurately, students lose the meaning at the sentence level and beyond. Sit beside the student with a 4 × 6 card. After the student reads one or two sentences, cover them and ask, "What did that say?" The student should paraphrase the meaning of what was just read. Praise the student's response and either elaborate on the response or offer a model summary, such as "I would add . . . " or "I would say . . . " Assure the student that many different responses are acceptable.

Move on to the next few sentences and repeat the process. As the student develops summarizing skills, ask the student to summarize longer selections of three or four sentences or a full paragraph. With this approach, the student's comprehension progresses from single sentence, to multisentence, to paragraph, and on to several paragraphs. As the text selection gets longer, remind the student to keep the oral summary to just one or two sentences.

- Reading to find out
  - This approach for improving understanding requires you to read the text and prepare ahead of time. Ask the student to read a certain amount of text (depending on the reader's skill level) and to find out a certain amount of information. The answer should not be found through common knowledge alone and should not rely on trivial details. The student can refer back to the text to substantiate the answer. Listen to the student's response, provide supportive feedback, and augment the student's response or offer a model one of your own, if necessary.
- Improving motivation
  - Students become motivated when they see achievement and greater understanding as a result of their efforts. By teaching students how to learn, rather than just specific skills, you help them apply a set of skills to solve tasks more effectively and efficiently in school as well as in nonacademic settings.

Students are also motivated when you give them a reason to read. Most students really want to succeed in school. Knowing how to read fluently and with understanding can be a powerful motivator for reading more and for pleasure.

## REWIRING THE BRAINS OF STRUGGLING READERS

Can the human brain be rewired for certain tasks? If so, is it possible to reroute the auxiliary circuits used by struggling readers to utilize the left posterior regions that are predisposed to rapid and automatic reading? Perhaps the most exciting news from neuroscience about reading has been the studies to determine whether such rewiring can occur as a result of using reading interventions. These imaging studies looked at children with difficult reading problems before and after they were subjected to an extensive phonologically based reading program.

In a study sponsored by Syracuse University, specially trained teachers provided second-grade and third-grade struggling readers with 50 minutes of individualized tutoring daily in activities related to the alphabetic principle. The tutoring, which lasted 8 months (105 hours), was in addition to the students' regular reading instruction. At the end of the yearlong intervention, all of the children improved their reading in varying degrees. The functional magnetic resonance imaging (fMRI) images taken immediately after the program showed the emergence of primary processing systems on the left side of the brain (like those used by good readers) in addition to the auxiliary pathways on the right side common to dyslexic and struggling readers. Furthermore, one year after the program intervention, fMRIs indicated there was additional development of the primary neural systems on the left rear side of the brain while the right front areas were less prominent (Figure 6.3). In other words, the program intervention appeared to have rewired the brains of struggling readers to more closely approximate the reading circuitry in the brains of typical readers, resulting in accurate and *fluent* readers (Shaywitz, 2003; Shaywitz et al., 2003).

A University of Washington fMRI study of shorter duration used a program based on phoneme and morpheme mapping with 10 children with dyslexia and 11 typical readers. After 28 hours of instruction, the fMRI scans showed changes in the brain functions of the children with dyslexia that closely resembled the neural processing characteristics of typical readers (Aylward et al., 2003).

Another study addressed the question of how much time the auditory system needs to correctly process the onset (or beginning) phoneme in a word. The only way to hear the difference between the words *bear* and *pear* is in the first 40 milliseconds of the onset of those sounds. You will recall from Chapter 5 that if the visual and auditory processing systems are not synchronized during reading, a child will have difficulty correctly matching phonemes to the letters that represent them. As a result, other brain regions are called into play in an effort to decode the words. Students with dyslexia are thus required to use a more labor-intensive set of neural pathways to recognize, decode, and comprehend the words they are reading.

**Figure 6.3**    These representative scans show the changes evident in the brains of struggling readers about one year after their involvement with effective reading interventions. Note that the interventions have helped the children develop reading areas (shown in white) that more closely resemble the areas used by typical readers.

**Changes in Brains of Struggling Readers**

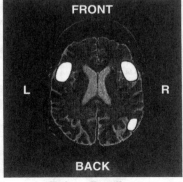
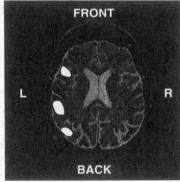

**Before Reading Interventions**          **After Reading Interventions**

The study involved 20 children with dyslexia aged 8 to 12 years (Temple et al., 2003). Their brains were scanned with functional MRIs before and after participating in an 8-week training program that focused on developing the alphabetic principle and phonemic practice. A control group of 12 students with typical reading abilities also had their brain scanned but did not participate in the training.

The pretraining scans were taken while the children were asked to identify letters that rhymed. During this exercise, children with typical reading abilities showed activity in the left temporal area (Broca's area, described in Chapter 1) as well as in the occipitotemporal region typical of skilled readers. The children with dyslexia, however, struggled with the task and showed activation mainly in the left and right frontal areas, similar to those shown for the reader with dyslexia (see Chapter 5).

The students with dyslexia then used a computer program called *Fast ForWord* for 100 minutes a day, 5 days a week. The program was designed to help students recognize the differences between onset sounds, especially those in words that rhyme. For example, the computer would show a picture of a boy and a toy. The computer voice would ask the student to point to the boy. At first, the computer voice asked the questions in a slow, exaggerated manner to help the student hear the differences in the /b/ and /t/ onset sounds. As the student progressed, the speed of the computer voice slowly increased.

After 8 weeks of training, the children were again given fMRIs while performing the rhyming activities. Their brain scans showed increased activity after remediation in the same areas that were activated in the typically reading children performing this task. As in other similar studies, the intense training in phonological awareness stimulated areas in the dyslexic brain that were not activated while reading prior to the training. There was also increased activity in right frontal brain regions not used by typical children. Apparently, the recovery of a more typical pathway also reactivated frontal areas that are used in children with dyslexia to compensate for their decoding difficulties. The researchers speculate that this activation pattern in the right frontal area might continue to change over time and come closer to that of typical readers (Habib, 2003).

The children who had dyslexia were retested after the training in several reading and language skills. In Figure 6.4, it is evident that their posttraining scores went up in the three reading areas tested by the Woodcock-Johnson Reading Mastery Test, namely, word identification, word attack, and passage comprehension.

Another study illustrates the effectiveness of focusing on the alphabetic principle when working with children with dyslexia (Richards & Berninger, 2008). The brains of 18 children with dyslexia and 21 without dyslexia were scanned with fMRI before and after the children with dyslexia received instructional treatment. All of the children performed a phoneme mapping task during the scanning, deciding whether letter(s) in a pair of pronounceable nonwords could stand for the same sound. Before treatment, a significant difference in fMRI scans was observed between children with dyslexia and those without in the brain areas similar to those in the left image of Figure 6.3.

The treatment for the children with dyslexia involved a 3-week instructional program that provided explicit instruction in linguistic

Figure 6.4   The graph shows the pretraining and posttraining average scores of the students with dyslexia on the word identification, word attack, and reading comprehension sections of the Woodcock-Johnson Reading Mastery Test (Temple et al., 2003).

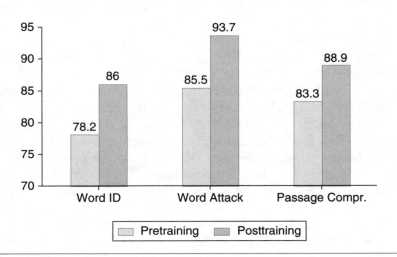

awareness, the alphabetic principle (taught in a way to maximize grapheme-phoneme associations), decoding and spelling, and a writers' workshop. After treatment, the fMRI scans showed that active areas in the brains of those children did not differ from the children without dyslexia in any of the brain clusters, suggesting that functional connectivity between the areas responsible for reading may normalize following targeted instructional treatment.

These and subsequent studies suggest that targeted and teacher-directed research-based reading programs that use computers to help students build phonemic awareness can substantially—and perhaps permanently—benefit struggling readers (e.g., Borman & Benson, 2006; Rouse & Krueger, 2004). The changes due to remediation brought the brain function of children with dyslexia closer to that seen in children without reading problems. Apparently, the commonly observed dysfunction in the brains of children with dyslexia can be at least partially improved through programs that focus on auditory processing and oral language training, resulting in improved language and reading ability.

## ✿ READING PROBLEMS AND TAKING TESTS

Tests are a difficult undertaking for students with reading problems, regardless of age. Teachers and schools, however, can make appropriate allowances and modifications that allow these students to show what they really know. Here are some accommodations to consider. Tailor the accommodations to meet the specific needs and age level of each student (Sams, 2003).

- When designing a test for these students, stick to a large simple type font (e.g., Arial), put key words in boldface, and provide plenty of space for answers.
- Make the purpose of the test clear to the student. If appropriate, also note that spelling, grammatical errors, and handwriting will not affect the test grade.
- Make sure you give clear and concise instructions.
- Allow additional time so that the test is a measure of what they know, not of the speed of their reading or writing.
- For essay exams, provide a model answer that shows the layout, paraphrasing, and conclusions expected in the answer. This helps students understand what is expected of them.
- Read out the questions, if needed, in areas such as mathematics and science since those are the areas being tested, not reading.
- For some children, have an adult record the child's answers, thereby allowing the child to focus on responses rather than on writing.
- Consider allowing the student to use a word processor to record answers.
- Use visual aids where appropriate since many struggling readers and students with dyslexia often have strong visual-spatial skills.
- Test in a location where students can work without being self-conscious about their work pace, rest breaks, or additional time.
- Consider alternative testing formats, such as an oral examination, PowerPoint presentations, or allowing the student to submit an audio recording with responses.

## ADVICE TO STUDENTS WITH ⚙ READING PROBLEMS

Here are some suggestions that parents and teachers can give to students with reading problems that can help them overcome many of the difficulties associated with this condition. Note that some of the advice is more appropriate for older children in that it relates to at-home situations where poor readers and students with dyslexia need practice in organizing and managing their affairs (Dehaene, 2009; DITT, 2001; Shaywitz, 2003).

*In general*

- Remember that your brain is adaptable and that problems you have now with reading could become less troublesome as you get older.
- Your brain is constantly changing and rebuilding itself as a result of your experiences. With appropriate practice, it *is* possible to overcome some or all of your reading difficulties.

*At home*

- Pack your school bag before you go to bed, ensuring a calm start to the next day.
- Put copies of your school schedule around the house, especially in the area where you do your homework. Make extra copies in case you lose them.

- Write down important information, such as class assignments, due dates for class work, tests, extracurricular activities, and other appointments.
- Know your body's rhythm. Avoid doing homework when you are hungry, tired, or feeling low.
- Keep the telephone numbers of at least two classmates who can tell you the homework assignment if you failed to record it accurately.
- When doing long assignments, break them down into smaller chunks and take frequent breaks to maintain your interest. Recognize that it will take you longer to read a passage than other students because your brain uses a pathway that is slower. But take the time you need and use your intellect and reasoning to understand the material fully and accurately.
- Do your homework in an area that is quiet and free from distractions.

*In school*

- Avoid taking too many courses that include a large amount of reading.
- Sit in the front of the class and away from windows to avoid being distracted.
- Develop your own shorthand so you can take notes during class to help you remember important information.
- If possible, record your classes and listen to the recording when you are more relaxed and can absorb more.
- Many textbooks are now available as audiobooks from Recording for the Blind and Dyslexic. Check out the organization's book list at www.rfbd.org.
- Get extra help from your teacher to develop your study skills, especially before tests.
- Ask your teacher if you can take a short essay test in place of a multiple-choice test. Multiple-choice tests do not give you enough context to decode unfamiliar words. Also, short essay responses give you a better opportunity to show what you have learned.
- Visualizing images probably comes easily to you. Whenever possible, design concept maps and use other types of graphic organizers to help you organize your work.
- Do not be afraid to tell your teacher that you do not understand something. Other students are likely to be in the same situation.
- Giving oral responses in the class may be difficult for you. Share this with your teachers to determine if there are other ways you can demonstrate your knowledge.
- Work on your computer skills because typing is a lot easier than writing. Be sure to proofread and spell-check your work.
- Being dyslexic may make your schoolwork seem hard, but it is no excuse for not putting forth the effort. Many dyslexics are successful and find ways to compensate for their circumstances (see, for example, the list of famous people with dyslexia in Chapter 5).
- Use the Internet to find out more about dyslexia and to get ideas on how to develop your study skills (see the "Resources" section for recommended sites on dyslexia).

# ADVICE FOR PARENTS OF CHILDREN ✿
# WITH READING PROBLEMS

Parents who learn that their child has reading problems, such as dyslexia, often experience blame, denial, guilt, fear, isolation, and anger. But by accepting that their child has a specific learning difficulty, they will be able to work on those strategies needed to allow their child to reach full potential. Here are some thoughts for parents of a child with reading problems to consider (Dehaene, 2009; DITT, 2001; Shaywitz, 2003):

- You know your child better than anyone else. If you suspect a reading problem, there probably is.
- Get professional help as soon as possible. Knowing exactly what is wrong will help you decide the best course of action for your child. Remember that not all struggling readers have dyslexia.
- Make your home an encouraging and safe place. To a child with reading problems, school can be a disheartening experience.
- Do not discuss your children's learning problems in front of them without including them in the discussion.
- Remember that, even if diagnosed with dyslexia, your child is more normal than different. Explain to the child that dyslexia means having a hard time learning to read. Emphasize that this has nothing to do with intelligence. Many people with this condition have learned to read and have become successful students and adults (see, for example, the list of famous people with dyslexia in Chapter 5). With effort and practice, the child will learn to read.
- Tell the child that struggling readers and people with dyslexia often have trouble hearing all the sounds in a word. They may only hear two sounds in a three-syllable word. Reassure the child that other children have this problem and that it can be overcome with proper instruction.
- You might even explain to older children about the different pathways that normal and dyslexic brains take when learning to read (see Chapter 5). Dyslexic children will learn to read, but it will take longer.
- Encourage the child to pursue areas of strength, such as music or sports, to experience the feelings of success in other areas of life.
- Teach your child how to pack the school bag for each day.
- Give your child the opportunity to tell you in a calm environment what happened in school and during the day. Sharing problems and concerns with a sympathetic listener can make them much less burdensome.
- Keep a record of how long it takes your child to do homework. Share this information with teachers who may be unaware of how much time your child needs to complete these tasks.
- Get in touch with the school periodically to discuss what strategies are being used to help your child. Use similar strategies at home when reading with your child.
- Remember that students who have difficulty reading often avoid doing it. But children learn to read by reading! Encourage your child

to continue reading so that those literacy skills develop and become automatic.

- Read assigned books and other materials to or with your child, explaining the meaning of new words and checking if your child understands what has been read.
- If the child asks questions about grammar or spelling when writing, give the answer so the child can move on. Dyslexic children often have problems with short-term memory, so supply the answer if they know the process.
- Seek out support groups for families with dyslexic children. They often can provide a lot of useful information about how to deal with learning difficulties.
- Finally, keep in mind that all of the recent research on dyslexia and other reading difficulties is encouraging, and that effective interventions are already here and more may come in the near future.

---

### Questions for Discussion/Reflection

- *What are the basic ingredients of early intervention programs?*
- *What types of intervention programs are more successful with older students?*
- *How have some interventions actually rewired the dyslexic brain?*
- *What advice should be given to struggling readers and students with dyslexia and their parents?*

---

## What's Coming?

The strategies and considerations presented in this chapter are designed to teach poor readers how to overcome their difficulties and become better readers. Such progress is particularly important as students in elementary school move up to middle and high school where reading of the course content becomes a vital part of successful learning. The strategies and techniques that teachers can use to help all students cope with the vast amount of reading required in secondary school content areas are the focus of the next chapter.

# 7

# Reading in the Content Areas

*One glance at a book and you hear the voice of another person, perhaps someone dead for 1,000 years. To read is to voyage through time.*

—Carl Sagan (1934–1996)

Students entering the intermediate grades, middle school, and high school are faced with an increased amount of reading and the expectation that they are able to comprehend the content in their texts. One of the challenges of the Common Core State Standards is for teachers to ensure that students have a strong vocabulary to express their work in clear and appropriate academic terminology in their different subject areas. Yet, little effort is made to determine either the reading ability of the students entering the class or the difficulty of the reading materials. Consequently, some students are doomed to failure from the start because they cannot read the course material, and they end up frustrated at both the teacher and the subject.

Many secondary teachers express concern about the reading and reading-related problems of their struggling students. Yet, except in English language arts, most content-area teachers do not view themselves as reading teachers, and they often express doubts about their ability to provide effective instruction in reading strategies. Studies show, however, that when content-area teachers take the time to teach and use reading strategies regularly, student achievement in the content area rises, especially in middle and high schools (e.g., Cantrell & Hughes, 2008; Greenleaf et al., 2011).

In their earlier years, students were taught developmental reading through the use of multilevel texts. However, content-area teachers usually teach from a single text written at a certain reading level. Furthermore, developmental reading emphasizes the process (learning to read) while content-area reading emphasizes application (reading to learn). In any particular class, the range of reading achievement among students often spans several grade levels. The challenge for the teacher, then, is to determine what strategies will help students acquire the content knowledge while trying to manage the wide range of differences in reading achievement.

For some students, the text itself is intimidating. High school science and history texts can easily run over 1,000 pages. Humorist Dave Barry once remarked that American students may not have the highest test scores in the world, but they sure have the biggest backpacks. Exactly how textbooks are chosen for a content-area course varies greatly among schools. In some cases, the text is chosen by one or more of the teachers who will be using it. Sometimes, it is chosen by the department chairperson, or the building principal, or a central office administrator. Regardless of who has this responsibility, the question arises as to what criteria were used to select the text. The selection process becomes particularly important now that textbook publishers are faced with addressing the Common Core State Standards and other standards. Texts need to be selected not by weight but by the likelihood that they will help students achieve the learning objectives of the content area.

Bruhn and Hasselbring (2013) suggest that those who are selecting a textbook consider the following questions:

- Questions About Content:
  - Is the textbook aligned with the appropriate state/district/Common Core standards?
  - Is the content accurate?
  - Is the content current?
  - Are cultural references accurate and free of stereotypes?
  - Is the language of the text appropriate for the students who will be using it?
  - Is the reading level appropriate for the students who will be using it?

- Questions About Instruction:
  - Does the text's organization convey a sense of purpose for each unit of study?
  - Does the textbook clarify the prerequisite knowledge that is required by the student?
  - Are common misconceptions identified and clarified?
  - Does the textbook show how the content relates to the real world?
  - Are the ideas developed to promote deep student understanding rather than fact memorization?
  - Do the activities in the text promote student thinking and reasoning?
  - Do formative and summative assessments accompany the text?
  - Are their supplemental materials available, such as videos, CDs, and online resources, to accompany the text?

If most of the answers to these questions are "yes," then the authors recommend considering the text. On the other hand, if the answers are mostly "no," then reject it.

Content-area teachers often assume that students come to their classes with the reading skills necessary to use the required text successfully. Moreover, these teachers may not recognize three major differences between the developmental reading that students were assigned in earlier grades and the expository reading required for the current course. The first difference is in learning new vocabulary. In developmental reading, vocabulary is taught in context, meaning is clarified, and words are rehearsed and practiced at a pace that most children can accomplish. In content-area courses, the vocabulary used in basic texts is highly specialized and technical, and often presented so quickly that students have little time to fully comprehend its meaning.

The second difference lies in the way concepts are introduced and explored. In developmental reading, teachers present concepts that are familiar, and they cover them at a pace that is appropriate for most children. In content courses, teachers present concepts that are unfamiliar and complex, usually at a rapid pace because there is so much to cover. The third difference is in the specialized type of reading that is needed for some courses, such as the ability to read charts, tables, graphs, maps, globes, and technical instruments (Baer & Nourie, 1993). Table 7.1 summarizes the main differences between developmental reading and reading in content areas.

It is important for content-area teachers to determine the level of reading difficulty in their course materials and the ability of their students to read them. By making some accommodations in materials and selecting appropriate strategies, all teachers can help more students succeed in learning the course content.

**Table 7.1**    Differences Between Developmental and Content-Area Reading

|  | Developmental | Content Area |
|---|---|---|
| *Texts* | Several multilevel texts. | Usually a single text at a fixed reading level. |
| *Teaching Approach* | Learning the process of reading (learning to read). | Learning to apply what has been read (reading to learn). |
| *Range of Reading Abilities* | Usually limited to a span of one or two grade levels. | Can span five or more grade levels. |
| *Vocabulary Acquisition* | Mostly general in nature. Presented at modest pace so students have time to practice words, clarify meanings, and reinforce comprehension. | Highly specific and technical. Presented quickly, so students have little time to practice words and develop meaning. |
| *Presentation of Concepts* | Concepts are usually familiar and presented at a modest pace. | Concepts are unfamiliar and complex, and presented at rapid pace with little time for thorough processing. |
| *Specialized Reading* | Limited mostly to printed text. | Can include reading charts, tables, graphs, maps, globes, and technical instruments. |

SOURCE: Baer and Nourie (1993).

## ✿ STRATEGIES FOR HELPING STUDENTS READ CONTENT MATERIAL

The brain-friendly strategies described here are intended to help students acquire course content successfully through reading and other methods. They are not intended to imply that the school can abdicate its ongoing responsibility to help students improve their reading skills at all grade levels. To some extent, every content teacher is also a teacher of reading, not of developmental reading, but by virtue of using a variety of techniques that allow students with reading problems to learn important content. The strategies include the following:

- Using direct instruction
- Conquering vocabulary
- Helping with comprehension
- Rewriting content material
- Incorporating supplemental textbooks
- Establishing in-class vertical files
- Using audiovisual aids and the Internet
- Promoting cooperative learning groups

### Using Direct Instruction

Students who have reading problems usually rely heavily on teacher explanations to grasp concepts and to identify what is essential to learn. Therefore, direct instruction can be a critical factor in their achievement. During direct instruction, do all of the following:

- Clearly identify important concepts. Some students think *everything* in the text is important and feel swamped.
- Explain why the students are learning the concepts. This helps establish meaning, a necessary component for long-term retention.
- Present the concepts in an organized manner. Many older students have poor organizational skills.
- Define and use unusual vocabulary words in context. The brain often needs to understand context if it is to establish meaning.
- Recommend a limited and specific reading textbook assignment that covers your presentation. Students often feel overwhelmed by the number and size of textbooks.
- Ask students to summarize orally and in their own words the main points you presented in the direct instruction segment. This is known as rehearsal, another important process for increasing retention (see Chapter 2).
- Consider asking the students to write out the summary as well. Writing requires more organization of thought and helps reveal misunderstandings or confusion.
- Suggest other print sources (of a lower reading level) that also explain the content.
- Explain and demonstrate how you read and study new material.

- Find ways to awaken student interest in upcoming topics. An interest-arousing pretest or a video clip on the Internet may be just enough to motivate students.
- Explain that all texts reflect the author's viewpoint and are thus subject to questioning and analysis.

## Conquering Vocabulary

Technical, unfamiliar, and unusual words are often stumbling blocks for students when reading course content. Familiar words used in a specialized context can also cause problems. Students encountering such words can learn them in any of four different ways:

- *Learning a new meaning for a known word.* The student recognizes the word but is learning a new meaning for it. For example, the student knows what a tree *branch* is, but is learning that the word can also describe a *branch* of government or *branch* of a river.

- *Learning the meaning of a new word to describe a known concept.* The student knows the concept but not this particular word to describe it. For example, the student has had experience with globes and baseballs but does not know they are examples of *spheres.*

- *Learning the meaning of a new word for an unknown concept.* The student is not familiar with the concept or the word that describes it, and must learn both. For example, the student is not familiar with the process or the word *osmosis.*

- *Clarifying and enriching the meaning of a known word.* The student is learning finer distinctions or connotations in the usage of what may seem like similar words. For example, understanding the distinctions among *dashing, jogging, running, sprinting,* and *trotting.*

All these types of learning vary in difficulty. The third type, learning the meaning of a new word for an unknown concept, is one of the most common, yet challenging. Much learning in the content areas involves this type of word learning. As students learn about *photosynthesis, secants,* and *oligarchies,* they may be learning new concepts as well as new words. Learning concepts and words in mathematics, social studies, and science may be even more difficult because each major concept is often linked to other new concepts. For example, the concept *oligarchy* can be associated with other unfamiliar concepts, such as *monarchy, plutocracy,* and *dictatorship. Photosynthesis* can be associated with *phototropism* and *osmosis.*

Identify these types of words in advance of assigning the reading. Work to develop students' word consciousness by calling their attention to the way writers choose words to convey meaning. Help the students research a word's origin or history and see if they can find examples of that word's usage in their everyday lives.

### Decoding New Words

Older students acquire more than half of the approximately 3,000 new words they learn each year through reading (Stahl, 2000). For English language learners, vocabulary knowledge is one of the most critical factors affecting their achievement in the content areas. Teachers cannot assume that English language learners possess the vocabulary needed to decode and comprehend the numerous word meanings they encounter in the course materials. Even though these students may possess proficient listening and speaking skills in English, it takes time and rereading to understand the formal aspects of English as used in secondary-level texts. Because knowledge of vocabulary is so closely linked to reading comprehension, students need to learn strategies for decoding new words that they encounter in the content texts. These strategies include decoding multisyllabic words and getting the meaning of unfamiliar words from context.

**Decoding Multisyllabic Words.** One strategy for decoding multisyllabic words takes just six steps. The teacher guides the student through the steps. Using a worksheet to analyze the word facilitates the process. Figure 7.1 illustrates one possible worksheet format with an example.

**Figure 7.1**   This chart helps students to decode new words through a six-step process. The word *transcontinental* is used here as an example.

Learning New Words

1. Write it down.

        transcontinental
        **WORD**

2. Split it up, if possible.

        X                         X

3. Find prefixes and suffixes.

        trans    continent    al
        **PREFIXES**    **ROOT**    **SUFFIXES**
                        **WORD**

4. Find the syllables in the root word and write down all word parts.

        trans    con    ti    nent    al
                        **SYLLABLES**

5. Write the whole word again and blend the sounds.

        transcontinental
        **WORD**

6. Use the word in a sentence.

        The transcontinental railroad connected the
        eastern and western parts of the United States.

1. The student first writes the whole word down, *transcontinental.*

2. If it is a compound word, such as *butterfingers,* the student writes down each word part, *butter* and *fingers.*

3. If it is not a compound word, the student puts an *x* on these lines and moves to the nest step, which is to write down the root word and any prefixes and suffixes so that *transcontinental* becomes *trans, continent,* and *al.*

4. Next, the student breaks down the root word into its syllables (*continent = con, ti,* and *nent*) and writes down all the word parts, *trans, con, ti, nent,* and *al.*

5. Now the student writes the whole word again while saying it aloud and blending the syllable sounds, *transcontinental.*

6. Finally, the student uses the new word in a sentence: *The transcontinental railroad connected the eastern and western parts of the United States.*

**Using Context Clues.** The context in which an unfamiliar word is used can often give hints as to its meaning. Help students use context clues by doing the following:

- Select an authentic text passage containing the unfamiliar words that can be defined through context. Ensure that the students have enough prior knowledge that they can reasonably determine the words' meanings.
- Model the process of using context clues to determine meaning by going through the steps of the Context Clues Strategy (see box).
- Think aloud as you use the strategy so that students can follow your reasoning.
- Explain how you used the clues to arrive at the meaning of the word.
- Identify the key words surrounding the target word that helped you decide on its meaning.
- Verify the word's meaning in the dictionary.
- Have students practice the model by giving them a page of text with three unknown words highlighted.

---

### Context Clues Strategy

1. When you come to a word you don't know, continue reading to a good stopping place.

2. Use the context to figure out the meaning of the new word.

3. Guess what the meaning might be.

4. Test your guess by asking if the meaning

   looks right;

   sounds right; and

   makes sense.

5. Check your guess in the dictionary.

## Helping With Comprehension

Students who are struggling readers often have difficulty comprehending what they are reading. Strategies that help students relate the content to their prior knowledge, practice mental imagery, and locate the main idea can be very effective aids to comprehension. Here is some general advice you can give students to help them with comprehension:

- Look over what you will be reading, noting words and phrases that are in boldface or italics. Look also for any charts, graphs, and pictures. Review any chapter summaries and related questions that are useful to guide your reading. Not everything in the text is equally important, so read to capture the main ideas.
- Take notes or draw diagrams while reading to help you remember main phrases and ideas. Use graphic organizers and mind maps, too.
- Read the text more than once.
- When you encounter an unknown word, try to guess its meaning by looking at the context. The sentences immediately before and after can give you good clues to determine meaning.
- Try to make connections between main ideas and their supporting details.
- Each time you finish a paragraph, stop and try to summarize it in your own words.
- Discuss what you have read with others who have read the same text.

**Narrative and Expository Text.** Some strategies need to be modified depending on the nature of the text. Narrative text is commonly associated with literature instruction and focuses on settings, characters, plots, conflicts, conflict resolution, and themes. Expository text is more commonly found in science and social studies texts and focuses on acquiring and processing information related to comparisons, cause and effect, and sequencing. In mathematics, expository text relates to the semantic and linguistics structures necessary to translate word problems into mathematical expressions.

### Using Prior Knowledge

Students bring with them a wide range of knowledge and experiences about many topics. Prior knowledge significantly influences a reader's comprehension of new topics, concepts, and vocabulary found in content-area texts. Comprehension of those texts relies heavily on the students' prior knowledge and their ability to apply it to the topics being covered in the content area. Reading difficult-content text can be made easier if students can relate the reading to what they already know. Before assigning a difficult text selection,

- preview the text with them;
- ask them what they already know about the content of the selection (a concept, time period, or topic);
- discuss and explain any unusual or technical words; and
- use visual aids whenever possible.

## Using Mental Imagery

You will recall from Chapter 2 that the visual recognition systems play a key role in learning to read. So it is no surprise that brain studies show substantial activity in other visual centers when someone is reading (Just, Newman, Keller, McEleney, & Carpenter, 2004). Readers often form mental images or pictures while reading. These visualizations help them remember and understand what they have read. Encourage students to form visual images of what they are reading by urging them to picture a character, a setting, a model in motion, or an event described in the text. Studies show that this strategy can be very effective, especially with slower readers (e.g. Center, Freeman, Robertson, & Outhred, 1999; Gambrell & Koskinen, 2002; Hibbing & Rankin-Erickson, 2003).

Imagery runs the gamut from simple concrete pictures to complex motor learning and multistep procedures. Because imagery is still not a common instructional strategy, it should be implemented early and gradually. These guidelines are adapted from Parrott (1986), Vesely and Gryder (2007), and West, Farmer, and Wolff (1991) for using imagery as a powerful aid to understanding text and retention.

- *Prompting.* Use prompts for telling students to form mental images of the content being learned. They can be as simple as "Form a picture in your mind of . . . " or more complex directions. Prompts should be specific to the content or task and should be accompanied by relevant photographs, charts, or arrays, especially for younger children.
- *Modeling.* Model imagery by describing your own image to the class and explaining how that image helps you recall and use the current learning. Also, model a procedure and have the students mentally practice the steps.
- *Interaction.* Strive for rich, vivid images where items interact. The richer the image, the more information it can include. If there are two or more items in the images, they should be visualized as acting on each other. If the recall is a ball and a bat, for example, imagine the bat hitting the ball.
- *Reinforcement.* Have students talk about the images they formed and get feedback from others on the accuracy, vividness, and interaction of the images. Talk provides mental rehearsal and helps students to remember the image for an extended period of time.
- *Add context.* Whenever possible, add context to the interaction to increase retention and recall. For example, if the task is to recall prefixes and suffixes, the context could be a parade with the prefixes in front urging the suffixes in the rear to catch up.
- *Avoid overloading the image.* Although good images are complete representations of what is to be remembered, they should not overload the working memory's capacity in older students of about seven items.

## Locating the Main Idea

Help students develop a strategy for locating the main idea in fiction and nonfiction passages.

- Model the procedure used in the Strategy for Locating the Main Idea (see box).
- After modeling, lead the students through guided, then independent, practice.
- Use graphic organizers that are appropriate for the passage.
- The paragraph summaries can take several forms, depending on whether you are using narrative or expository text. Have students identify which type of text they are reading, since they are different in form and intent.
- Narrative text:

Start by giving them some sentence fragments, such as the following:

"This story takes place_____."

"_____is a character who_____."

"A problem occurs when_____."

"The problem is finally solved when_____."

"At the end of the story_____."

- Expository text:

Main idea/Topic:_____.

Subtopic:_____.

Detail 1:_____.

Detail 2:_____.

Subtopic:_____.

Detail 1:_____.

Detail 2:_____.

- Consider using cooperative learning for this activity, because it gives students opportunities to share and critique their summaries. This oral rehearsal aids in retention of important ideas, concepts, and details.
- If students have difficulty, provide summaries that are partially filled in and let the students furnish the missing details.

### Strategy for Locating the Main Idea

1. Look at the title, headings, and picture. What do you already know about this topic?

2. Predict what the author might say about this topic.

3. Read the passage to find out the significant details or facts. Reread the passage to clarify any questions.

4. Modify your thoughts about the main idea as you review each detail.

5. Think about what the details or facts have in common.

6. Decide on the main idea.

7. Write a summary paragraph that includes the author's essential points and supporting details.

## *Paraphrasing for Comprehension*

Paraphrasing is commonly thought of as copying information from a text source and changing a few words. That process rarely results in retention of learning because the copying act can be done almost automatically and without much conscious thought. If the purpose of paraphrasing is to give students opportunities to get a deeper understanding of the text, to make connections to what they already know, and to enhance remembering, then a much more systematic process must be followed.

Effective paraphrasing incorporates reading, writing, listening, and speaking, thereby activating the brain's frontal lobe and leading to a fuller comprehension of the course material. It can be used in all content areas and with students in the upper elementary grades and beyond, and it can help students learn from many different types of texts, including fiction and nonfiction.

The process encourages active student participation; provides for mental, oral, and written rehearsal of newly learned material; and enhances comprehension and retention. At the same time, it develops reading, communication, and creative skills (Fisk & Hurst, 2003). See the box on this page for the guidelines and steps for using paraphrasing successfully in the classroom.

---

### Paraphrasing for Comprehension

**Guidelines:**

This strategy is appropriate for upper elementary grades and beyond. It can be used in all content areas and with all types of texts, including fiction and nonfiction. It is effective because it uses all modes of communication: reading, writing, listening, and speaking. The process encourages active student participation; provides for mental, oral, and written rehearsal of newly learned material; and enhances comprehension and retention. At the same time, it develops reading, communication, and creative skills.

A good paraphrase must convey the original meaning of the author but in the student's own words and phrasing. The voice of the author also should be maintained. If the original work is humorous, satirical, sarcastic, or melancholy, the paraphrase should be also. Students should therefore identify the author's meaning and voice before they start writing.

The teacher should explain the purpose and benefits of paraphrasing. Students already do some paraphrasing when they take notes in class, write a book report, or give a speech. Outside examples can include telling someone about a trip taken, or a news reporter summarizing an interview.

**Steps:**

This general scheme has four steps. Modify the steps as appropriate for the age level of the students and the nature of the material being read.

1. *First reading and discussion.* Read aloud the text to be paraphrased while students follow along in their own texts. Have the students suggest possible definitions for any unfamiliar words. After clarifying the vocabulary, ask the students to identify the main idea and the author's tone.

*(Continued)*

(Continued)

> **Paraphrasing for Comprehension**
>
> 2. *Second reading and note taking.* Students read the text on their own and take detailed notes when they finish a paragraph. The notes should capture the main idea and supporting details, but should be in the students' own words. Students may want to use a thesaurus to help them with difficult or technical words.
>
> 3. *Written paraphrase.* When finished with the note taking, the students put the original text away so it will not to influence the next step. Using only their notes, the students write their paraphrased version that communicates the main ideas with the same voice of the original text.
>
> 4. *Sharing paraphrases.* When the paraphrases are completed, the students form pairs and compare the similarities and differences between their respective paraphrases. They are also asked to decide how the author's voice is communicated in their versions.

SOURCE: Adapted from Fisk and Hurst (2003).

### *Reading Aloud to the Class*

Consider reading certain parts of the text to the class, especially those parts that use difficult or highly technical words or describe complex situations. Remember that many students can understand something when they hear it even though they may not be able to read about it themselves. This is particularly true for English language learners who often understand oral language much better than written words. Reading aloud can also be used to make connections between texts, to develop background information, or for enjoyment. Where appropriate, the oral reading can be done by other students, school volunteers, or parents. Another option is for you or a student to record certain text sections and have the recordings available for student use in the school's media center.

Teachers sometimes underestimate the effectiveness of read-aloud activities. Yet research studies show that, when used on a regular basis, especially in the elementary grades, they can boost students' comprehension as well as increase the students' knowledge and vocabulary in the content areas (Santoro, Chard, Howard, & Baker, 2008).

### Rewriting Content Material

Some course materials may have a particularly high level of reading difficulty. Rewriting the material at a reading level closer to that of the students who are having problems allows those students to gain confidence in their ability to understand the content despite their reading difficulties. Another possibility is to have students who do understand the course material rewrite it for their classmates. Students often rewrite content in language that their peers are more likely to understand. This approach reinforces both reading and writing skills. Of course, the teacher should check these rewrites for accuracy.

## Incorporating Supplemental Textbooks/Internet Sites

Identify textbooks and Internet sites that cover the same material as the course text but are written at a lower reading level. This may require using several sources because it is unlikely that one source will cover all the course content. Trade books are another possibility. They also present concepts covered in the primary textbook but are generally at a lower reading level. Furthermore, trade books help students recognize that the study of content subjects is not limited to school textbooks. By presenting concepts in many different ways, supplemental texts and appropriate Internet sites enhance student learning (Fenty & Barnett, 2013).

## Using Audiovisual Aids and Technology

Audiovisual aids and technology are a great help to students with reading problems. Many students today have grown up in and become acclimated to a multimedia environment. Whenever possible, use videotapes/DVDs, audiotapes/CDs, television, computer programs, and other technology to supplement and accompany direct instruction. All students benefit from the use of these materials because they increase interest and participation. However, care must be taken that the content delivered by the technology is targeted to the lesson's learning objective. Otherwise, manipulating the technology becomes the focus of attention, rather than the subject matter.

## Promoting Cooperative Learning Groups and Differentiated Instruction

Cooperative learning (Johnson, Johnson, & Holubec, 2008) and differentiated instruction (Sousa & Tomlinson, 2011) remain two of the most effective strategies in classes that have a wide range of student abilities, including reading. Cooperative learning allows students to work in teams and to be assigned tasks that match their ability and that contribute to the whole group effort. As the team members interact, students have opportunities to share and learn the concepts being studied. In differentiated instruction, the teacher adjusts the activities aimed at acquiring the learning objective to meet the different needs of individual students. Numerous studies have shown both strategies to be effective in significantly increasing student comprehension of subject-area content.

# SEQUENCING THE READING STRATEGIES    ✿

Now that we have discussed some of the strategies content-area teachers can use to help their students comprehend course materials, the next step is to look at the sequence in which the strategies should be presented for maximum effect on student comprehension. The sequence can be divided into three phases: activities before, during, and after reading the content-area text (Isakson, Isakson, & Windham, 2011).

## Phase 1: Before Reading

The purpose of these activities is to activate the learner's prior knowledge and to stimulate the brain's memory recall and imagery systems to spark curiosity, to motivate, and to facilitate retention of learning. Deciding which strategies to use depends on the material to be read and the background knowledge of the students.

• *Getting a feel for the text.* Students can learn quite a bit from the way a text is organized. Suggest that they look carefully at the title, headings, and introduction. The first sentence of each section or paragraph usually reveals what the ensuing text is about. Also, study any visuals, such as graphs and tables, and look for any vocabulary words that may be in bold type. Questions at the end of a section or chapter are good for review and summary.

• *Questions to ask.* Using questions to engage students in a dialogue about something they are about to read can clarify their thinking, stimulate interest, and help them determine what to expect from reading the material.

  o Make connections between the learner's background knowledge and the reading. "This passage is about_____. What do you already know about this?"
  o State a purpose for reading the passage. "This section is about_____. What are some things we could learn about this?"
  o Make predictions. "This passage is about_____. What do you think this could be about? What might happen to you if you_____?"

• *Select core vocabulary.* Choose the words that are likely to be unfamiliar and difficult and present them on the board or on paper. These words are often written in bold or italic type. Ask students to write a definition, even if it is only a guess. Collect and return the papers at the end of Phase 3 to complete by filling in the correct definitions. Then ask the students to use the word in a sentence to ensure they understand its meaning.

• *Write out the predictions.* Ask students to write out what they think the passage will be about and what they might learn from it.

• *Analogies and visual images.* Relate the material in the new reading to knowledge the students already possess. Ask them to think about what they know that is similar to what they think will be in the passage.

• *Concept maps.* Concept maps used before reading help students identify important concepts and ideas and how they are related to each other. By understanding these relationships in advance, students are more likely to comprehend their text readings.

## Phase 2: During Reading

These strategies are designed to address two difficulties that poor readers have with content-area texts: (1) The students spend far more time struggling with individual words than constructing meaning from text. (2) The main ideas in a text are often deeply embedded, and often too many concepts are superficially presented at once.

- *Questions to ask.* These questions help students review what they are learning while reading, confirm or change their predictions, and make connections to prior readings.

  o Clarify and review what has happened so far. "What are some things you have already learned about_____?"
  o Confirm or create new predictions. "Now that you have learned_____, will you keep or change your predictions?"
  o Make connections to other readings.

- *Reciprocal teaching techniques.* As explained earlier, this is a powerful technique because students assume a dominant role in their own learning. It includes the four strategies of questioning, clarifying, summarizing, and predicting. Teachers and students become partners in improving the students' understanding of the content material and their ability to monitor their own comprehension. Although the technique was developed years ago, it is not part of the common practice of secondary content-area teachers, mainly because they have not experienced it. When it is used, however, research studies have demonstrated that students who worked with reciprocal teaching increased their group participation and use of the strategies taught, learned from the passages studied, and increased their learning when reading independently. Furthermore, the studies showed that the technique could be used in various settings at different grade levels, and that the students maintained the reading gains they achieved (e.g., Gruenbaum, 2012; Schünemaum, Spörer, & Brunstein, 2013; Slater & Horstman, 2002; Yang, 2010).

The technique takes about 10 days to teach, during which time the teacher is doing a lot of modeling. Eventually, the teacher increasingly hands over responsibility to the students who assume the role of teacher/ leader and lead group discussions with other students. The teacher monitors the groups and intervenes to keep the students on task and to facilitate the discussion. See the box on the next page for an explanation of the steps and procedures involved in reciprocal teaching.

- *Summary notes.* Students write down a summary of each section of the passage as soon as they finish it. The summary should include the main idea and supporting details. Concept maps can help.

## Phase 3: After Reading

The strategies here are to help students rehearse, analyze, and extend their reading to increase the chances they will remember what they have read. Questioning and vocabulary prediction are important parts of this process.

- *Questions to ask.* These questions foster retention of learning by reinforcing the concepts in the reading and encouraging critical thinking and personal response.

  o Reinforce the concept. "Have you had any of the experiences mentioned in the passage? If so, how did you feel about them?"
  o Model ways of thinking through the information the students have read. "What events are described in this passage? What caused them? How do you know that?"

o Encourage critical thinking and personal response. "What do you think might have happened if___? Why did the author___?"

o Build awareness of common themes. "What else have we read that is similar to this? What parts are the same, and what parts are different?"

- *Vocabulary prediction.* Redistribute the vocabulary prediction forms from Phase 1 and have the students write in the definitions based on their reading. Ask them to discuss what they learned about the meaning and use of the vocabulary words.

- *Analyze good and bad examples of writing.* Ask the students to view, analyze, and discuss good and bad examples of chapter summaries. Ask them to explain the characteristics of good and bad summaries and to write their own, using the criteria for the good summaries.

- *Other readings related to the course text.* Suggest other resources for the students to read that relate to the text. Trade books or magazines at the appropriate reading level should be available in class or at the school's library media center.

### Reciprocal Teaching

**Guidelines:**

The teacher explains the four supporting strategies used in this technique: *Questioning* focuses the students' attention on main ideas and provides a means for checking their understanding of what they are reading. *Clarifying* requires students to work on understanding confusing and ambiguous sections of text. *Summarizing* requires students to determine what is important in the text and what is not. *Predicting* requires students to rehearse what they have learned and to begin the next section of text with some expectation of what is to come.

The teacher models the sequence of strategies. Eventually, the teacher increasingly hands over responsibility to the students who now assume leadership roles in group discussion. The teacher monitors the groups to keep students on task and to facilitate the discussion.

**Specific Steps:**

1. The leader reads aloud a short segment of text.

2. Questioning: The leader or other group members generate several questions related to the passage just read, and group members answer the questions. For example, "What was the problem here?" "What was the cause?" "What was the solution?" or "What was the chain of events?"

3. Clarifying: The leader and group members clarify any problems or misunderstandings. For example, "What does the word___mean?" or "What did the author mean when he said____?"

4. Summarizing: After all problems have been clarified, the leader and group members summarize the text segment.

5. Predicting: Based on the discussion and the reading thus far, the leader and group members make predictions about the contents of the upcoming text.

**Reciprocal Teaching**

6. This sequence is repeated with subsequent sections of the text. With daily practice, struggling readers will master the four supporting strategies and will use them for all their independent reading in other content-area courses.

7. Some cautions:

Start with simple questions at the beginning. But as students gain more practice, model open-ended questions that are thought-provoking:

"Explain why___."
"Explain how___."
"What is a new example of___?"
"What conclusions can you draw from___?"
"What do you think causes___? Why?"
"What evidence do you have to support your answer?"
"What are the strengths and weaknesses of___?"
"Compare___and___with regard to___."

Do not hesitate to provide more modeling and direct explanation, when needed, throughout the reciprocal teaching process.

SOURCE: Adapted from Cibrowski (1993); Slater and Horstman (2002).

# GRAPHIC ORGANIZERS AND COMPREHENSION OF CONTENT-AREA READING

**Graphic organizers** have been mentioned in previous chapters as valuable tools for organizing and representing knowledge and for illustrating relationships between concepts. Even though graphic organizers have been mentioned in pedagogical literature for more than 30 years, content-area teachers have been slow to incorporate them as a routine instructional tool. Yet, research studies have shown them to be particularly effective in helping typical students as well as those with reading problems and other learning disabilities to learn content area material (e.g., Dexter & Hughes, 2011; Swanson, Edmonds, Hairrell, Vaughn, & Simmons, 2011). Studies also have found that reading assignments requiring students to complete graphic organizers in lieu of answering traditional study guide questions can significantly increase reading comprehension as well (Barton-Arwood & Little, 2013; Scammacca et al., 2007). With this evidence in mind, let's spend some time discussing the reasons why graphic organizers can be effective and present some different types of organizers for consideration.

Graphic organizers are effective because they do all of the following:

- Show the organization or structure of concepts as well as relationships between and among concepts
- Make it more clear to students what they are expected to know and do, and allow students to focus on what is important
- Provide a mental framework for helping students to organize knowledge and build the framework piece by piece, linking it to

other learned frameworks, thereby enhancing neural networks in long-term memory

- Show how each item on the graphic can serve as a link to remembering related information discussed in class
- Reduce the cognitive demands on the learner by showing (as opposed to just telling) students how the information is structured, allowing the teacher to present information at more sophisticated and complex levels
- Develop literacy and thinking skills because the quality of the students' writing improves not only in the organization of ideas, but also in fluency and in other areas such as writing mechanics (punctuation, spelling, capitalization, etc.)
- Encourage students to use information processing and higher-order thinking skills, such as using cues to recognize important information, making decisions about what is important or essential, consolidating information, identifying main ideas and supporting details, and making decisions about the best way to structure the information
- Stimulate students who have constructed different organizers to discuss their diagrams and debate the importance of various points, draw conclusions, make connections to other ideas, and form inferences, predictions, or forecasts
- Result in an almost immediate improvement in performance on classroom tests for many students, whereas increased scores on standardized achievement tests occur more gradually as students gain skills using graphic organizers strategically
- Serve as excellent instruments for formative assessments

Some teachers resist using graphic organizers because they believe it takes too much class time to draw them. But now there are many free and inexpensive computer programs (e.g., Inspiration Software [see "Resources"]) that help students construct and print different types of organizers in just minutes.

## Types of Organizers

Graphic organizers come in several different forms, depending on the nature of the associated material to be learned. Among the most common types of graphic organizers are the following:

- Concept mapping
- Flowchart
- Venn diagram
- Matrix
- Webbing

### Concept Mapping

One of the first types of graphic organizers to be developed, concept maps were originally used in the late 1970s to help students learn complex concepts in science. As research studies revealed how much more science children learned through using concept maps, they spread slowly to other subject areas (Hyerle & Alper, 2011). Studies show that concept mapping also improves content-area text comprehension and summarization for intermediate, middle, and high school students—including those with reading and learning difficulties (e.g., Gajria, Jitendra, Sood, & Sacks, 2007)—as well as improves these students' retention and transfer of learning (e.g., Nesbit & Adesope, 2006). Concept maps are now becoming more popular. There are multiple Internet sites that offer numerous examples of concept maps in many subject areas.

Concept maps are used to do each of the following:

- Develop an understanding of a body of knowledge
- Explore new information and relationships
- Access prior knowledge
- Gather new knowledge and information
- Share knowledge and information generated

Share the guidelines included in the box on tips for making a concept map. Computer programs that build graphic organizers would be more efficient than paper-and-pencil versions, but both are equally effective at improving learning. Cooperative learning teams find Post-its are very useful because they allow items to be moved around on a board or chart until the students are satisfied that they have the best arrangement. The Post-its also make revisions easy. Once completed, the scheme can be put into a computer template.

---

### Tips for Making a Concept Map

Before students get started with their concept map, they should answer the following questions:

- What is the central word, concept, research question, or problem around which to build the map?
- What are the concepts, items, descriptive words, or important questions that one can associate with the concept, topic, research question, or problem?

Here are some suggestions that will help them construct the map:

- Consider using a computer program, such as *Inspiration*, to construct the map. If that is not available, Post-its are handy and allow you to move the concepts around a board easily.
- Use a top-down approach, working from general to specific, or use a free association approach by brainstorming items and then develop the links and explain the relationships.
- If possible, use different colors and shapes for items and links to identify different types of information.
- Use different-colored items to identify prior and new information.
- Experiment with a variety of different layouts until you find one that is compelling, understandable, and attractive.
- Be prepared to revise the map several times. This is another reason why computer software is helpful.

Before getting started on their concept maps, the students should get their research materials, class notes, and related articles together to use as their database for constructing the map. They should also ask themselves questions about the learning, such as these:

- What is the central word, concept, research question, or problem around which to build the map?
- What are the concepts, items, descriptive words, or important questions that I can associate with the concept, topic, research question, or problem?

Procedure. Classroom instruction about the major topic usually takes place first. Armed with their new knowledge, the students gather their resources. Working independently, in teams, or as a whole class, the students start selecting the items, identifying the relationships, and choosing the descriptive words that will describe the relationships. After making the first chart, they review it to determine if the relationships are correctly labeled, and whether some other arrangement would make the map clearer or more attractive. Remember, there is rarely only one way to do a concept map. Later, students with different maps can discuss their variations and debate their differences. Figure 7.2 shows a concept map built around the process of photosynthesis. All the basic steps are included. The map can be made more attractive with pictures of plants, a sun, or a glass of water placed near the appropriate item.

Figure 7.2    This is an example of a concept map built around the process of photosynthesis. As long as the basic steps are included, there are many different configurations that this map could take. It is important that the student write the relationship between any two items near the arrow that links them.

**Concept Map on Photosynthesis**

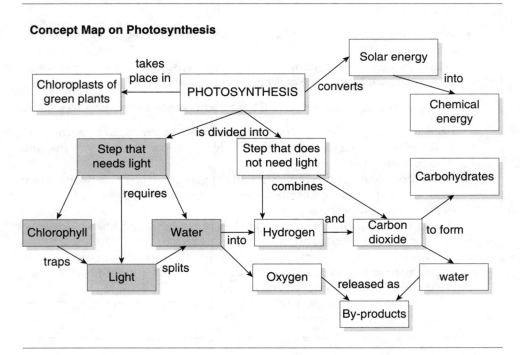

## Flowchart

A flowchart is used typically to depict a sequence of events, stages, phases, actions, and outcomes. This organizer is good to use with young children and as a first step in developing linear relationships. The questions to ask before completing the chart are as follows:

- What is the name of the event, procedure, or person that will be described?
- What are the specific stages, steps, phases, or events?
- Are the events in the correct sequence?
- How do the stages, steps, phases, or events relate to one another?
- What is the final outcome?

After the important steps have been identified, the students fill in the flowchart in the proper sequence. In some situations, the flowchart can represent a part of a cycle, as in the case of the example on the left side of Figure 7.3. The flowchart shows the five steps in reciprocal teaching for a passage of text read aloud. After completing the steps in the first passage, the process is repeated for the second passage, and so on.

## Venn Diagrams

John Venn first used these diagrams in the late 1800s to show relationships in mathematics. They are now used across many content areas to compare

Figure 7.3   On the left is a flowchart organizer depicting the steps in the reciprocal reading process. The arrow from Step 5 to Step 1 shows the process is repeated for each passage of text. On the right is a Venn diagram comparing characteristics of fish and whales. Common characteristics are in the area where the circles overlap.

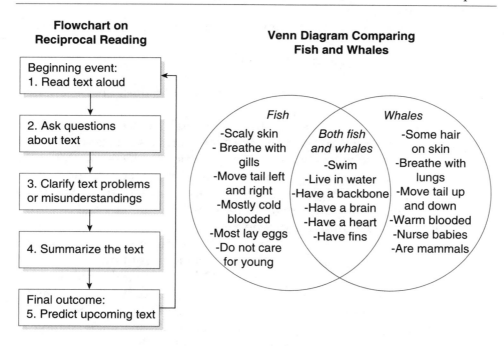

and contrast the qualities of two or three items, such as people, places, events, stories, ideas, situations, and things. Use a double Venn diagram to work with two items and a triple Venn diagram for three items. The questions to ask when preparing to use a Venn diagram are as follows:

- What items do you want to compare?
- What characteristics do the items have in common (intersecting portions)?
- What characteristics do the items not have in common (nonintersecting portions)?

The Venn diagram on the right in Figure 7.3 shows some of the similarities and differences between fish and whales. Characteristics that are common to both fish and whales are shown in the area where the two circles overlap.

### Matrixes

When comparing the characteristics of more than three items, Venn diagrams become too difficult to construct. In this instance, the matrix is a much easier organizer to use, and it can be adapted to a variety of learning activities. Among the most common types are the following three:

- Comparison matrix
- K-W-H-L chart
- Content grids

**Comparison Matrix.** This matrix is used to describe and compare attributes and characteristics of two or more items, such as people, places, events, stories, ideas, situations, and things. One distinct advantage of this matrix is that there is no limit to the number of items or characteristics that can be included.

The questions to ask when preparing the matrix chart are as follows:

- What items do you want to compare?
- What characteristics do you want to compare?
- How are the items similar or different based on these characteristics?

In constructing the matrix, the student generally places the items to be compared down the left column and the characteristics across the top row. After defining the specific characteristic, the student places an "X" in the box to indicate if that item possesses the characteristic. For example, if we wanted to expand the fish and whale comparisons used in the Venn diagram in Figure 7.3 to include other animals, such as humans and dogs, the matrix pictured in Figure 7.4 is one possibility.

**K-W-H-L Chart.** This is an expansion of the more familiar K-W-L matrix in that it includes a step whereby the students identify how they plan to find out the needed information. The K-W-H-L chart's familiarity does not detract from its usefulness. Although it is more commonly used in elementary schools, it is an effective memory device at all grade levels (Figure 7.5). With this matrix, students plan and gather initial information on a topic or theme, identify primary and secondary resources they need to access,

Figure 7.4    A comparison matrix of different characteristics belonging to several types of animals.

| Animal | Characteristics | | | | | | | |
|---|---|---|---|---|---|---|---|---|
| | Swim | Breathe air with lungs | Have fins | Have a brain | Have a backbone | Warm blooded | Most lay eggs | Are mammals |
| Fish | X | | X | X | X | | X | |
| Whales | X | X | X | X | X | X | | X |
| Humans | X | X | | X | X | X | | X |
| Dogs | X | X | | X | X | X | | X |

Figure 7.5    This type of matrix takes advantage of the students' prior knowledge and encourages them to monitor their own learning. This example is a lesson on the characteristics of plants.

| K | W | H | L |
|---|---|---|---|
| What do we **K**now? | What do we **W**ant to find out? | *How can we find out what we need to learn?* | What did we **L**earn? |
| Plants are living things. | What do plants need to live? | Biology books | Plants need sunlight, water, and nutrients to survive. |
| Many plants are green. | Why are plants green? | Biology books Internet search | Plants are green because they contain chlorophyll. |
| Some plants grow tall. | What are some plants that grow tall? | Internet search Field trips | Sunflowers and corn are plants that grow tall. |
| Some animals eat plants. | What do we call animals that eat just plants? | Biology books Encyclopedia | Animals that eat only plants are called herbivores. |
| Attributes we need to use: plant size, color, location | | | |

SOURCE: Adapted from Bender and Larkin (2003).

develop a plan for accessing resources, and identify the attributes and characteristics they will need to research.

The questions to ask when preparing to use a K-W-H-L chart are as follows:

- What do we already know?
- What do we want to find out?
- How are we going to find out? What primary and secondary resources can we access?
- What attributes or characteristic should we focus on?
- What have we learned?

After reading the text and learning the material, the students go back to the "K" column to determine if any of their prior knowledge was inaccurate. They should note any of the statements that are inaccurate, according to the text, and rewrite them so that they are correct. Then they go to the "W" column and check any of their questions that the text did not answer. Students should be prepared to bring these unanswered questions up in class, or tell how they will find answers to them and where they will look to get the answers.

**Content Grids.** This type of matrix helps students to think about and evaluate certain characteristics of people, places, events, and things. It may include making a decision about who was the bravest person in recent history, the best type of computer to buy, or the greatest environmental threat of the twenty-first century. Before beginning, the students should decide on the items to be included as well as the set of criteria that will be used to determine their decisions. Then they write in each block their judgment and rationale about how well or how poorly each item (person, place, thing, etc.) meets each criterion. Students can complete this matrix alone first and discuss their decisions later in groups, or they can complete the matrix together as part of a cooperative learning activity. Either way, the process leads students to higher-order thinking in that they must analyze and judge competing items against the same set of criteria. Figure 7.6 shows examples of different types of course content matrices.

**Figure 7.6**   These are two examples of content grids, one from a world history class and one from an environmental science class. The students must decide on the items and criteria before filling in the matrix with their judgments and rationale.

| Who Was the Bravest Leader of the Twentieth Century? | | | | |
|---|---|---|---|---|
| | Fought against evil | Improved people's lives | Persistent | Trustworthy |
| Winston Churchill | | | | |
| Mahatma Gandhi | | | | |
| Franklin Roosevelt | | | | |
| Your choice | | | | |

| What Is the Greatest Environmental Threat of the Twenty-First Century? | | | | |
|---|---|---|---|---|
| | Degree of danger | Economic impact | Length of danger | Number of people affected |
| Acid rain | | | | |
| Climate change | | | | |
| Dumping toxic chemicals in the ground | | | | |
| Ozone layer depletion | | | | |

## Webbing

Webs come in many varieties, but webbing is generally used for brainstorming ideas about something that has been read and for solving problems in content areas. They are effective memory devices because they translate printed words into vivid visual images of relationships between items that the slower reader may not detect in the text. Brainstorming webs integrate the language components of the brain's left hemisphere with the visual and spatial talents of the right hemisphere—a "whole brain" approach that is important in learning and remembering. Creativity is also an essential component here because the brain's frontal lobe makes free associations and begins to build a holistic picture from seemingly isolated items. As the process continues, the brain reorganizes concepts into images that can be communicated to others. Thus, brainstorming webs are excellent discussion tools that stimulate higher-order thinking and processing.

Although brainstorming webs involve free associations, they are not unguided activities that just consume time, as some teachers think. Rather, the brainstorming process is always guided by specific questions, such as the following:

- What is the topic to be brainstormed?
- Is the process of brainstorming clear?
- What should be the final product?

Brainstorming webs are usually made individually when a student is mapping out relationships that appear in the content-area reading. When working individually, students produce a wider range of ideas and patterns than when working in a group. They do not have to worry about other people's opinions and can therefore be more creative.

For problem solving, brainstorming in cooperative learning groups is very effective because it uses the brain power and experiences of everyone in the group. When individual members reach their limit on an idea, another member's background knowledge or experience may take the idea to another stage. In this manner, group brainstorming tends to produce web diagrams that include more subtle and deeper relationships. Figure 7.7 is an example of a web developed by a cooperative learning group based on some of the characteristics of vertebrates.

# READING PATTERNS ✿
# IN THE CONTENT AREAS

Recall from earlier chapters that the human brain seeks patterns in order to interpret its environment. This same pattern-seeking trait applies to reading content-area material. As the brain reads content-area text, such as science or social studies, it looks for patterns of thought that can be connected with past experience and comprehended. Each content area comprises unique patterns of organized knowledge that the reader must identify in order to successfully understand that particular subject. When content-area teachers clearly identify the types of patterns that students should look for

**Figure 7.7**    This web diagram depicts some of the characteristics of vertebrates. The web could be expanded by adding more characteristics and giving specific examples of each type.

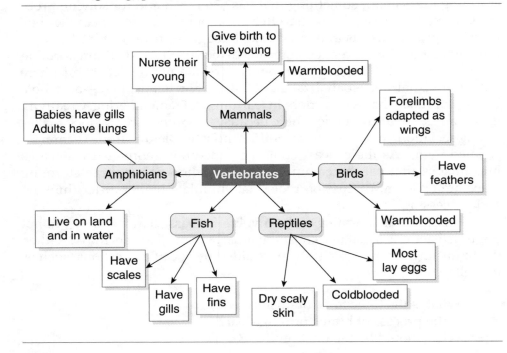

when they read the subject text, they help their students establish the mind-set their brains need to make sense of the printed text. But have content-area teachers been trained to do this?

### Disciplinary Literacy

We often hear the expression "Every teacher is a reading teacher." But do content-area teachers have the skills to fulfill this expectation? Many subject-area teachers were required to take courses in reading and writing in their content area during their preservice training. These courses usually focus on general reading comprehension or developing study skills related to the subject matter. However, little attention has been paid to the literary dimensions of their subject. In addition to the actual content knowledge, each discipline has specialized vocabulary, standards of what constitutes quality and precision in the field, and the specialized reading and writing needed to communicate its content and discoveries. A study of disciplinary literacy found that experts from mathematics, chemistry, and history read their respective texts quite differently (Shanahan & Shanahan, 2008). These content-area experts discussed the findings with college teachers who prepare secondary teachers in these areas and recommended different comprehension strategies for work with adolescents. Table 7.2 summarizes their findings and shows how experts and researchers in the disciplines do, in fact, approach the reading of their texts very differently.

The Common Core State Standards for English Language Arts present a set of goals for integrating advanced literacy instruction into content areas in middle and high schools. How will the states and school districts

Table 7.2    Differences in Reading Patterns Among Disciplines

|  | History | Chemistry | Mathematics |
|---|---|---|---|
| *Text source or author's view* | Thorough consideration of author's view | Text source a factor, but not that informative | Actively avoids using source as factor |
| *Consider when text written and its influence* | Important factor: what did authors know and when did they know it | When text written very important given rapid changes in science | Context not important |
| *How text agrees or disagrees with others in field* | Connections to other texts important to determine perspective | Text checked against others to determine any outcome differences | Reader's knowledge focuses attention and limits misinterpretation |
| *Organization of information in text* | Organization reveals relationship between narratives and author's arguments | Organization supports understanding and helps locate information | Organization supports understanding and helps locate information |
| *Consider graphics: pictures, tables, charts, etc.* | Evaluate graphics same as text | Graphics help translate and compare overlapping information | Both graphics and text must be unified and interpreted together |
| *Critique of text* | Critical analysis needed to determine author's credibility | Examines credibility of information and its congruence with other scientific evidence | Strong emphasis on accuracy rather than credibility |
| *Rereading or close reading* | Close reading important and rereading of essential information | Close reading important and rereading of essential information | Intensive rereading needed to weigh all information |
| *Interest* | Selects texts that match reader's interests and uses personal perspective to evaluate author's perspective | Selects texts that match reader's scientific interests and gives greater attention to new information | Selects texts that match reader's mathematical interests and gives greater attention to new information |

SOURCE: Adapted from Shanahan and Shanahan (2008).

meet these challenges? Professional development programs across the country are now trying to prepare teachers for these tasks. Properly executed, these programs can give teachers the strategies that lead to increased student achievement in both reading comprehension skills and subject content learning (e.g., Greenleaf et al., 2011).

The recent release of the Next Generation Science Standards also places new demands on the nature of science, technology, and engineering instruction (Achieve, 2013). These standards focus on a smaller set of core concepts in each discipline, exchanging the time now spent on the rote memorization of facts with an emphasis on deeper understanding and application of the content. They also include cross-cutting concepts that are integrated with the Common Core State Standards for English Language Arts and Mathematical Practice.

Here are some of the patterns of organized knowledge that comprise some of the school's curriculum areas.

### Art/Music/Drama

- Dialogue that describes, visualizes, and portrays actions
- Interpreting language through movement
- Readers' theatre to link oral and written language
- Role-playing to practice and interpret dialogue
- Understanding the perspective of the artist, composer, or writer

### Literature

- Describing and visualizing the setting
- Character development of main and supporting characters, their authenticity, and their relationships
- Distinguishing plot and episodes
- Understanding the literary piece's genre
- Discovering the moral, theme, or message

### Mathematics

- Patterns and key words for solving word problems
- Symbolic relationships and operators
- Searching for evidence and reasoning
- Understanding graphic relationships

### Science

- Types of classification
- Experimental procedures
- Cause and effect
- Steps in problem solving
- Definitions and explanations, with or without diagrams

### Social Studies

- Definitions and explanations
- Cause and effect
- Chronological or sequential events
- Comparing and contrasting
- Distinguishing fact and opinion

Studies indicate that a large number of students of all ethnic backgrounds are functioning below grade level in their reading (NAEP, 2011). This is a particularly difficult problem for students reading in the content areas where they are reading to acquire knowledge and skills in subjects such as mathematics, health, science, and social studies. In these subjects, the vocabulary used in the texts is often technical and written at a more difficult readability level. In this chapter, I have offered numerous tested strategies that could be used to aid these students in acquiring and understanding vocabulary and in gaining a more accurate and deeper comprehension of the content they read. My hope is that teachers willing and determined to make "reading to learn" a successful experience for their students will consider adding these strategies to their repertoire.

---

### Answer to Test Question #9

**Question:** There is little that secondary school content-area teachers can do to improve the comprehension skills of their students who are poor readers.

**Answer:** *False.* Content-area teachers can use numerous tested strategies that aid poor readers in understanding vocabulary and in gaining a more accurate and deeper comprehension of the content they read.

---

## Teaching English Language Learners in the Content Areas

Working with older English language learners (ELLs) in the content areas is especially challenging because the students are attempting to learn both conversational English and academic English at the same time. Despite these challenges, it can be done successfully. For a full explanation and instructional suggestions of how to teach ELLs in the content areas, see *How the ELL Brain Learns* (Sousa, 2011b).

---

### QUESTIONS FOR DISCUSSION/REFLECTION

- *What are some successful strategies for helping students comprehend content material?*
- *In what sequence should these strategies be used?*
- *What are some patterns that exist in the organization of content in different subject areas?*

---

## What's Coming?

The next and last chapter looks at the basic components of a successful reading program. It summarizes what students need to know as they learn to read and what teachers need to do to make that process more successful for all students. The chapter also suggests professional development activities for teachers and school principals, presents some ways of closing the reading achievement gap, and discusses the importance of implementing action research in schools and classrooms.

# 8

# Putting It All Together

*I think it's the books that you read when you're young that live with you forever.*

—J. K. Rowling (1965–)

## THE BASICS OF A SUCCESSFUL ⚙ READING PROGRAM

Surely by now it is clear that learning to read is no easy task. Unlike spoken language, there are no areas of the brain prewired for reading. Thus, there is no reason to consider reading to be a natural ability like speaking. Human beings have been talking for thousands of years, while reading is a relatively recent and quite artificial accomplishment. Toddlers seem to be preprogrammed to talk, and they usually learn to do so without formal instruction. On the other hand, the fact that large numbers of adults never do learn to read suggests that this ability is not in the same category.

Of course, some children learn to read with minimal instruction. These children, however, do not as a result read stories in a qualitatively different way than children taught via systematic phonics. The only difference seems to be that they have managed to crack the phonetic code on their own, without much teaching. How they learned the letter-sound correspondences seems to make no difference to the end result. Children who have become good readers through the whole-language approach have no advantage over children who have become good readers through systematic phonics. There is no harm in some children learning to read on their own.

The problem is that the vast majority do not. Consequently, one of the major long-term goals of schools is to graduate students who are lifelong and highly competent readers.

Successfully achieving that long-term goal is not easy, because some barriers need to be overcome. These include teachers uninformed about the new understandings of how the brain learns to read, outdated materials for teaching reading, outdated methods for teaching reading, and the overemphasis on test scores. Moreover, to accomplish a long-term goal, short-term goals must first be achieved. I offer here some suggested short-term goals that I hope educators will consider. They are based on the current state of research on how we learn to read and on studies of effective instruction in reading.

## Expose Teachers to Current Scientific Knowledge About How the Brain Learns to Read

During the past 15 years, research developments in neuroscience and cognitive psychology have added greatly to our understanding of how the brain learns to read and the nature of the problems that can arise during that process. We now know enough from this research to put many myths about reading to rest. We have a better idea of which instructional strategies will increase the likelihood that more children will learn to read successfully. The research supports the continued use of some strategies while doubting the effectiveness of others. Armed with this knowledge, teachers can make better choices in reading programs and in their own instructional methods. That is the good news. The bad news is that the implications of this research for our practice are not getting to many classroom teachers fast enough. Nevertheless, teachers of early reading are aware that there is a growing body of newer research on reading, so word is slowly getting out.

Teachers of reading must have access to the summaries of findings from a broad base of research on reading-related topics. They also need to recognize different types of studies. For example:

- *Experimental studies* provide generalizations that offer sound advice based on trends.
- *Correlational studies* usually provide reasoned hypotheses about how two variables can affect each other.
- *Case studies* help teachers consider new methods for instruction and assessment.

The responsibility of the school district is to engage teachers in ongoing study of the changing knowledge base produced by discoveries in scientific research on the reading process. Teachers need to be a vital part of the decision-making process in schools because it is through their work that children learn to read. With this approach, teachers recognize that teaching is not just an art form anymore; it is now a *science* and an art form. By staying abreast of scientific developments, they can make informed decisions and contribute to locally developed, scientifically based programs of instruction and assessment in reading.

*Teacher Preparation*

Because phonemic awareness (PA) is a critical component of acquiring the alphabetic principle, it is important that teachers in this area be well trained in the concept of phonemic awareness and how to teach it. Yet research in best practices suggests that prospective elementary teachers need more instruction in phonemic awareness in their teacher preparation courses. One study examined the phonemic awareness knowledge of 223 first-year teachers who were certified in elementary education, special education, and early childhood education (Cheesman, McGuire, Shankweiler, & Coyne, 2009). The study revealed that a large number of first-year teachers "(a) have limited understanding of what constitutes PA instruction, (b) cannot reliably distinguish PA and phonics, and (c) cannot reliably identify or count phonemes in written words when the spelling is not transparent" (Cheesman et al., 2009, p. 285).

This disconcerting finding may be due in part to the lack of knowledge that some teacher educators possess regarding the linguistic characteristics of the English language. In one major study, researchers first administered a survey of language concepts to 78 college and university instructors who taught reading education classes to prospective reading teachers (Joshi et al., 2009). The instructors were familiar with syllabic knowledge, but they performed poorly on concepts relating to phonemes and morphemes. In a second part of this study, the researchers interviewed 40 more instructors about best practices in teaching the five components (phonological awareness, phonics, fluency, vocabulary, and comprehension) identified by the National Reading Panel. Eighty percent of instructors incorrectly defined phonological awareness and did not mention phonics instruction as a desirable method to use for beginning readers, particularly for students who were at risk for reading difficulties.

If university programs are not adequately preparing teachers of reading, then this responsibility falls on school districts who must incorporate scientifically based research strategies into their professional development programs. District administrators who hire prospective reading teachers might consider discussing this situation with college administrators who supervise the teacher preparation courses in reading.

## Develop a Scientifically Based Reading Program and Stick With It

The scientific evidence is clear: Learning to read successfully requires the ability to manipulate sounds into words, to break down words into their component sounds, and to match sounds with the letters that represent them. A scientifically based reading program, therefore, will focus on developing phonological awareness, and then on the more sophisticated phonemic awareness (see Chapter 2). Children need to know and recognize the alphabet in print and be able to match those letters with the sounds they represent. Mastering the alphabetic principle is essential to becoming a proficient reader, and instructional methods that explicitly teach this principle are more effective than those that do not. Learning phonics is especially important for children who are at risk for not learning to read (see also Chapter 2). In addition to phonics instruction, using whole-language activities as a *supplement* helps to make reading enjoyable and meaningful (see Chapter 3). The reading program should emphasize vocabulary building, and the rules of grammar and syntax, and include activities that lead to reading fluency and comprehension.

Reading programs that overemphasize extensive and repetitive drills in phonics will bore students, and programs that overemphasize guessing how words sound and what they mean will be a source of frustration for students, especially those at risk of not learning to read. Phonological awareness, phonemic awareness, and the alphabetic principle should be taught in interesting and innovative ways, using a variety of materials. Usually, the program begins with coded texts to reinforce letter-sound correspondences. But teachers should select other high-interest sources of reading that maintain student attention and demonstrate that learning to read can be enjoyable.

### Does Technology Affect Motivation to Read?

Concerns abound about whether the technologically centered gadgets that children play with today, including computers, tablets, and smartphones, will lessen their motivation to read. The concerns are unfounded, because a major portion of computer interactions still involves reading and writing, and that will continue to be the case for the near future. Studies show that elementary students using laptops display increased intrinsic motivation and persistence in completing schoolwork (e.g., Mouza, 2008). These students often go beyond the requirements of assignments, therefore improving the quality of their finished work product. When used appropriately either in our out of school, technology allows students to direct their own learning at their own pace, and engage in deeper examination of the topics through reading. Parents and teachers need to find ways of using the attraction of the technology to lure children into working with programs that will help them learn to read and read to learn.

Once a program with these components has been developed or selected, stick with it. Too much energy, teacher goodwill, and resources are wasted when districts leap from one reading program to another, based on the latest political favorite or on which publisher has made the greatest offer. Consistency is essential if we expect the program to have a lasting impact on developing the reading skills of students in the early grades.

### What Skills Should Be in Place by Grade 3?

Most researchers agree that reading skills have to be in place by the end of third grade if the student is to cope successfully with the increasing reading requirements of the ensuing grades. What reading skills should our students have acquired at that time to demonstrate that they can continue to progress as successful readers? The Common Core State Standards for English Language Arts, among other sets of reading standards, suggest that by the end of third grade, students should acquire critical literacy, which includes the skill and will to use language in all its forms as well as to solve problems and communicate effectively (NGA & CCSSO, 2010). To do so, children need to

- know and apply grade-level phonics and word analysis skills in decoding words (the alphabetic principle);

- identify and know the meaning of the most common prefixes and derivational suffixes;
- decode words with common Latin suffixes;
- decode multisyllable words;
- read grade-appropriate irregularly spelled words;
- read with sufficient accuracy and fluency to support comprehension;
- read grade-level text with purpose and understanding;
- read grade-level prose and poetry orally with accuracy, appropriate rate, and expression on successive readings; and
- use context to confirm or self-correct word recognition and understanding, rereading as necessary.

## Offer Ongoing Professional Development That Includes Teaching Strategies Based on the New Research

Because all reading programs are not the same, teachers must be educated in how to evaluate the different programs to determine which ones are based on strong evidence. Preservice and in-service programs need to provide teachers with the training necessary to select, develop, and implement the most appropriate reading program. Systematic phonics instruction is a necessary and vital component of learning to read, but it is not the only component. A total reading program should include instruction in phonemic awareness, vocabulary development, fluency, and comprehension (NRP, 2000).

Beginning teachers are in extra need of in-service support. Too often their preservice courses did not provide them with sufficient knowledge and skills to help all children become successful readers. Studies of teacher preparation programs show that too little time is allocated to the teaching of reading and that there is wide variance in the content of these programs (Cheesman et al., 2009; NRP, 2000).

Every day, teachers try to help students learn to read. For some children, learning to read comes quickly, usually because of exposure to frequent language experiences during the preschool years. But for other children, learning to read is a struggle, and this is when teachers really *do* make a difference. Recent studies bear this out. An extensive analysis of student achievement and teacher training concluded that teacher experience was a major factor in determining student success in elementary reading (Harris & Sass, 2007).

When early literacy teachers do participate in training to learn about research-based practices, the results can be impressive. For example, one study involved a yearlong project in which first- and second-grade teachers participated in scientifically based instruction on phonemic awareness, phonics, and fluency, and were coached by professional mentors (Podhajski, Mather, Nathan, & Sammons, 2009). The reading achievement of their first-grade students exceeded that of students in the control group in letter name fluency, phonemic segmentation, nonsense word fluency, and oral reading. Students in the second grade achieved better than the control students in phonemic segmentation. A similar study involving the training and coaching of kindergarten teachers also showed improved achievement in student literacy (Kretlow, Wood, & Cooke, 2011).

> **What Beginning Readers Need to Learn**
>
> *Phonological awareness:* Rhyming, alliteration, deleting, and substituting sounds, sound patterns
>
> *Phonemic awareness:* Segmenting words into individual sounds, manipulating phonemes
>
> *Visual perception of letters:* Understanding the names of the letters of the alphabet and recognizing them in print
>
> *Alphabetic principle:* Correlating letter-sound patterns with specific text
>
> *Word recognition:* Learning words that occur most often in language and that are needed in writing
>
> *Orthographic awareness:* Understanding spelling rules and writing conventions
>
> *Syntax:* Understanding rules affecting the word order in phrases and sentences
>
> *Fluency in oral reading:* Rereading texts to develop fluency

Children who come to school with phonics skills already developed and who can apply them correctly do not need the same intensity and level of phonics instruction as children who are just beginning to learn to read. Professional development should help teachers assess the needs of individual children and tailor instruction to meet these needs.

### Remember the Content-Area Teachers

To some degree, all teachers are teachers of reading. Yet, we often overlook content-area teachers when designing professional development programs to enhance reading instruction. If the content-area teachers assume that the English department bears the responsibility for teaching reading and writing skills, then they will see no reason to assume this task. Furthermore, whenever I have discussed literacy instruction with content-area teachers, they often reply that they know little about teaching reading or how to get their students to read the subject matter more fluently. Of course, they are correct. The Common Core State Standards include goals for integrating advanced literacy instruction into the content areas in middle and high school. If these goals are to be met, districts should provide meaningful training to content-area teachers that includes simple yet effective strategies they can use to help their students better comprehend their content material (see Chapter 7 for suggested strategies).

Even modest training times can be effective. Studies (e.g., Concannon-Gibney & McCarthy, 2012; Torgesen, Houston, & Rissman, 2007) show that whenever content-area teachers participate in a professional development program to enhance the reading outcomes of the struggling readers in their classrooms, the following findings consistently emerge:

- Before the professional development, content-area teachers are generally not cognizant of the reading difficulties their students display and are often overwhelmed by these challenges.

- Content-area teachers welcome in-service training on the comprehension strategies, insisting on substantial modeling, engaging in biweekly support meetings, and taking time in class to implement the strategies.
- The teachers see positive effects from the strategies through improvements in students' vocabulary decoding and use, reading comprehension, and graph interpretations.
- Middle school is the last chance for struggling readers to get the support they need in reading to learn. Content-area teachers at this level who are knowledgeable in how to use research-based interventions can have a major impact on the reading success of their students.

## Teach Reading Through the Students' Strengths

Difficulties with reading frequently mask a student's strengths in other cognitive areas. Because struggling readers have problems with their phonologic module's ability to interpret the meaning of individual words, they will miss details in the text. Furthermore, they have difficulty remembering extended lists of unfamiliar words long enough to comprehend complex sentences. You will recall from Chapter 5 that dyslexics deal with this situation by calling upon their brain's right frontal lobe during reading to interpret the overall meaning of a passage. Consequently, the dyslexic students' reliance on the right frontal lobe develops other cognitive strengths, such as creativity, problem solving, critical thinking, concept formation, and reasoning (Shaywitz, 2003; Vlachos, Andreou, & Delliou, 2013).

Although overall cognitive ability may not influence the acquisition of phonemic awareness or of understanding phonics, reasoning and verbal skills can help dyslexic children and other struggling readers comprehend what they are reading. By using their bank of vocabulary words, personal experiences, and other knowledge, these students can use their cognitive skills to identify unfamiliar words in text. Teachers can work with these students to expose them to opportunities that bolster their strengths through enhancing their vocabularies, expanding their storehouse of knowledge, and enriching their worldly experiences. This approach allows students with reading difficulties to use their other strengths to overcome their phonological weakness.

| What Teachers Need to Know About Teaching Reading |
|---|
| How the brain learns to read |
| The relationship between spoken language and reading |
| How to provide direct instruction in phonics |
| How to provide direct instruction in the alphabetic principle |
| The relationship between phonology and morphology in relation to spelling |

*(Continued)*

(Continued)

| What Teachers Need to Know About Teaching Reading |
| --- |
| How to diagnose spelling and reading skills |
| How to use strategies that help students gain fluency |
| How to help students understand the rules of syntax |
| The dependence of reading comprehension on other aspects of reading and on language skills |
| Procedures for ongoing in-class assessment of children's reading abilities |
| How to modify instructional strategies based on in-class assessments |
| Understanding the needs of students with disabilities and those with limited English proficiency |
| How to use a variety of reading intervention strategies to address different learning styles and cultures |
| How to apply research judiciously to their practice and how to update their knowledge base |

## Offer Professional Development in Reading to Building Principals

Principals are the instructional leaders of their school. They need to become familiar with the latest scientific research on reading, especially with the implementation of the Common Core State Standards. Learning to read is far too important a goal to be left to discretionary programs and individual teacher decisions about what approach to take. The challenge for the principal is to maintain consistency of instruction while still encouraging the unique contributions of teachers. In the end, however, principals must insist that the district select a scientifically based reading program, ensure that all teachers of beginning reading follow it, and stress the development of phonological awareness.

Effective reading instruction in kindergarten and the primary grades should be one of the principal's top priorities (Torgesen et al., 2007). Below is a brief survey that may help principals and teachers determine the extent to which the school's reading program is meeting the needs of all children.

When you have completed the chart, add up the values of the circled numbers to get a total score. The highest possible score is 63. Take a close look at any component with a score of 1. Why is that the case? What can you do about it?

### Preparing for the Common Core State Standards

Adopting the Common Core State Standards will require principals at all grade levels to prepare their faculty and staff for implementation. For the

**Components of Our Reading Program**

**Directions:** Circle the number that most closely describes the extent to which a component is present in your school's reading program. When finished, connect the circles with straight lines to get a profile of your reading program. Add up the values of the circled numbers (highest score is 63). Discuss the importance of any individual component that receives a score of 1.

| Component | Little or None | Some | Significant |
|---|---|---|---|
|  | 1 | 2 | 3 |
| Program is research based | 1 | 2 | 3 |
| Teachers have been trained in research-based strategies related to the program | 1 | 2 | 3 |
| Emphasis on phonemic awareness | 1 | 2 | 3 |
| Systematic instruction and practice in phonics | 1 | 2 | 3 |
| Systematic instruction in the alphabetic principle | 1 | 2 | 3 |
| Activities and practice to enhance word decoding | 1 | 2 | 3 |
| Activities and practice on word recognition | 1 | 2 | 3 |
| Activities and practice on semantics | 1 | 2 | 3 |
| Activities and practice on syntax | 1 | 2 | 3 |
| Writing activities are coordinated with reading instruction | 1 | 2 | 3 |
| Activities for building vocabulary growth | 1 | 2 | 3 |
| Strategies that use morphology to build spelling skills and enhance vocabulary growth | 1 | 2 | 3 |
| Instructional practices develop the children's ability to monitor their reading comprehension | 1 | 2 | 3 |
| Activities for improving reading fluency | 1 | 2 | 3 |
| Activities for improving reading comprehension | 1 | 2 | 3 |
| Strategies for improving content area reading | 1 | 2 | 3 |
| In-service opportunities connected to the program | 1 | 2 | 3 |
| Other literature sources are integrated into the program | 1 | 2 | 3 |
| Instructional practices in middle grades build on reading and literacy growth in the primary grades | 1 | 2 | 3 |
| Interventions for helping teachers diagnose and address reading difficulties | 1 | 2 | 3 |
| Constructive communication about the program is maintained with parents | 1 | 2 | 3 |

English Language Arts standards, principals may wish to consider the following steps, among others (NAESP, 2013):

- Engage teacher leaders so that teachers buy into the process.
- Take the small step necessary to help teachers adjust to the rigor and expectations of the standards.
- Allow plenty of time for teachers to discuss and reflect on the implementation.
- Inform parents of the coming curriculum changes.
- Create an ongoing, job-embedded professional development program for English language arts that emphasizes rigor, text complexity, and use of research/evidence-based strategies.
- Discuss implications for social studies and science courses.
- Discuss the intent and types of assessments and the need to document the evidence of student achievement.
- Develop plans for struggling students.

The details for facilitating these steps will vary, of course, depending, for example, on the degree to which each school has unique populations—such as the number of English language learners and students with special needs—the socioeconomic level of the school's community, and the rate of teacher turnover.

---

**Answer to Test Question #10**

**Question:** The Common Core State Standards for English Language Arts include a basic curriculum and a selection of assessment instruments.

**Answer:** *False.* The standards are a list of knowledge and skill goals. What content and what instructional methods are used to achieve the goals are left to the states and school districts to decide. Stakeholders are discussing how the standards are to be assessed.

---

## Working With Parents and Students

Principals provide a great community service when they talk to parents of newborns and alert them to the importance of the early preschool years in developing a child's literacy. Given the evidence that the brain's ability to acquire spoken language is at its peak in the early years, parents should create a rich environment that includes lots of communication activities, such as talking, singing, and reading aloud. In schools, this means addressing any language-learning problems quickly to take advantage of the brain's ability to rewire improper connections during this important period of growth. It also means that parents and teachers should not assume that children with language-based problems are going to be limited in cognitive thought processes as well.

Principals can also ensure that the school's reading program will help students associate reading with pleasure. For readers having difficulties, principals can develop a library of specially recorded books that have a slow pace, clear phrasing, and small amounts of material per audiovisual recording. Struggling readers need to listen to the recording and to follow along.

## Close the Achievement Gap in Reading

We hear a lot these days about closing the achievement gap between low-income and minority children, and other students. Despite the continuing concern, money, and effort, the gap in reading scores refuses to narrow. What causes this unfortunate situation depends on who you ask. Adults often say these students achieve poorly because they don't eat breakfast, they are too poor, their parents don't care, or they don't have any books at home. This focuses blame on the children and their families. But talking with students often produces different reasons. They talk about teachers who are not qualified in what they are teaching, about counselors who underestimate their potential, about principals who dismiss their concerns, and of a curriculum that is boring and irrelevant to their needs.

No one argues that issues like poverty, family stability, and home environment do not matter, because clearly they do. But if educators assume that unfortunate social and economic conditions will affect how *much* a child learns, then we end up not challenging the child. As a result, these students become the object of a self-fulfilling prophecy: We expect less of them, so we give them less, and they produce less in return.

Educators are not usually able to change what happens to children outside of school, but they can ensure that what happens *in school* really matters. Closing the achievement gap, in my opinion, requires concerted effort in four areas:

- *Establish and maintain high standards, and expect all students to meet them.* People rise and fall to the level of expectations we set for them. Too often in high-poverty schools there is little expectation that students can meet the reading standards. We misinterpret their lack of literacy as an inability to acquire literacy. Schools must be clearly committed to the notion that standards are for everyone and that everyone *can* reach them with appropriate instruction and, if needed, systematic interventions.

- *Design a challenging reading curriculum that is aligned with the standards.* Assume that all students can learn phonemic awareness and the alphabetic principle, although some students may take longer. Keep the practice consistent and challenging and introduce interesting literature as appropriate to enhance comprehension.

- *Provide systematic research-based additional help for struggling readers.* Many schools have programs, such as Title I, designed to offer additional help to disadvantaged students. But these sessions can subject the students to more of the same outdated strategies that did not work in their regular classrooms. For some children, the school day just does not provide enough time to include the activities they need to catch up. More effort should be made to provide help through an extended school day, on weekends, before school, during vacation periods, and in the summer. Districts that have implemented these extended instructional times for struggling readers are reporting significant improvements in reading achievement.

- *Ensure that teachers thoroughly know the subjects they are teaching.* In many states, 15 to 30 percent of middle school and high school teachers are teaching outside their areas of college study (Hill, 2011). That number increases dramatically in high-poverty schools because fully qualified teachers often find those positions less desirable and succeed in avoiding them. Numerous research studies over decades have shown that the classroom teacher remains the single greatest factor that determines most students' success in learning. As I have stated in my other books, the quality of learning rarely exceeds the quality of teaching. When we have fully qualified teachers with high expectations and an updated knowledge base of how to teach reading, we can make great headway in closing the reading achievement gap.

## Encourage Teachers to Be Researchers

Teachers cannot be mere consumers of the knowledge emerging from scientific research. They must position themselves as active participants in the research community. One way to do this is through action research. Action research gives the practitioner a chance to be a researcher and to investigate specific problems that affect teaching and learning. Unlike traditional education research, where teachers are studied by outsiders, action research is conducted by teachers themselves to study their own classroom practices. It is a systematic investigation into some aspect of the school pursued by educators out of a desire to improve what they do. Action research expands the role of a teacher as an inquirer into teaching and learning through systematic classroom research.

Teachers of reading can test whether a particular strategy they want to use is effective by trying it with some students and not with others. By setting up a small research project in the classroom, teachers can determine how well the students using the strategy (test group) learned compared with those who did not use the strategy (control group).

Action research is well suited to schools because of its democratic methodology, inclusiveness, flexibility of approach, and potential for changing practice. Action research uses a solution-oriented approach that is characterized by six cycles (Figure 8.1):

- Identifying the problem ("Will this strategy be more effective than other ones I have used?")
- Systematically collecting data ("How will I know if it worked?")
- Analyzing the data ("Did it improve the students' learning? How?")
- Taking action on the data ("What changes should I make?")
- Redefining the problem, if necessary ("Is there something else I should try?")
- Sharing the results with colleagues

Because the teacher who is responsible for implementing changes also does the research, a real fit is created between the needs of a specific learner and the action taken. Teachers of reading should understand that their own honing of proven instructional strategies through reflection and systematic monitoring of their students' progress is a critical component of a scientifically based reading program. Action research provides a means to that end.

Figure 8.1    This diagram illustrates the six steps in the action research cycle, starting with identifying or redefining the problem.

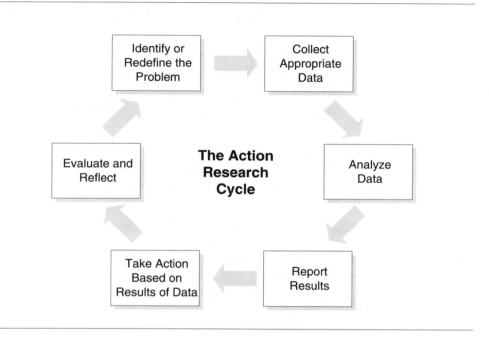

Action research also provides teachers with opportunities to gain knowledge and skills in research methods and applications and to become more aware of the possibilities and options for change. Teachers using action research are likely to be receptive and supportive of systemic changes that school leaders may be seeking. We teach our students that inquiry is a tool of scientists. By engaging in action research, teachers extend their knowledge of reading instruction through inquiry. They carefully observe, generate and test hypotheses, collect data, and draw conclusions based on evidence that are shared with other reading teachers and researchers.

## CONCLUSION    ✿

Here are some of the major points I have presented in this book:

- Despite the variations among how and the rates at which children learn, they all have similar brains. Although the brain is not innately wired for reading, the neural circuits for visual recognition and spoken language processing can be taught to make connections between the sounds of language and the letters that represent them (the alphabetic principle), an absolutely necessary skill in order to learn to read competently.

- The size of a child's spoken vocabulary is a key predictor of later success in reading.

- Although decoding is an essential skill for beginning readers, acquiring vocabulary is also important so that children can learn the way English words are formed (root words, prefixes, and suffixes). This is particularly crucial for those students with a low-literacy background or whose native language is not English.

- We must identify as soon as possible children who are at risk for reading difficulties and have standardized and scientifically based screening tests for dyslexia. Children with these challenges should get intensive phonological training in small groups.

- Thanks to the brain's amazing plasticity, dyslexia can be circumvented through research-based programs that develop alternative cerebral pathways for reading.

- Educators, parents, and psychologists can no longer ignore the recent scientific discoveries about how the brain learns to read, especially those that indicate which teaching methods may be more effective, and which ones less effective.

- Neuroscience has made significant contributions to our understanding of the reading process, but it will not solve all language learning problems. That will take the work of dedicated and enlightened educators who arouse a child's interest in reading, and who employ creative and effective strategies based on updated knowledge of how the brain learns to read fluently and with comprehension.

Teaching children to read is not an easy task. This is especially true in the typical primary classroom where teachers welcome children from an ever-increasing variety of home situations, cultures, and native languages. Given these variables, successful teachers of reading are flexible rather than rigid in their approach, and they know through experience what they need to do to make learning to read exciting and meaningful. They also acknowledge that the findings of scientific studies are clear: Explicit instruction in phonemic awareness is essential because it helps the beginning reader understand the alphabetic principle and apply it to reading and writing. Enriched text complements—but does not replace—this process to provide relevant and enjoyable reading experiences.

This approach recognizes that learning to read and write are complex activities requiring at least seven levels of brain processing that must eventually be integrated:

- Phonological—knowing the sound system of language, phonemic awareness, and sound-letter correspondences
- Graphic—visually perceiving letters and symbols
- Lexical—recognizing words and their component parts, such as prefixes and suffixes
- Syntactic—understanding rules of grammar and discourse
- Semantic—comprehending meaning and detecting thematic structures
- Communicative—expressing purposes and intentions
- Cultural—communicating shared beliefs and knowledge

Effective reading programs and reading teachers should address all these levels of processing because each level supports the others. At the same time, children must be encouraged to use all the resources available to them in their efforts to decode, comprehend, and compose text. During this process, teachers need to have the skills to quickly recognize reading problems that arise and be able to select tested strategies to help students overcome those problems. Studies show that effective classroom instruction alone can substantially reduce reading failure (e.g., Joshi et al., 2009; Podhajski et al., 2009).

There is little doubt that the knowledge, strength, and sophistication of the teacher is what really matters in helping children learn to read successfully. It is to that end that this book was written, and it is my hope that teachers and parents who read it will feel more empowered to help their children gain the literacy skills they need to be productive citizens of the world.

---

### QUESTIONS FOR DISCUSSION/REFLECTION

- *What are the basics of a successful reading program?*
- *What do beginning readers need to learn?*
- *What do teachers need to know about teaching reading?*

# Resources

**Note: All Internet sites were active at time of publication.**

## All About Adolescent Literacy

Website: www.adlit.org

This site offers information and resources to parents and educators of struggling adolescent readers and writers. It includes research papers and reports, classroom strategies, and other valuable resources on adolescent literacy.

## American Speech-Language-Hearing Association

Website: www.asha.org

This association represents speech, language, and hearing professionals. The site provides information for teachers and parents about normal speech development as well as how to detect problems during early childhood.

## Content Area Reading Special Interest Group

Website: www.ucmo.edu/carsig

A subgroup of the International Reading Association, this group was formed to provide information on research and successful practices related to content-area reading. The site offers valuable suggestions in several different subject areas.

## Council for Exceptional Children

2900 Crystal Drive

Suite 1000

Arlington, VA 22202-3557

Tel.: 1-888-CEC-SPED (888-232-7733)

Website: www.cec.sped.org

The CEC site has many suggestions for teachers and parents of children with learning disabilities as well as those who are gifted.

### Florida Center for Reading Research

Website: www.fcrr.org

This center was established by the state of Florida to analyze reading curricula and materials. The site offers assessment reports on various reading programs.

### Graphic Organizers

Website: www.graphic.org

This site has examples of different types of graphic organizers and suggestions on how to use them in lessons at all grade levels.

### Head Start

Website: www.acf.hhs.gov/programs/ohs

Head Start is a federally funded program that promotes school readiness in young children by supporting efforts in language and literacy, cognition and general knowledge, physical development and health, social and emotional development, and approaches to learning.

### Inspiration Software, Inc.

Website: http://inspiration.com

This company produces software that helps students construct all types of visual organizers for improving comprehension and building thinking skills. *Kidspiration* is designed for Grades K–5, and *Inspiration* is for Grade 6 and higher. Demonstration versions can be downloaded from the site, and it offers activities for tablets.

### International Dyslexia Association

40 York Road, 4th Floor

Baltimore, MD 21204

Tel.: (410) 296-0232

Website: www.interdys.org

The International Dyslexia Association (IDA) studies the various treatments for dyslexia as well as related language-based learning differences. It is the oldest such organization in the United States serving individuals with dyslexia. Its website offers publications, research references, and other useful information.

## International Reading Association

800 Barkdale Road

P.O. Box 8139

Newark, DE 19714-8139

Tel.: 1-800-336-READ (1-800-336-7323)

Website: www.reading.org

The world's largest association devoted to reading maintains a rich source of information, including useful advice to parents and teachers who are helping children learn to read. This site also offers access to research articles and studies related to reading.

## KidsHealth—Understanding Dyslexia

Website: www.kidshealth.org/parent/medical/learning/dyslexia.html

This site offers information on the nature and treatment of dyslexia, written mainly for parents.

## Literacy Information and Communication System (LINCS, formerly known as the National Institute for Literacy)

Website: www.lincs.ed.gov

This learning community supported by the U.S. government promotes activities to strengthen literacy for people of all ages, and has several reports available online that review scientific research studies in reading.

## Literature Circles Resource Center

Website: www.litcircles.org

Maintained by Seattle University's College of Education, this site offers educators many resources, suggestions, and sample lessons for using literature circles as part of a balanced literacy program.

## National Association for the Education of Young Children

1313 L Street, Suite 500

Washington, DC 20005

Tel.: 1-800-424-2460

Website: www.naeyc.org

This long-standing organization supports efforts to improve professional practice and opportunities in the education of children from birth through third grade.

### National Center for Learning Disabilities

Website: www.ncld.org

Since 1977, this organization has provided parents and teachers with evidence-based tools, programs, and events that focus on helping individuals with learning disabilities. The site provides links to all these resources along with free e-newsletters with new information.

### National Clearinghouse for English Language Acquisition and Language Instruction Educational Programs

Website: www.ncela.gwu.edu

This site has information, articles, and Web resources for reading instruction and other important topics in the education of English language learners.

### National Reading Panel

Website: www.nationalreadingpanel.org

The NRP report is available in its entirety or as an abbreviated 33-page summary from the panel's website.

### Organization for Human Brain Mapping

Website: www.humanbrainmapping.org

This organization of scientists and clinicians is involved in using brain imaging to understand more about the structures and functions of the brain. The site provides information about the organization as well as research abstracts from some of their seminars.

### Parents as Teachers

Website: www.parentsasteachers.org

This site helps professionals and organizations work with parents to provide developmentally appropriate resources to help their children learn and grow from birth to kindergarten. It lists training programs and resources, and provides research information about the effectiveness of such programs.

### Reading Partners

Website: http://readingpartners.org

This national nonprofit organization recruits and trains volunteers to work one-on-one with elementary students who are struggling readers, using research-based strategies.

## Reading Recovery Council of North America

1926 Kenny Road, Suite 100

Columbus, OH 43210-1069

Tel.: 614-292-7111

Website: www.readingrecovery.org

The official site of the Reading Recovery program has been used in numerous school districts for nearly two decades to help beginning struggling readers. The site provides information and leads to many resources on reading and literacy.

## Reading Rockets

http://readingrockets.org

This site is sponsored by WETA, a Washington, D.C., public television station, and includes lots of information to support struggling readers. It offers research studies, classroom strategies, lessons, and activities to assist teachers, parents, and other educators.

## Success for All Foundation

200 West Towsontown Boulevard

Baltimore, MD 21204-5200

Tel.: 1-800-584-4998

Website: www.successforall.org

Here is all the information one needs to understand the history, components, implementation, and effectiveness of the Success for All program.

## U.S. Department of Education

600 Maryland Avenue SW

Washington, DC 20202

Tel.: 1-800-USA-LEARN (872-5327)

Website: www.ed.gov

This site includes access to the ERIC databases and the National Center for Education Statistics, as well as descriptions of all the other activities that are the responsibility of the Department of Education.

## What Works Clearinghouse

Tel.: 1-866-503-6114

Website: http://ies.ed.gov/ncee/wwc

This site is part of the U.S. Department of Education's Institute of Education Sciences. It examines the research on various programs, practices, policies, and products in education, including literacy, to determine if they are of high quality so educators can make decisions based on valid research evidence.

## Yale Center for Dyslexia and Creativity

Website: http://dyslexia.yale.edu

Founded by famed dyslexia researchers Drs. Sally and Bennett Shaywitz, this information-rich site offers advice to parents, teachers, and policy makers on the nature of treatment of dyslexia. It includes stories of famous people with dyslexia and answers many questions that people with dyslexia frequently ask.

# COMMON CORE STATE STANDARDS ✿
# FOR ENGLISH LANGUAGE ARTS

Listed below are the Common Core Anchor Standards for Reading and the chapters where you can find information and strategies related to each standard.

## Key Ideas and Details

1. Read closely to determine what the text says explicitly and to make logical inferences from it; cite specific textual evidence when writing or speaking to support conclusions drawn from the text. See Chapters 4, 7, and 8.

2. Determine central ideas or themes of a text and analyze their development; summarize the key supporting details and ideas. See Chapters 4 and 7.

3. Analyze how and why individuals, events, and ideas develop and interact over the course of a text. See Chapters 4, 7, and 8.

## Craft and Structure

4. Interpret words and phrases as they are used in a text, including determining technical, connotative, and figurative meanings, and analyze how specific word choices shape meaning or tone. See Chapters 2, 3, 4, 7, and 8.

5. Analyze the structure of texts, including how specific sentences, paragraphs, and larger portions of the text (e.g., a section, chapter, scene, or stanza) relate to each other and the whole. See Chapters 4, 7, and 8.

6. Assess how point of view or purpose shapes the content and style of a text. See Chapters 4, 7, and 8.

## Integration of Knowledge and Ideas

7. Integrate and evaluate content presented in diverse media and formats, including visually and quantitatively, as well as in words. See Chapters 2, 3, 4, 7, and 8.

8. Delineate and evaluate the argument and specific claims in a text, including the validity of the reasoning as well as the relevance and sufficiency of the evidence. See Chapters 4, 7, and 8.

9. Analyze how two or more texts address similar themes or topics in order to build knowledge or to compare the approaches the authors take. See Chapters 4, 6, 7, and 8.

## Range of Reading and Level of Text Complexity

10. Read and comprehend complex literary and informational texts independently and proficiently. **See Chapters 2, 3, 4, 7, and 8.**

SOURCE: © Copyright 2010. National Governors Association Center for Best Practices and Council of Chief State School Officers. All rights reserved.

# Glossary

**Academic language.** The ability to know, understand, and use subject-area content and skills and communicate these to others.

**Acoustic analysis.** The process that separates relevant word sounds from background noise, decodes the phonemes of the word, and translates them into a phonological code that can be recognized by the mental lexicon.

**Affix.** Letters attached to the beginning (prefix) or end (suffix) of a word.

**Alphabetic principle.** The understanding that spoken words can be broken down into phonemes, and that written letters represent the phonemes of spoken language.

**Angular gyrus.** A fold at the base of the brain's left parietal lobe that is involved in semantic processing, number processing, memory, and cognition.

**Aphasia.** The impairment or loss of language abilities following damage to the brain.

**Automaticity.** The instant decoding of letters (and other stimuli), such that the brain processing involved in the decoding process is automatic.

**Blending.** Combining the phonemes of a spoken word into a whole word, as in blending /d/, /o/, and /g/ into *dog.*

**Blocking.** A linguistic principle that prevents a rule from applying to a word that already has an irregular form. For example, the existence of *stood* blocks a rule from adding *-ed* to *stand,* thus preempting *standed.*

**Broca's area.** A region of the brain located behind the left temple that is associated with speech production, including vocabulary, syntax, and grammar.

**Cerebellum.** Meaning "little brain," this structure at the rear of the cerebrum and above the brain stem is mainly responsible for learning and coordinating voluntary movements, but also plays a role in memory and cognition.

**Cerebral cortex.** The thin layer of gray tissue covering the outer portion of the cerebrum.

**Cerebrum.** The largest part of the brain, accounting for about two-thirds of the brain's total mass. It is involved in thinking, producing and understanding language, perception, planning, and organization, among other cognitive functions.

**Chunking.** The ability of the brain to perceive a coherent group of items as a single item or chunk.

**Collaborative strategic reading (CSR).** A technique to improve reading comprehension by using heterogeneous groups in multilevel classes.

**Comprehension.** The ability to understand and attribute meaning to what is heard or read.

**Content-area reading.** Reading in curriculum areas where students learn course content, such as facts and concepts, rather than learning skills.

**Corpus callosum.** The bridge of nerve fibers that connects the left and right cerebral hemispheres and allows communication between them.

**Decoding.** The ability to use the alphabetic principle to sound out a word by recognizing which phonemes are represented by the letters, and then blending those phonemes into a legitimate word.

**Dendrite.** The branched extension from the cell body of a neuron that receives impulses from nearby neurons through synaptic contacts.

**Deep orthography.** A language writing system, such as English, that does not have a one-to-one correspondence between the spoken phonemes and the letters that represent them. The same phoneme can be represented by different letters in words, and the same letters can represent different phonemes.

**Digraph.** A phoneme consisting of two successive letters that is pronounced as a single sound, as the *-ea* in *clean,* the *ch-* in *child,* or the *-ng* in *song*.

**Dyslexia.** A persistent developmental problem in learning to read. In 2002, the International Dyslexia Association adopted the following definition: "Dyslexia is a specific learning disability that is neurological in origin. It is characterized by difficulties with accurate and/or fluent word recognition and by poor spelling and decoding abilities. These difficulties typically result from a deficit in the phonological component of language that is often unexpected in relation to other cognitive abilities and the provision of effective classroom instruction. Secondary consequences may include problems in reading comprehension and reduced reading experience that can impede the growth of vocabulary and background knowledge."

**Educational neuroscience.** Also called *Mind, Brain, and Education* or *Neuroeducation*, this is a new area of scientific inquiry exploring the relationships and applications of discoveries in neuroscience and psychology to educational practice (pedagogy).

**Encoding.** The ability to attach sounds to letter combinations to spell and write words.

**Event-related potential (ERP).** An electrical signal emitted by the brain in response to a stimulus such as a picture or a word. The signals are detected by electrodes pasted to the scalp.

**Fixation.** The period of time when our eyes stop after making rapid movements across the page during reading. It is during these fixations of about 200 to 250 milliseconds that the eyes actually acquire information from the text.

**Fluency.** The ability to read a text orally with speed, accuracy, and proper expression.

**Frontal lobe.** The front part of the brain that monitors higher-order thinking, directs problem solving, and regulates the excesses of the emotional system.

**Functional magnetic resonance imaging (fMRI).** A process that measures blood flow to the brain to record areas of high and low neural activity.

**Genetic material.** The chromosomes and genes present in all body cells that direct one's growth and development.

**Gist.** An interpretation and mental representation of the meaning of a phrase, sentence, paragraph, passage, and so on.

**Grapheme.** The smallest part of written language that represents a single phoneme in the spelling of a word. A grapheme may be just one letter, such as *b, d, g,* or *s,* or several letters, as in *ck, sh, igh,* and *th.*

**Graphic organizer.** A visual representation of knowledge, concepts, or ideas, such as with charts, diagrams, and timelines.

**Gray matter.** The thin layer of cells that cover the surface of the cerebrum, also called the cerebral cortex.

**Gyrus.** Plural: *gyri.* A ridge (hill) in the cerebral cortex generally surrounded by sulci.

**Hippocampus.** Meaning "seahorse" because of its shape, it is part of the brain's limbic (emotional) system and plays an important role in consolidating information from working memory to long-term memory and in spatial navigation.

**Immediate memory.** A temporary memory where information is processed briefly (in seconds) and subconsciously, then either blocked or passed on to working memory.

**Invented spelling.** The creation of plausible spellings of real words using one's knowledge of letter names and sounds.

**Lexicon.** A person's mental dictionary consisting of words and their meanings.

**Limbic system.** An area located at the base of the cerebrum containing the structures that contribute to memory and emotional processing.

**Long-term storage.** The areas of the brain where memories are stored permanently.

**Magnetic resonance imaging (MRI).** A process that uses radio waves to disturb the alignment of the body's atoms in a magnetic field to produce computer-processed, high-contrast images of internal structures.

**Meta-analysis.** A statistical process that combines the results of different studies to look for patterns of agreement and disagreement among those results, and any other interesting relationships. The results are usually reported as effect sizes.

**Millisecond (ms).** A unit of time that represents one one-thousandth of a second.

**Morpheme.** The smallest units into which words can be divided that have meaning, as in *un-in-habit-able* (four morphemes).

**Morphology.** The component of grammar that studies how words are built from pieces called morphemes, and how affixes change the meaning of words in predictable ways.

**Neuron.** The basic cell making up the brain and nervous system, consisting of a cell body, a long fiber (axon) that transmits impulses, and many shorter fibers (dendrites) that receive them.

**Nonword.** A string of letters that cannot be pronounced and that have no meaning, such as *ndwsb* or *tgzaq.*

**Occipital lobe.** Located at the rear of the brain, this area is mainly responsible for visual processing.

**Occipitotemporal area.** The area of the brain that overlaps portions of the occipital and temporal lobes where all the important information about a word is stored, including its spelling, pronunciation, and meaning.

**Onset.** The initial consonant sound of a syllable, such as the *t-* sound in *tag,* or the *sw-* sound in *swim.*

**Oral reading accuracy (ORA).** A measurement calculated by subtracting the number of word errors during reading (not counting repetitions or self-corrected errors) from the total number of words read, and dividing that result by the total number of words. The resulting decimal is multiplied by 100 to yield a percentage.

**Oral reading fluency (ORF).** Also known as **words correct per minute (WCPM)**, this measure is calculated by subtracting the number of word errors during one minute of reading (not counting repetitions or self-corrected errors) from the total number of words read.

**Orthography.** The written system that describes a spoken language. Spelling and punctuation represent the orthographic features of written English.

**Overlearning.** The ability to perform a task with little attention or conscious thought.

**Parietal lobe.** Located between the occipital and frontal lobe, this area integrates sensory information, and helps in determining spatial sense and navigation.

**Parietotemporal area.** The area of the brain that overlaps portions of the parietal and temporal lobes where word analysis is thought to occur during reading.

**Positron emission tomography (PET).** A process that traces the metabolism of radioactively-tagged sugar in brain tissue, producing a color image of cell activity.

**Phoneme.** The smallest units of sound that make up a spoken language. For example, the word *go* has two phonemes, *guh* and *oh.* The English language has about 44 phonemes. Some phonemes are represented by more than one letter.

**Phonemic awareness.** The ability to hear, identify, and manipulate phonemes in spoken syllables and words.

**Phonics.** The understanding that there is a predictable relationship between the sounds of *spoken* language (phonemes) and the letters that represent those sound in *written* language (graphemes).

**Phonologic memory.** The ability to retain verbal bits of information (phonemes) in working memory.

**Phonological awareness.** In addition to phonemic awareness, it includes the ability to recognize that sentences comprise words, words comprise syllables, and syllables comprise onsets and rimes that can be broken down into phonemes.

**Phonology.** The component of grammar that studies the sound patterns of a language, including how phonemes are combined to form words, as well as patterns of timing, stress, and intonation.

**Plasticity.** The ability of the brain to reorganize itself and form new neural networks as a result of changes in its environment.

**Prefrontal cortex.** The part of the brain located in the frontal lobe that lies just behind the forehead and that carries out executive functions, such as assessing options, predicting outcomes, and suppressing unacceptable social and emotional urges.

**Prosody.** The unique rhythm, cadence, accent patterns, and pitch of a language when spoken.

**Pseudoword.** A string of letters that can be pronounced but has no meaning (also called nonsense or invented words), such as *gebin* or *splor.*

**Regression.** The movement of the eyes backward over a written line to reread text.

**Rehearsal.** The reprocessing of information in working memory.

**Rime.** A part of a syllable that contains the vowel and all that follows it, as the *-ag* sound in *tag* or the *-im* sound in *swim.*

**Semantics.** The study of how meaning is derived from words and other text forms.

**Shallow orthography.** A language writing system, such as Italian, Spanish, or Finnish, that has a consistent correspondence between the spoken phonemes and the letters that represent those phonemes in writing.

**Silent sustained reading (SSR).** A strategy in which students are assigned to do silent reading for a specified number of minutes each day. Despite its continued usage, its effectiveness has not been proved.

**Sulcus.** Plural: **sulci.** A crevice (valley) on the surface of the brain.

**Syllable.** A word part that contains a vowel or vowel sound pronounced as a unit: *speak-er, a-lone.*

**Synapse.** The junction between two neurons consisting of a minute gap where impulses pass from one neuron to the next.

**Syntax.** The rules and conventions that govern the order of words in phrases, clauses, and sentences.

**Temporal lobe.** Located behind the ears, this region is involved in visual memory, auditory processing, and comprehending language.

**Visual word form area (VWFA).** Located at the boundary of the occipital and temporal lobes on the left side of the brain, this region plays an essential role in the visual analysis of letter and word shape.

**Wernicke's area.** The region of the brain, usually located in the left hemisphere, thought to be responsible for sense and meaning in one's native language(s).

**Whole-language method.** An approach to reading instruction that emphasizes the recognition of words as wholes and de-emphasizes letter-sound relationships.

**Word blindness.** The inability to read words even when a person's eyes are optically normal.

**Word form.** The neural model that encompasses the spelling, pronunciation, and meaning of a word.

**Working memory.** The temporary memory of limited capacity where information is processed consciously.

# References

Achieve. (2013). *Next generation science standards.* Washington, DC: Author.

Adlof, S. M., Catts, H. W., & Lee, J. (2010). Kindergarten predictors of second versus eighth grade reading comprehension impairments. *Journal of Learning Disabilities, 43*(4), 332–345.

Ahmed, S. T., & Lombardino, L. J. (2000). Invented spelling: An assessment and intervention protocol for kindergarten children. *Communication Disorders Quarterly, 22,* 19–28.

Alvermann, D. E., & Mallozzi, C. A. (2010). Primary and elementary/middle grades reading. In P. Peterson, E. Baker, & B. McGaw (Eds.), *International encyclopedia of education* (3rd ed., Vol. 1, pp. 464–467). Oxford, UK: Academic Press.

American Speech-Language-Hearing Association. (2013). *How does your child hear and talk?* Retrieved from http://www.asha.org/public/speech/development/chart.htm

Andrews, S., & Lo, S. (2013, April). Is morphological priming stronger for transparent than opaque words? It depends on individual differences in spelling and vocabulary. *Journal of Memory and Language, 68*(3), 279–296.

Argus, L. (2012, January). Shake it up with reading. *Science Scope, 35*(5), 51.

Armbruster, B. (1996). Schema theory and the design of content-area textbooks. *Educational Psychologist, 21,* 253–276.

August, D., & Shanahan, T. (2006). *Developing literacy in second-language learners: Report of the national literacy panel on language minority children and youth.* Mahwah, NJ: Erlbaum.

Aylward, E., Richards, T., Berninger, V., Nagy, W., Field, K., Grimme, A., Richards, A., Thomson, J., & Cramer, S. C. (2003, June). *Instructional treatment associated with changes in brain activation in children with dyslexia.* Paper presented at the conference of the Organization for Human Brain Mapping, New York, NY.

Bach, S., Brandeis, D., Hofstetter, C., Martin, E., Richardson, U., & Brem, S. (2010, November). Early emergence of deviant frontal fMRI activity for phonological processes in poor beginning readers. *NeuroImage, 53,* 682–693.

Baer, G. T., & Nourie, B. L. (1993). Strategies for teaching reading in the content areas. *The Clearing House, 67,* 121–122.

Bailet, L. L., Repper, K., Murphy, S., Piasta, S., & Zettler-Greeley, C. (2011). Emergent literacy intervention for prekindergarteners at risk for reading failure: Years 2 and 3 of a multiyear study. *Journal of Learning Disabilities, 46*(2) 133–153.

Baillieux, H., Vandervliet, E. J. M., Manto, M., Parizel, P. M., De Deyn, P. P., & Mariën, P. (2009, February). Developmental dyslexia and widespread activation across the cerebellar hemispheres. *Brain and Language, 108*(2), 122–132.

Barton-Arwood, S. M., & Little, M. A. (2013). Using graphic organizers to access the general curriculum at the secondary level. *Intervention in School and Clinic, 49*(1), 6–13.

Beach, K. D., & O'Connor, R. E. (2013, July 12). Early response-to-intervention measures and criteria as predictors of reading disability in the beginning of third grade. *Journal of Learning Disabilities* [Published online ahead of print], 1–28. doi:10.1177/0022219413495451

Bear, D., Invernizzi, M., Templeton, S., & Johnston, F. (2008). *Words their way: Word study for phonics, vocabulary, and spelling instruction* (4th ed.). Upper Saddle River, NJ: Pearson.

Beauchamp, M. S., Lee, K. E., Argall, B. D., & Martin, A. (2004). Integration of auditory and visual information about objects in superior temporal sulcus. *Neuron, 41*(5), 809–823.

Beck, I. L., McKeown, M. G., Hamilton, R. L., & Kugan, L. (1997). *Questioning the author: An approach for enhancing student engagement with text.* Newark, DE: International Reading Association.

Bender, W. N., & Larkin, M. J. (2003). *Reading strategies for elementary students with learning difficulties.* Thousand Oaks, CA: Corwin Press.

Benítez-Burraco, A. (2010). Neurobiology and neurogenetics of dyslexia. *Neurología* [English edition], 25(9), 563–581.

Berninger, V. W., Nielsen, K. H., Abbott, R. D., Wijsman, E., & Raskind, W. (2008, April). Gender differences in severity of writing and reading disabilities. *Journal of School Psychology, 46*(2), 151–172.

Bhatt, R. S., Hayden, A., Reed, A., Bertin, E., & Joseph, J. (2006). Infants' perception of information along object boundaries: Concavities versus convexities. *Journal of Experimental Child Psychology, 94*(2), 91–113.

Bialystok, E., McBride-Chang, C., & Luk, G. (2005, November). Bilingualism, language proficiency, and learning to read in two writing systems. *Journal of Educational Psychology, 97*(4), 580–590.

Biemiller, A. J., & Boote, C. (2006). An effective method of building meaning vocabulary in primary grades. *Journal of Educational Psychology, 98*(1), 44–62.

Birsh, J. R. (2005). *Multisensory teaching of basic language skills* (2nd ed.). Towson, MD: Brookes.

Bischoff-Grethe, A., Proper, S. M., Mao, H., Daniels, K. A., & Berns, G. S. (2000). Conscious and unconscious processing of nonverbal predictability in Wernicke's area. *Journal of Neuroscience, 20,* 1975–1981.

Bloch, C., Kaiser, A., Kuenzli, E., Zappatore, D., Haller, S., Franceschini, R., Luedi, G., Radue, E.-E., & Nitsch, C. (2009). The age of second language acquisition determines the variability in activation elicited by narration in three languages in Broca's and Wernicke's area. *Neuropsychologia, 47*(3), 625–633.

Bolton, F., & Snowball, D. (1993). *Ideas for spelling.* Portsmouth, NH: Heinemann.

Borman, G. D., & Benson, J. (2006). *Can brain research and computers improve literacy? A randomized field trial of the* Fast ForWord® Language *computer-based training program* (WCER working paper no. 2006–5). Madison: University of Wisconsin–Madison, Wisconsin Center for Education Research.

Bowers, P. N., Kirby, J. R., & Deacon, S. H. (2010, May). The effect of morphological instruction on literacy skills: A systematic review of the literature. *Review of Educational Research, 80*(2), 114–179.

Brady, S., & Moats, L. (1997). *Informed instruction for reading success: Foundations for teacher preparation.* Baltimore, MD: International Dyslexia Association.

Brasseur-Hock, I. F., Hock, M. F., Kieffer, M. J., Biancarosa, G., & Deshler, D. D. (2011, August). Adolescent struggling readers in urban schools: Results of a Latent Class Analysis. *Learning and Individual Differences, 21*(4), 438–452.

Brown, W. E., Eliez, S., Menon, V., Rumsey, J. M., White, C. D., & Reiss, A. L. (2001). Preliminary evidence of widespread morphological variations of the brain in dyslexia. *Neurology, 27,* 781–783.

Bruhn, A. L., & Hasselbring, T. S. (2013). Increasing student access to content area textbooks. *Intervention in School and Clinic, 49*(1), 30–38.

Brunswick, N., Martin, G. N., & Rippon, G. (2012, February). Early cognitive profiles of emergent readers: A longitudinal study. *Journal of Experimental Child Psychology, 111*(2), 268–285.

Burke, M. D., Hagan-Burke, S., Kwok, O., & Parker, R. (2009, February). Predictive validity of early literacy indicators from the middle of kindergarten to second grade. *Journal of Special Education, 42*(4), 209–226.

Burman, D. D., Bitan, T., & Booth, J. R. (2008). Sex differences in neural processing of language among children. *Neuropsychologia, 46*(5), 1349–1362.

Burnham, D., Kitamura, C., & Vollmer-Conna, U. (2002). What's new pussycat? On talking to babies and animals. *Science, 296,* 1435.

Bushnell, C., Kemp, N., & Martin, F. H. (2011). Text-messaging practices and links to general spelling skill: A study of Australian children. *Australian Journal of Educational & Developmental Psychology, 11,* 27–38.

Byrne, B. (1991). Experimental analysis of the child's discovery of the alphabetic principle. In L. Riehen & C. Perfetti (Eds.), *Learning to read: Basic research and its implications* (pp. 75–84). Hillsdale, NJ: Erlbaum.

Calderón, M., Hertz-Lazarowitz, R., & Slavin, R. (1998). Effects of Bilingual Cooperative Integrated Reading and Composition on students making the transition from Spanish to English reading. *The Elementary School Journal, 99,* 153–166.

Calderón, M., & Minaya-Rowe, L. (2003). *Designing and implementing two-way bilingual programs.* Thousand Oaks, CA: Corwin Press.

Callender, W. A. (2007). The Idaho results-based model: Implementing response to intervention statewide. In S. R. Jimerson, M. K. Burns, & A. M. VanDerHeyden (Eds.), *Handbook of response to intervention: The science and practice of assessment and intervention* (pp. 331–342). New York, NY: Springer.

Cantrell, S. C., & Hughes, H. K. (2008). Teacher efficacy and content literacy implementation: An exploration of the effects of extended professional development with coaching. *Journal of Literacy Research, 40,* 95–127.

Caplan, D. (2006). Why is Broca's area involved in syntax? *Cortex, 42*(4), 469–471.

Carbo, M. (2003, September). How principals can do it all in reading—Part III. *TEPSA Instructional Leader, 16,* 1–3.

Carnine, D. W., Silbert, J., & Kame'enui, E. J. (1997). *Direct instruction reading.* Upper Saddle River, NJ: Prentice Hall.

Carretti, B., Borella, E., Cornoldi, C., & De Beni, R. (2009, June). Role of working memory in explaining the performance of individuals with specific reading comprehension difficulties: A meta-analysis. *Learning and Individual Differences, 19*(2), 246–251.

Castles, A., Coltheart, M., Wilson, K., Valpied, J., & Wedgwood, J. (2009, September). The genesis of reading ability: What helps children learn letter-sound correspondences? *Journal of Experimental Child Psychology, 104*(1), 68–88.

Center, Y., Freeman, L., Robertson, G., & Outhred, L. (1999, October). The effect of visual imagery training on the reading and listening comprehension of low listening comprehenders in Year 2. *Journal of Research in Reading, 22*(3), 241–256.

Chait, M., Eden, G., Poeppel, D., Simon, J. Z., Hill, D. F., & Flowers, D. L. (2007, July). Delayed detection of tonal targets in background noise in dyslexia. *Brain and Language, 102*(1), 80–90.

Chard, D. J., & Osborn, J. (1998). *Suggestions for examining phonics and decoding instruction in supplementary reading programs.* Austin, TX: Texas Education Agency.

Cheesman, E. A., McGuire, J. M., Shankweiler, D., & Coyne, M., (2009, August). First-year teacher knowledge of phonemic awareness and its instruction. *Teacher Education and Special Education, 32*(3), 270–289.

Cheour, M., Ceponiene, R., Lehtokoski, A., Luuk, A., Allik, J., Alho, K., & Näätänen, R. (1998, September). Development of language-specific phoneme representations in the infant brain. *Nature Neuroscience, 1,* 351–353.

Chouinard, P. A., & Goodale, M. A. (2010). Category-specific neural processing for naming pictures of animals and naming pictures of tools: An ALE meta-analysis. *Neuropsychologia, 48*(2), 409–418.

Christakis, D. A., Gilkerson, J., Richards, J. A., Zimmerman, F. J., Garrison, M. M., Xu, D., Gray, S., & Yapanel, U. (2009). Audible television and decreased adult words, infant vocalizations, and conversational turns: A population-based study. *Archives of Pediatric and Adolescent Medicine, 163*(6), 554–558.

Cibrowski, J. (1993). *Textbooks and students who can't read them.* Cambridge, MA: Brookline Books.

Clark-Edmands, S. (2000, July). Screening checklists: Early identification of children at risk for reading failure, handwriting difficulties, and spelling error analysis. *Learning Disabilities Journal, 10*(3), 14–18.

Clements, A. M., Rimrodt, S. L., Abel, J. R., Blankner, J. G., Mostofsky, S. H., Pekar, J. J., Denckla, M. B., & Cutting, L. E. (2006). Sex differences in cerebral laterality of language and visuospatial processing. *Brain and Language, 98*(2), 150–158.

Cohen, L., Dehaene, S., Naccache, L., Lehérich, S., Dehaene-Lambertz, G., Hénaff, M., & Michel, F. (2000). The visual word form area: Spatial and temporal characterization of an initial stage of reading in normal subjects and posterior split-brain patients. *Brain, 123,* 291–307.

Cohen, L., Lehéricy, S., Henry, C., Bourgeois, M., Larroque, C., Sainte-Rose, C., Dehaene, S., & Hertz-Pannier, L. (2004, December). Learning to read without a left occipital lobe: Right-hemispheric shift of visual word form area. *Annals of Neurology, 56*(6), 890–894.

Cole, P. G., & Mengler, E. D. (1994). Phonemic processing of children with language deficits: Which tasks best discriminate children with learning disabilities from average readers? *Reading Psychology, 15,* 223–243.

Collins, A. M., & Loftus, E. F. (1975). A spreading-activation theory of semantic processing. *Psychological Review, 82,* 407–428.

Compton, D. L., Fuchs, D., Fuchs, L. S., & Bryant, J. D. (2006). Selecting at-risk readers in first grade for early intervention: A two-year longitudinal study of decision rules and procedures. *Journal of Educational Psychology, 98,* 394–409.

Concannon-Gibney, T., & McCarthy, M. J. (2012). The explicit teaching of reading comprehension in science class: A pilot professional development program. *Improving Schools, 15*(1), 73–88.

Daly, E., Chafouleas, S., & Skinner, C. (2005). *Interventions for reading problems: Designing and evaluating effective strategies.* New York, NY: Guilford.

Damasio, H., Grabowski, T. J., Tranel, D., Hichwa, R. D., & Damasio, A. (1996). A neural basis for lexical retrieval. *Nature, 380,* 499–505.

Dapretto, M., & Bookheimer, S. Y. (1999). Form and content: Dissociating syntax and semantics in sentence comprehension. *Neuron, 2,* 427.

Davies, M. (2012). *The corpus of contemporary American English: 450 million words, 1990–2012.* Retrieved from http://corpus.byu.edu/coca

de Haan, M., Johnson, M. H., & Halit, H. (2003). Development of face-sensitive event-related potentials during infancy: A review. *International Journal of Psychophysiology, 51*(1), 45–58.

Dehaene, S. (2009). *Reading in the brain.* New York, NY: Viking.

Dehaene-Lambertz, G. (2000). Cerebral specialization for speech and non-speech stimuli in infants. *Journal of Cognitive Neuroscience, 12,* 449–460.

Dennis, D. V. (2013). Heterogeneity or homogeneity: What assessment data reveal about struggling adolescent readers. *Journal of Literacy Research, 45*(1), 3–21.

Deshler, D. D., Ellis, E. S., & Lenz, B. K. (1996). *Teaching adolescents with learning disabilities: Strategies and methods.* Denver, CO: Love.

Dexter, D. D., & Hughes, C. A. (2011). Graphic organizers and students with learning disabilities: A meta-analysis. *Learning Disability Quarterly, 34*(1), 51–72.

Duke, N. K., & Block, M. K. (2012). Improving reading in the primary grades. *The Future of Children, 22*(2), 55–72.

Duncan, J. (2004). *How to read critically.* Retrieved from http://ctl.utsc.utoronto.ca/twc/sites/default/files/CriticalReading.pdf

Durán, R. P. (2008, February). Assessing English-language learners' achievement. *Review of Research in Education, 32*(2), 292–327.

Dyslexia International—Tools and Technology (DITT). (2001). *Language shock—Dyslexia across cultures.* Brussels, Belgium: Author.

Eckert, M. M., Leonard, C. M., Richards, T. L., Aylward, E. H., Thomson, J., & Berninger, V. W. (2003). Anatomical correlates of dyslexia: Frontal and cerebellar findings. *Brain, 126,* 482–494.

Edelen-Smith, P. J. (1998). How now brown cow: Phoneme awareness activities for collaborative classrooms. *Intervention in School and Clinic, 33,* 103–111.

Edmonds, M. S., Vaughn, S., Wexler, J., Reutebuch, C., Cable, A., Tackett, K. K., & Schnakenberg, J. W. (2009, Spring). A synthesis of reading interventions and effects on reading comprehension outcomes for older struggling readers. *Review of Educational Research, 79*(1), 262–300.

Ehri, L. (1998). Grapheme-phoneme knowledge is essential for learning to read words in English. In J. Metsala & L. Ehri (Eds.), *Word recognition in beginning literacy* (pp. 3–40). Mahwah, NJ: Erlbaum.

Ehri, L., & Roberts, T. (2006). The roots of learning to read and write: Acquisition of letters and phonemic awareness. In D. Dickinson & S. Neuman (Eds.), *Handbook of early literacy research* (Vol. 2, pp. 113–130). New York, NY: Guilford.

Escamilla, K. (1994). Descubriendo la Lectura: An early intervention literacy program in Spanish. *Literacy, Teaching, and Learning, 1,* 57–70.

Fedorenko, E., Gibson, E., & Rohde, D. (2006, May). The nature of working memory capacity in sentence comprehension: Evidence against domain-specific working memory resources. *Journal of Memory and Language, 54*(4), 541–553.

Fenty, N. S., & Barnett, K. N. (2013, September). Using alternate texts to support comprehension of core curriculum. *Intervention in School and Clinic, 49*(1), 21–29.

Fisher, S. E., & DeFries, J. C. (2002). Developmental dyslexia: Genetic dissection of a complex cognitive trait. *Nature Reviews Neuroscience, 30,* 767–780.

Fisk, C., & Hurst, B. (2003). Paraphrasing for comprehension. *The Reading Teacher, 57,* 182–185.

Foorman, B. R., Francis, D. J., Fletcher, J. M., Schatschneider, C., & Mehta, P. (1998). The role of instruction in learning to read: Preventing reading failure in at-risk children. *Journal of Educational Psychology, 90,* 37–55.

Frith, U. (1985). Beneath the surface of developmental dyslexia. In K. E. Patterson, J. C. Marshall, & M. Coltheart (Eds.), *Surface dyslexia: Cognitive and neuropsychological studies of phonological reading* (pp. 301–330). Hillsdale, NJ: Erlbaum.

Gajria, M., Jitendra, A. K., Sood, S., & Sacks, G. (2007, May/June). Improving comprehension of expository text in students with LD: A research synthesis. *Journal of Learning Disabilities, 40*(3), 210–225.

Galuske, R. A. W., Schlote, W., Bratzke, H., & Singer, W. (2000). Interhemispheric asymmetries of the modular structure in human temporal cortex. *Science, 289,* 1946–1949.

Gambrell, L. B., & Koskinen, P. S. (2002). Imagery: A strategy for enhancing comprehension. In C. C. Block & M. Pressley (Eds.), *Comprehension instruction: Research-based best practices* (pp. 305–318). New York, NY: Guilford.

Gathercole, S. E. (2008). Working memory. *Learning and Memory: A Comprehensive Reference, 2,* 33–51.

Gazzaniga, M. S., Ivry, R. B., & Mangun, G. R. (2002). *Cognitive neuroscience: The biology of the mind* (2nd ed.). New York, NY: Norton.

Georgiewa, P., Rzanny, R., Gaser, C., Gerhard, U. J., Vieweg, U., Freesmeyer, D., Mentzel, H. J., Kaiser, W. A., & Blanz, B. (2002). Phonological processing in dyslexic children: A study combining functional imaging and event related potentials. *Neuroscience Letters, 318*(1), 5–8.

Gernsbacher, M. A., Robertson, R. R. W., Palladino, P., & Werner, N. K., (2004). Managing mental representations during narrative comprehension. *Discourse Processes, 37*(2), 145–164.

Gersten, R., Compton, D., Connor, C., Cimino, J., Santoro, L., Linan-Thompson, S., & Tilly, W. (2009). *Assisting students struggling with reading: Response to intervention and multitier intervention in the primary grades. A practice guide* (NCEE 2009–4045). Washington, DC: U.S. Department of Education. Retrieved from http://ies.ed.gov/ncee/wwc/PracticeGuide.aspx?sid=3

Geva, E., & Yaghoub-Zadeh, Z. (2006). Reading efficiency in native English-speaking and English-as-a-second-language children: The role of oral proficiency and underlying cognitive-linguistic processes. *Scientific Studies of Reading, 10,* 31–57.

Glezer, L. S., Jiang, X., & Riesenhuber, M., (2009, April). Evidence for highly selective neuronal tuning for whole words in the "visual word form area." *Neuron, 62,* 199–204.

Goldberg, E. (2001). *The executive brain: Frontal lobes and the civilized mind.* New York, NY: Oxford University Press.

Graham, S. A., & Fisher, S. E. (2013). Decoding the genetics of speech and language. *Current Opinion in Neurobiology, 23*(1), 43–51.

Graham, S., & Hebert, M. A. (2010). *Writing to read: Evidence for how writing can improve reading. A Carnegie Corporation Time to Act Report.* Washington, DC: Alliance for Excellent Education.

Grainger, J., & Ziegler, J. (2007). Cross-code consistency effects in visual word recognition. In E. L. Grigorenko & A. J. Naples (Eds.), *Single-word reading: Biological and behavioral perspectives* (pp. 129–158). New York, NY: Erlbaum.

Grande, M., Meffert, E., Huber, W., Amunts, K., & Heim, S. (2011, August). Word frequency effects in the left IFG in dyslexic and normally reading children during picture naming and reading. *NeuroImage, 57*(3), 1212–1220.

Greenleaf, C. L., Litman, C., Hanson, T. L., Rosen, R., Boscardin, C. K., Herman, J., Schneider, S. A., Madden, S., & Jones, B. (2011, June). Integrating literacy and science in biology: Teaching and learning impacts of reading apprenticeship professional development. *American Educational Research Journal, 48*(3), 647–717.

Gruenbaum, E. A. (2012, Spring). Common literacy struggles with college students: Using the reciprocal teaching technique. *Journal of College Reading and Learning, 42*(2), 110–116.

Guiller, J., & Durndell, A. (2007, September). Students' linguistic behaviour in online discussion groups: Does gender matter? *Computers in Human Behavior, 23,* 2240–2255.

Gunn, B., Biglan, A., Smolkowski, K., & Ary, D. (2000). The efficacy of supplemental instruction in decoding skills for Hispanic and non-Hispanic students in early elementary school. *The Journal of Special Education, 34,* 90–103.

Guthrie, J. T., McRae, A., Coddington, C. S., Klauda, S. L., Wigfield, A., & Barbosa, P. (2009, May/June). Impacts of comprehensive reading instruction on diverse outcomes of low- and high-achieving readers. *Journal of Learning Disabilities, 42*(3), 195–214.

Habib, M. (2003). Rewiring the dyslexic brain. *Trends in Cognitive Science, 7,* 330–333.

Hagaman, J. L., Casey, K. J., & Reid, R. (2012). The effects of paraphrasing strategy on the reading comprehension of young students. *Remedial and Special Education, 33*(2), 110–123.

Häikiö, T., Bertram, R., Hyönä, J., & Niemi, P. (2009, February). Development of the letter identity span in reading: Evidence from the eye movement moving window paradigm. *Journal of Experimental Child Psychology, 102*(2), 167–181.

Hale, A. D., Hawkins, R. O., Sheeley, W., Reynolds, J. R., Jenkins, S., Schmitt, A. J., & Martin, D. A. (2010). An investigation of silent versus aloud reading comprehension of elementary students using Maze assessment procedures. *Psychology in the Schools, 48,* 4–14.

Harn, B. A., Linan-Thompson, S., & Roberts, G. (2008, March/April). Intensifying instruction: Does additional instructional time make a difference for the most at-risk first graders? *Journal of Learning Disabilities, 41,* 115–125.

Harris, D. N., & Sass, T. R. (2007). *Teacher training, teacher quality, and student achievement.* Washington, DC: National Center for Analysis of Longitudinal Data in Education Research.

Hart, B., & Risley, T. R. (2003). The early catastrophe: The 30 million word gap by age 3. *American Educator, 27,* 4–9.

Hart, E. R., & Speece, D. L. (1998). Reciprocal teaching goes to college: Effects of postsecondary students at risk for academic failure. *Journal of Educational Psychology, 90,* 670.

Hasbrouck, J., & Tindal, G. A. (2006). Oral reading fluency norms: A valuable assessment tool for reading teachers. *The Reading Teacher, 59*(7), 636–644.

Helenius, P., Salmelin, R., Richardson, U., Leinonen, S., & Lyytinen, H. (2002). Abnormal auditory cortical activation in dyslexia 100 msec after speech onset. *Journal of Cognitive Neuroscience, 14,* 603–617.

Hernandez, A. E., & Li, P. (2007, July). Age of acquisition: Its neural and computational mechanisms. *Psychological Bulletin, 133,* 638–650.

Hibbing, A. N., & Rankin-Erickson, J. L. (2003). A picture is worth a thousand words: Using visual images to improve comprehension for middle school struggling readers. *The Reading Teacher, 56*(8), 758–770.

Hill, J. G. (2011). *Education and certification qualifications of departmentalized public high school-level teachers of core subjects: Evidence from the 2007–08 schools and staffing survey* (NCES 2011–317). Washington, DC: U.S. Department of Education, Institute of Education Sciences, National Center for Education Statistics. Retrieved from http://nces.ed.gov/pubsearch

Howes, N., Bigler, E. D., Burlingame, G. M., & Lawson, J. S. (2003). Memory performance of children with dyslexia: A comparative analysis of theoretical perspectives. *Journal of Learning Disabilities, 36,* 230–246.

Hyerle, D. N., & Alper, L. S. (2011). *Student successes with thinking maps: School-based research, results, and models for achievement using visual tools.* Thousand Oaks, CA: Corwin.

Individuals with Disabilities Education Improvement Act (IDEA), 20 U.S.C. § 1400 *et seq.* (2004).

International Dyslexia Association (IDA). (2003). *Common signs of dyslexia.* Baltimore, MD: Author.

Isakson, M. B., Isakson, R. L., & Windham, I. (2011). *Learn more & read faster.* Provo, UT: BYU Press.

Jaušovec, N., & Jaušovec, K. (2009, November). Gender related differences in visual and auditory processing of verbal and figural tasks. *Brain Research, 1300,* 135–145.

Jenkins, J. R., Hudson, R. F., & Johnson, E. S. (2007). Screening for service delivery in an RTI framework: Candidate measures. *School Psychology Review, 36,* 560–582.

Jenkins, J. R., Schiller, E., Blackorby, J., Thayer, S. K., & Tilly, W. D. (2013). Responsiveness to intervention in reading: Architecture and practices. *Learning Disability Quarterly, 36*(1), 36–46.

Jeynes, W. H. (2008, January). A meta-analysis of the relationship between phonics instruction and minority elementary school student academic achievement. *Education and Urban Society, 40*(2), 151–166.

Johnson, D. W., Johnson, R. T., & Holubec, E. J. (2008). *Cooperation in the classroom* (Rev. ed.). Edina, MN: Interaction Book Company.

Johnson, E. S., Jenkins, J. R., Petscher, Y., & Catts, H. W. (2009, November). How can we improve the accuracy of screening instruments? *Learning Disabilities Research & Practice, 24*(4), 174–185.

Johnson, D. W., & Johnson, R. T. (1989). Cooperative learning: What special educators need to know. *The Pointer, 33,* 5–10.

Joseph, L. M. (2007). Best practices on interventions for students with reading problems. In A. Thomas & J. Grimes (Eds.), *Best practices in school psychology V* (pp. 1163–1180). Bethesda, MD: National Association of School Psychologists.

Joshi, R. M., Binks, E., Hougen, M., Dahlgren, M. E., Ocker-Dean, E., & Smith, D. L. (2009). Why elementary teachers might be inadequately prepared to teach reading. *Journal of Learning Disabilities, 42*(5), 392–402.

Just, M. A., Newman, S. D., Keller, T. A., McEleney, A., & Carpenter, P. A. (2004, January). Imagery in sentence comprehension: An fMRI study. *NeuroImage, 21*(1), 112–124.

Kaminen, N., Hannula-Jouppi, K., Kestila, M., Lahermo, P., Muller, K., Kaaranen, M., Myllylouma, B., Voutilainen, A., Lyytinen, H., Nopola-Hemmi, J., & Kere, J. (2003, May). A genome scan for developmental dyslexia confirms linkage to chromosome 2pll and suggests a new locus on 7q32. *Journal of Medical Genetics, 40,* 340–345.

Kemp, N., & Bushnell, C. (2011, February). Children's text messaging: Abbreviations, input methods and links with literacy. *Journal of Computer Assisted Learning, 27*(1), 18–27.

Kibby, M. Y., Pavawalla, S. P., Fancher, J. B., Naillon, A. J., & Hynd, G. W. (2009, April). The relationship between cerebral hemisphere volume and receptive language functioning in dyslexia and attention-deficit hyperactivity disorder (ADHD). *Journal of Child Neurology, 24*(4), 438–448.

Kirby, J. R., Silvestri, R., Allingham, B. H., Parrila, R., & La Fave, C. B. (2008). Learning strategies and study approaches of postsecondary students with dyslexia. *Journal of Learning Disabilities, 41*(1), 85–96.

Klingner, J. K., Vaughn, S., & Schumm, J. S. (1998). Collaborative strategic reading during social studies in heterogeneous fourth grade classrooms. *Elementary School Journal, 99,* 3–22.

Kortteinen, H., Närhi, V., & Ahonen, T. (2009). Does IQ matter in adolescent's reading disability? *Learning and Individual Differences, 19*(2), 257–261.

Kraebel, K. S., West, R. N., & Gerhardstein, P. (2007). The influence of training views on infants' long-term memory for simple 3D shapes. *Developmental Psychobiology, 49*(4), 406–420.

Kretlow, A. G., Wood, C. L., & Cooke, N. L. (2011). Using in-service and coaching to increase kindergarten teachers' accurate delivery of group instructional units. *Journal of Special Education, 44*(4), 234–246.

Kuhl, P. K. (2004). Early language acquisition: Cracking the speech code. *Nature Reviews Neuroscience, 5*(11), 831–843.

Kuhn, M. R., & Stahl, S. A. (2003). Fluency: A review of developmental and remedial practices. *Journal of Educational Psychology, 95,* 3–21.

Labov, W. (2003). When ordinary children fail to read. *Reading Research Quarterly, 38,* 128–131.

Lai, C. S., Fisher, S. E., Hurst, J. A., Vargha-Khadem, F., & Monaco, A. P. (2001). A forkhead-domain gene is mutated in a severe speech and language disorder. *Nature, 413,* 519–523.

Larson, K. (2004). *The science of word recognition.* Retrieved from http://www.microsoft.com/typography/ctfonts/WordRecognition.aspx

Laycock, R., Crewther, D. P., & Crewther, S. G. (2012, July). Abrupt and ramped flicker-defined form shows evidence for a large magnocellular impairment in dyslexia. *Neuropsychologia, 50*(8), 2107–2113.

Leppänen, P. H. T., Hämäläinen, J. A., Salminen, H. K., Eklund, K. M., Guttorm, T. K., Lohvansuu, K., Puolakanaho, A., & Lyytinen, H. (2010, November–December). Newborn brain event-related potentials revealing atypical processing of sound frequency and the subsequent association with later literacy skills in children with familial dyslexia. *Cortex, 46*(10), 1362–1376.

Lesaux, N., & Siegel, L. (2003). The development of reading in children who speak English as a second language. *Developmental Psychology, 39*, 1005–1019.

Lesnick, J., Goerge, R., Smithgall, C., & Gwynne J. (2010). *Reading on grade level in third grade: How is it related to high school performance and college enrollment?* Chicago, IL: Chapin Hall at the University of Chicago.

Mahony, D., Singson, M., & Mann, V. A. (2000). Reading ability and sensitivity to morphophonological situations. *Reading and Writing: An Interdisciplinary Journal, 12*(3/4), 191–218.

Mann, V. A. (2000). Introduction to special issue on morphology and the acquisition of alphabetic writing systems. *Reading and Writing: An Interdisciplinary Journal, 12*(3/4), 143–147.

Marupaka, N., Iyer, L. R., & Minai, A. A. (2012, August). Connectivity and thought: The influence of semantic network structure in a neurodynamical model of thinking. *Neural Networks, 32*, 147–158.

Maurer, U., Brem, S., Bucher, K., & Brandeis, D. (2005). Emerging neuropsychological specialization for letter strings. *Journal of Cognitive Neuroscience, 17*(10), 1532–1552.

Maurer, U., Brem, S., Kranz, F., Bucher, K., Benz, R., Halder, P., Steinhausen, H. C., & Brandeis, D. (2006). Coarse neural tuning for print peaks when children learn to read. *NeuroImage, 33*(2), 749–758.

McCandliss, B. D., Cohen, L., & Dehaene, S. (2003, July). The visual word form area: Expertise for reading in the fusiform gyrus. *Trends in Cognitive Sciences, 7*, 293–299.

McCrory, E. J., Mechelli, A., Frith, U., & Price, C. J. (2005). More than words: A common neural basis for reading and naming deficits in developmental dyslexia? *Brain, 128*, 261–267.

McGee, L., & Ukrainetz, T. (2009). Using scaffolding to teach phonemic awareness in preschool and kindergarten. *The Reading Teacher, 62*, 599–603.

Mehler, J., Jusczyk, P., Lambertz, G., Halsted, N. M., Bertoncini, J., & Amiel-Tison, C. (1988). A precursor of language acquisition in young infants. *Cognition, 29*, 143–178.

Mendelsohn, A. L., Berkule, S. B., Tomopoulos, S., Tamis-LeMonda, C. S., Huberman, H. S., Alvir, J., & Dreyer, B. P. (2008). Infant television and video exposure associated with limited parent-child verbal interactions in low socioeconomic status households. *Archives in Pediatric and Adolescent Medicine, 162*(5), 411–417.

Meng, H., Smith, S. D., Hager, K., Held, M., Liu, J., Olson, R., . . . & Gruen, J. R. (2005). DCDC2 is associated with reading disability and modulates neuronal development in the brain. *Proceedings of the National Academy of Sciences USA, 102*(47), 17053–17058.

Menzies, H. M., Mahdavi, J. N., & Lewis, J. L. (2008). Early intervention in reading: From research to practice. *Remedial and Special Education, 29*(2), 67–77.

Mesmer, H. E. (2006). Beginning reading materials: A national survey of primary teachers' reported uses and beliefs. *Journal of Literacy Research, 38*(4), 389–425.

Moats, L. C. (2005, Winter). How spelling supports reading: And why it is more regular and predictable than you think. *American Educator, 29*(4), 12–22, 42–43.

Morais, J., Cary, L., Alegria, J., & Bertelson, P. (1979). Does awareness of speech as a sequence of phonemes arise spontaneously? *Cognition, 7*, 323–331.

Morris, D., Bloodgood, J. W., Lomax, R. G., & Perney, J. (2003). Developmental steps in learning to read: A longitudinal study in kindergarten and first grade. *Reading Research Quarterly, 38*, 302–328.

Morris, J., & Stockall, L. (2012). Early, equivalent ERP masked priming effects for regular and irregular morphology. *Brain and Language, 123*(2), 81–93.

Mouza, C. (2008). Learning with laptops: Implementation and outcomes in an urban, under-privileged school. *Journal of Research on Technology in Education, 40*(4), 447–473.

Munro, J., & Dalheim, B. (2008). Checklist for identifying reading difficulties at each of the levels of text. *Studies in Exceptional Learning and Gifted Education.* University of Melbourne Graduate School of Education.

National Assessment of Educational Progress (NAEP). (2011). *The nation's report card: Reading 2011–2012.* Washington, DC: Author.

National Assessment of Educational Progress (NAEP). (2012). *Long-term trend reading assessments.* Washington, DC: Author.

National Association for the Education of Young Children (NAEYC). (1998, July). Learning to read and write: Developmentally appropriate practices for young children. *Young Children, 53*(4), 30–46.

National Association of Elementary School Principals (NAESP). (2013). *Common Core implementation checklist.* Alexandria, VA: Author.

National Early Literacy Panel (NELP). (2008). *Developing early literacy: Report of the National Early Literacy Panel.* Washington, DC: National Institute for Literacy.

National Governors Association (NGA) Center for Best Practices & the Council of Chief State School Officers (CCSSO). (2010). *Common Core State Standards for English language arts & literacy in history/social studies, science, and technical subjects.* Washington, DC: Author. Retrieved from http://www.corestandards .org/ELA-Literacy

National Institute for Literacy (NIFL). (2001). *Put reading first: The research building block for teaching children to read.* Jessup, MD: Author.

National Reading Panel (NRP). (2000). *Teaching children to read: An evidence-based assessment of the scientific research literature and its implications for reading instruction.* Washington, DC: National Institute of Child Health and Human Development.

Nesbit, J. C., & Adesope, O. O. (2006, Fall). Learning with concept and knowledge maps: A meta-analysis. *Review of Educational Research, 76*(3), 413–448.

Ness, M. K. (2009). Reading comprehension strategies in secondary content area classrooms: Teacher use of and attitudes towards reading comprehension instruction. *Reading Horizons, 49*(2), 143–166.

Nicolson, R. I., Fawcett, A. J., & Dean, P. (2001, September). Developmental dyslexia: The cerebellar deficit hypothesis. *Trends in Neuroscience, 24,* 508–511.

O'Connor, R. E., Bocian, K., Beebe-Frankenberger, M., & Linklater, D. L. (2010, February). Responsiveness of students with language difficulties to early intervention in reading. *Journal of Special Education, 43*(4), 220–235.

Olson, J., Larsen, L., Bolton, L., & Verhelst, S. (2007). *Guided reading strategies to improve students' critical thinking skills in grades three, four and five.* Saskatoon, SK: Dr. Stirling McDowell Foundation for Research into Teaching.

Ouellette, G., & Sénéchal, M. (2008). Pathways to literacy: A study of invented spelling and its role in learning to read. *Child Development, 79*(4), 899–913.

Palincsar, A. S., & Brown, A. L. (1984). The reciprocal teaching of comprehension-fostering and comprehension-monitoring activities. *Cognition and Instruction, 1,* 117–175.

Paloyelis, Y., Rijsdijk, F., Wood, A. C., Asherson, P., & Kuntsil, J. (2010). The genetic association between ADHD symptoms and reading difficulties: The role of inattentiveness and IQ. *Journal of Abnormal Child Psychology, 38*(8), 1083–1095.

Paracchini, S., Thomas, A., Castro, S., Lai, C., Paramasivam, M., Wang, Y., . . . & Monaco, A. P. (2006). The chromosome 6p22 haplotype associated with dyslexia reduces the expression of KIAA0319, a novel gene involved in neuronal migration. *Human Molecular Genetics, 15*(10), 1659–1666.

Paris, S. G., Carpenter, R. D., Paris, A. H., & Hamilton, E. E. (2004). Spurious and genuine correlates of children's reading comprehension. In S. G. Paris & S. A. Stahl (Eds.), *Children's reading comprehension and assessment* (pp. 131–160). Mahwah, NJ: Erlbaum.

Parker, R., Hasbrouck, J. E., & Denton, C. (2002a). How to tutor students with reading problems. *Preventing School Failure, 47,* 42–44.

Parker, R., Hasbrouck, J. E., & Denton, C. (2002b). How to tutor students with comprehension problems. *Preventing School Failure, 47,* 45–47.

Parrott, C. A. (1986). Visual imagery training: Stimulating utilization of imaginal processes. *Journal of Mental Imagery, 10,* 47–64.

Parviainen, T., Helenius, P., Poskiparta, E., Niemi, P., & Salmelin, R. (2006). Cortical sequence of word perception in beginning readers. *Journal of Neuroscience, 26*(22), 6052–6061.

Pascalis, O., Scott, L. S., Kelly, D. J., Shannon, R. W., Nicholson, E., Coleman, M., & Nelson, C. A. (2005). Plasticity of face processing in infancy. *Proceedings of the National Academy of Sciences, 102*(14), 5297–5300.

Paterson, K. B., & Jordan, T. R. (2010). Effects of increased letter spacing on word identification and eye guidance during reading. *Memory & Cognition, 38,* 502–512.

Pearson, P. D., & Duke, N. K. (2002). Comprehension instruction in the primary grades. In C. C. Block & M. Pressley (Eds.), *Comprehension instruction: Research-based best practices* (chap. 16). New York, NY: Guilford.

Peereman, R., Content, A., & Bonin, P. (1998). Is perception a two-way street: The case of feedback consistency in visual word recognition. *Journal of Memory and Language, 39,* 151–174.

Pennington, B. F. (1990). The genetics of dyslexia. *Journal of Child Psychology and Psychiatry, 31,* 193–201.

Petscher, Y., Kim, Y.-S., & Foorman, B. R. (2011). The importance of predictive power in early screening assessments: Implications for placement in the response to intervention framework. *Assessment for Effective Instruction, 36*(3), 158–166.

Phillips, B. M., Clancy-Menchetti, J., & Lonigan, C. J. (2008). Successful phonological awareness instruction with preschool children. *Topics in Early Childhood Special Education, 28*(1), 3–17.

Phillips, B., & Torgesen, J. (2006). Phonemic awareness and reading: Beyond the growth of initial reading accuracy. *Handbook of early literacy research* (Vol. 2, pp. 101–113). New York, NY: Guilford.

Pinker, S. (1994). *The language instinct: How the mind creates language.* New York, NY: William Morrow.

Pinker, S. (1999). *Words and rules: The ingredients of language.* New York, NY: Basic Books.

Podhajski, B., Mather, N., Nathan, J., & Sammons, J. (2009, September/October). Professional development in scientifically based reading instruction: Teacher knowledge and reading outcomes. *Journal of Learning Disabilities, 42*(5), 403–417.

Porcaro, C., Zappasodi, F., Barbati, G., Salustri, G., Pizzella, V., Rossini, P. M., & Tecchio, F. (2006, July). Fetal auditory responses to external sounds and mother's heart beat: Detection improved by Independent Component Analysis. *Brain Research, 1101,* 51–58.

Posner, M. I., Rothbart, M. K., & Sheese, B. E. (2007). Attention genes. *Developmental Science, 10,* 24–29.

Priebe, S. J., Keenan, J. M., & Miller, A. C. (2012, January). How prior knowledge affects word identification and comprehension. *Reading and Writing, 25*(1), 131–149.

Prior, S. M., Fenwick, K. D., Saunders, K. S., Ouellette, R., O'Quinn, C., & Harvey, S. (2011). Comprehension after oral and silent reading: Does grade level matter? *Literacy Research and Instruction, 50,* 183–194.

Puranik, C., & Apel, K. (2010). Effect of assessment task and letter writing ability on preschool children's spelling performance. *Assessment for Effective Intervention, 36*(1), 46–56.

Rayner, K. (2009). Eye movements and attention in reading, scene perception, and visual search. *Quarterly Journal of Experimental Psychology, 62*(8), 1457–1506.

Rayner, K., Foorman, B. R., Perfetti, C. A., Pesetsky, D., & Seidenberg, M. S. (2001, November). How psychological science informs the teaching of reading. *Psychological Science in the Public Interest, 2*, 31–74.

Rayner, K., Slattery, T. J., & Bélanger, N. N. (2010). Eye movements, the perceptual span, and reading speed. *Psychonomic Bulletin & Review, 17*(6), 834–839.

Renvall, H., & Hari, R. (2002). Auditory cortical responses to speech-like stimuli in dyslexic adults. *Journal of Cognitive Neuroscience, 14*, 757–768.

Reutzel, D. R., Fawson, P. C., & Smith, J. A. (2008). Reconsidering silent sustained reading: An exploratory study of scaffolded silent reading. *Journal of Educational Research, 102*(1), 37–50.

Reyna, V. F., Estrada, S. M., DeMarinis, J. A., Myers, R. M., Stanisz, J. M., & Mills, B. A. (2011). Neurobiological and memory models of risky decision making in adolescents versus young adults. *Journal of Experimental Psychology: Learning, Memory, and Cognition, 37*, 1125–1142.

Richards, T. L., & Berninger, V. W. (2008, July). Abnormal fMRI connectivity in children with dyslexia during a phoneme task: Before but not after treatment. *Journal of Neurolinguistics, 21*(4), 294–304.

Rimrodt, S. L., Peterson, D. J., Denckla, M. B., Kaufmann, W. E., & Cutting, L. E. (2010, June). White matter microstructural differences linked to left perisylvian language network in children with dyslexia. *Cortex, 46*(6), 739–749.

Ring, J. J., Barefoot, L. C., Avrit, K. J., Brown, S. A., & Black, J. L. (2013, March/April). Reading fluency instruction for students at risk for reading failure. *Remedial and Special Education, 34*(2), 102–112.

Robinson, A. J., & Pascalis, O. (2004). Development of flexible visual recognition memory in human infants. *Developmental Science, 7*(5), 527–533.

Rolstad, K., Mahoney, K., & Glass, G. (2005). The big picture: A meta-analysis of program effectiveness research on English language learners. *Educational Policy, 19*, 572–594.

Rouse, C. E., & Krueger, A. B. (2004). Putting computerized instruction to the test: A randomized evaluation of a "scientifically based" reading program. *Economics of Education Review, 23*(4), 323–338.

Rumsey, J., Horwitz, B., Donohue, B. C., Nace, K. L., Maisog, J. M., & Andreason, P. (1999). A functional lesion in developmental dyslexia: Left angular gyral flow predicts severity. *Brain and Language, 70*, 187–204.

Sams, G. (2003). *Dyslexia and exams.* Retrieved from http://www.dyslexia-parent.com

Santoro, L. E., Chard, D. J., Howard, L., & Baker, S. K. (2008). Making the *very* most of classroom read-alouds to promote comprehension and vocabulary. *The Reading Teacher, 61*(5), 396–408.

Scammacca, N., Roberts, G., Vaughn, S., Edmonds, M., Wexler, J., Reutebuch, C. K., & Torgesen, J. K. (2007). *Interventions for adolescent struggling readers: A meta-analysis with implications for practice.* Portsmouth, NH: RMC Research Corporation, Center on Instruction.

Schlagel, B. (2007). Best practices in spelling and handwriting. In S. Graham, C. MacArthur, & J. Fitzgerald (Eds.), *Best practices in writing instruction* (pp. 179–201). New York, NY: Guilford.

Schlaggar, B. L., & Church, J. A. (2009, February). Functional neuroimaging insights into the development of skilled reading. *Current Directions in Psychological Science, 18*(1), 21–26.

Schulte-Körne, G., & Bruder, J. (2010, November). Clinical neurophysiology of visual and auditory processing in dyslexia: A review. *Clinical Neurophysiology, 121*(110), 1794–1809.

Schünemann, N., Spörer, N., & Brunstein, J. C. (2013, October). Integrating self-regulation in whole-class reciprocal teaching: A moderator–mediator analysis of incremental effects on fifth graders' reading comprehension. *Contemporary Educational Psychology, 38*(4), 289–305.

Scientific Learning Corporation (SLC). (2000). *Fast ForWord reading: Why it works.* Oakland, CA: Author.

Scull, J. (2010). Embedding comprehension within reading acquisition processes. *Australian Journal of Language and Literacy, 33*(2), 87–107.

Shanahan, T., & Lonigan, C. J. (2010, May). The national Early Literacy Panel: A summary of the process and the report. *Educational Researcher, 39*(4), 279–285.

Shanahan, T., & Shanahan C. (2008). Teaching disciplinary literacy to adolescents: Rethinking content-area literacy. *Harvard Educational Review, 78*(1), 40–59.

Shankweiler, D., & Fowler, A. E. (2004). Questions people ask about the role of phonological processes in learning to read. *Reading and Writing, 18,* 483–515.

Shaywitz, S. E. (1996, November). Dyslexia. *Scientific American, 275,* 98–104.

Shaywitz, S. E. (2003). *Overcoming dyslexia: A new and complete science-based program for reading problems at any level.* New York, NY: Knopf.

Shaywitz, B., Shaywitz, S., Blachman, B., Pugh, K. R., Fulbright, R., Skudlarski, P., . . . Gore, J. (2003, June). *Development of left occipito-temporal systems for skilled reading following a phonologically-based intervention in children.* Paper presented at the conference of the Organization for Human Brain Mapping, New York, NY.

Shaywitz, B. A., Shaywitz, S. E., & Gore, J. (1995). Sex differences in the functional organization of the brain for languages. *Nature, 373,* 607–609.

Shelley-Tremblay, J., Langhinrichsen-Rohling, J., & Eyer, J. (2012, September). Attention therapy improves reading comprehension in adjudicated teens in a residential facility. *Journal of Correctional Education, 63*(2), 49–67.

Singh, L. (2008, February). Influences of high and low variability on infant word recognition. *Cognition, 106,* 833–870.

Singson, M., Mahony, D., & Mann, V. A. (2000). The relation between reading ability and morphological skills: Evidence from derivational suffixes. *Reading and Writing: An Interdisciplinary Journal, 12*(3/4), 219–252.

Siok, W. T., Spinks, J. A., Jin, Z., & Tan, L. H. (2009, October). Developmental dyslexia is characterized by the co-existence of visuospatial and phonological disorders in Chinese children. *Current Biology, 19*(19), R890–R892.

Sipe, L. R. (2001). Invention, convention, and intervention: Invented spelling and the teacher's role. *The Reading Teacher, 55,* 264–273.

Slater, W. H., & Horstman, F. R. (2002). Teaching reading and writing to struggling middle school and high school students: The case for reciprocal teaching. *Preventing School Failure, 46,* 163–166.

Slavin, R. E. (1995). *Cooperative learning: Theory, research and practice* (2nd ed.). Boston, MA: Allyn & Bacon.

Slavin, R. E., & Cheung, A. (2003). *Effective programs for English language learners: A best-evidence synthesis.* Baltimore, MD: Johns Hopkins University, CRESPAR.

Slavin, R. E., & Cheung, A. (2005). A synthesis of research on language of reading instruction for English language learners. *Review of Educational Research, 75*(2), 247–284.

Slavin, R. E., Lake, C., Davis, S., & Madden, N. A. (2009, June). *Effective programs for struggling readers: A best-evidence synthesis.* Retrieved from http://www.bestevidence.org/word/strug_read_Jun_02_2010.pdf

Smith, F., & Goodman, K. S. (1971). On the psycholinguistic method of teaching reading. *Elementary School Journal, 71,* 177–181.

Snow, C. E., Burns, M. S., & Griffin, P. (Eds.). (1998). *Preventing reading difficulties in young children.* Washington, DC: National Academies Press.

Solan, H. A., Shelley-Tremblay, J., Ficarra, A., Silverman, M., & Larson, S. (2003). Effect of attention therapy on reading comprehension. *Journal of Learning Disabilities, 36,* 556–563.

Solan, H. A., Shelley-Tremblay, J. F., Hansen, P. C., & Larson, S. (2007, May/June). Is there a common linkage among reading comprehension, visual attention, and magnocellular processing? *Journal of Learning Disabilities, 40*(3), 270–278.

Solis, M., Ciullo, S., Vaughn, S., Pyle, N., Hassaram, B., & Leroux, A. (2012). Reading comprehension interventions for middle school students with learning disabilities: A synthesis of 30 years of research. *Journal of Learning Disabilities, 45*(4), 327–340.

Sommer, I. E., Aleman, A., Somers, M., Boks, M. P., & Kahn, R. S. (2008, April). Sex differences in handedness, asymmetry of the planum temporale and functional language lateralization. *Brain Research, 1206,* 76–88.

Son, J. Y., Smith, L. B., & Goldstone, R. L. (2008). Simplicity and generalization: Shortcutting abstraction in children's object categorizations. *Cognition, 108*(30), 626–638.

Sousa, D. A. (2007). *How the special needs brain learns* (2nd ed.) Thousand Oaks, CA: Corwin.

Sousa, D. A. (2011a). *How the brain learns* (4th ed.). Thousand Oaks, CA: Corwin.

Sousa, D. A. (2011b). *How the ELL brain learns.* Thousand Oaks, CA: Corwin.

Sousa, D. A., & Tomlinson, C. A. (2011). *Differentiation and the brain: How neuroscience supports the learner-friendly classroom.* Bloomington, IN: Solution Tree Press.

Southgate, V., Csibra, G., Kaufman, J., & Johnson, M. H. (2008). Distinct processing of objects and faces in the infant brain. *Journal of Cognitive Neuroscience, 20*(4), 741–749.

Southwest Educational Development Laboratory (SEDL). (2001). *The cognitive foundations of learning to read.* Austin, TX: Author.

Speece, D. L., & Mills, C. (2003). Initial evidence that letter fluency tasks are valid indicators of early reading skill. *Journal of Special Education, 36,* 223–233.

Stahl, K. A. D. (2004, April). Proof, practice, and promise: Comprehension strategy instruction in the primary grades. *The Reading Teacher, 57*(7), 598–609.

Stahl, S. A. (2000). *Promoting vocabulary development.* Austin, TX: Texas Education Agency.

Steinbrink, C., Vogt, K., Kastrup, A., Müller, H.-P., Juengling, F. D., Kassubek, J., & Riecker, A. (2008, November). The contribution of white and gray matter differences to developmental dyslexia: Insights from DTI and VBM at 3.0 T. *Neuropsychologia, 46*(13), 3170–3178.

Stinson, E. (2003). *Best practices in reading instruction.* Nashville, TN: NPT Educational Services.

Stone, G. O., Vanhoy, M., & Van Orden, G. C. (1997). Perception is a two-way street: Feedforward and feedback phonology in visual word recognition. *Journal of Memory and Language, 36,* 337–359.

Strong, A. C., Wehby, J. H., Falk, K. B., & Lane, K. L. (2004). The impact of a structured reading curriculum and repeated reading on the performance of junior high students with emotional and behavioral disorders. *School Psychology Review, 33,* 561–581.

Swaab, T. Y., Baynes, K., & Knight, R. T. (2002, September). Separable effects of priming and imageability on word processing: An ERP study. *Cognitive Brain Research, 15,* 99–103.

Swanborn, M. S. L., & de Glopper, K. (1999). Incidental word learning while reading: A meta-analysis. *Review of Educational Research, 69,* 261–285.

Swanson, E., Edmonds, M. S., Hairrell, A., Vaughn, S., & Simmons, D. C. (2011). Applying a cohesive set of comprehension strategies to content-area instruction. *Intervention in School and Clinic, 46*(5), 266–272.

Tallal, P., Miller, S. L., Bedi, G., Byma, G., Wang, X., Nagarajan, S., Schreiner, C., Jenkins, W. M., & Merzenich, M. M. (1996, January). Fast-element enhanced speech improves language comprehension in language-learning impaired children. *Science, 271,* 81–84.

Tan, A., & Nicholson, T. (1997). Flashcards revisited: Training poor readers to read words faster improves their comprehension of text. *Journal of Educational Psychology, 89,* 276–288.

Taylor, B. M., Pearson, P. D., Clark, K. F., & Walpole, S. (2000). Effective schools and accomplished teachers: Lessons about primary reading instruction in low-income schools. *Elementary School Journal, 101,* 121–166.

Temple, E., Deutsch, G. K., Poldrack, R. A., Miller, S. L., Tallal, P., Merzenich, M. M., & Gabrieli, J. D. E. (2003, March). Neural deficits in children with dyslexia ameliorated by behavioral remediation: Evidence from functional MRI. *Proceedings of the National Academy of Sciences, 100,* 2860–2865.

Therrien, W. J. (2004). Fluency and comprehension gains as a result of repeated reading: A meta-analysis. *Remedial and Special Education, 25,* 252–261.

Tiu, R. D., Jr., Thompson, L. A., & Lewis, B. A. (2003). The role of IQ in a component model of reading. *Journal of Learning Disabilities, 36,* 424–436.

Tomopoulos, S., Dreyer, B. P., Berkule, S., Fierman, A. H., Brockmeyer, C., & Mendelsohn, A. L. (2010). Infant media exposure and toddler development. *Archives of Pediatric and Adolescent Medicine, 164*(12), 1105–1111.

Torgesen, J. K., Houston, D., & Rissman, L. (2007). *Improving literacy instruction in middle and high schools: A guide for principals.* Portsmouth, NH: RMC Research Corporation.

Trainin, G., & Andrzejczak, N. (2006). *Readers' theatre: A viable reading strategy?* Lincoln: University of Nebraska, Great Plains Institute of Reading and Writing.

Turkeltaub, P. E., Gareau, L., Flowers, D. L., Zeffiro, T. A., & Eden, G. F. (2003). Development of neural mechanisms for reading. *Nature Neuroscience, 6*(7), 767–773.

Uhry, J. (1999). Invented spelling in kindergarten: The relationship with finger-point reading. *Reading and Writing, 11,* 441–464.

Underwood, T., & Pearson, D. P. (2004). Teaching struggling adolescent readers to comprehend what they read. In T. L. Jetton & J. A. Dole (Eds.), *Adolescent literacy research and practice* (pp. 135–161). New York, NY: Guilford.

Vandenberghe, R., Nobre, A. C., & Price, C. J. (2002). The response of left temporal cortex to sentences. *Journal of Cognitive Neuroscience, 14*(4), 550–560.

van der Mark, S., Klaver, P., Bucher, K., Maurer, U., Schulz, E., Brem, S., Martin, E., & Brandeis, D. (2011, February). The left occipitotemporal system in reading: Disruption of focal fMRI connectivity to left inferior frontal and inferior parietal language areas in children with dyslexia. *NeuroImage, 54*(3), 2426–2436.

Vandermosten, M., Boets, B., Luts, H., Poelmans, H., Wouters, J., & Ghesquière, P. (2011, March–April). Impairments in speech and nonspeech sound categorization in children with dyslexia are driven by temporal processing difficulties. *Research in Developmental Disabilities, 32*(2), 593–603.

van Ermingen-Marbach, M., Grande, M., Pape-Neumann, J., Sass, K., & Heim, S. (2013). Distinct neural signatures of cognitive subtypes of dyslexia with and without phonological deficits. *NeuroImage: Clinical, 2,* 477–490.

Vannest, K. J., Harrison, J. R., Temple-Harvey, K., Ramsey, L., & Parker, R. I. (2011). Improvement rate differences of academic interventions for students with emotional and behavioral disorders. *Remedial and Special Education, 32*(6), 521–534.

Vaughn, S., Wanzek, J., Linan-Thompson, S., & Murray, C. (2007). Monitoring response to intervention for students at-risk for reading difficulties: High and low responders. In S. R. Jimerson, M. K. Burns, & A. M. VanDerHeyden (Eds.), *The handbook of response to intervention: The science and practice of assessment and intervention* (pp. 234–243). New York, NY: Springer.

Vellutino, F. R., Fletcher, J. M., Snowling, M. J., & Scanlon, D. M. (2004). Specific reading disability (dyslexia): What have we learned in the past four decades? *Journal of Child Psychology and Psychiatry, 45*(1), 2–40.

Vellutino, F. R., Scanlon, D. M., Zhang, H., & Schatschenider, C. (2008). Using response to kindergarten and first grade intervention to identify children at-risk for long-term reading difficulties. *Reading and Writing, 21,* 437–480.

Vesely, P., & Gryder, N. (2007, Summer). Teaching visual imagery for vocabulary learning. *Academic Exchange Quarterly, 11*(2), 51–55.

Vlachos, F., Andreou, E., & Delliou, A. (2013, May). Brain hemisphericity and developmental dyslexia. *Research in Developmental Disabilities, 34*(5), 1536–1540.

Voegtline, K. M., Costigan, K. A., Pater, H. A., & DiPietro, J. A. (2013). Near-term fetal response to maternal spoken voice. *Infant Behavior and Development, 36*(4), 526–533.

Wagovich, S. A., Pak, Y., & Miller, M. D. (2012, May). Orthographic word knowledge growth in school-age children. *American Journal of Speech-Language Pathology, 21,* 140–153.

Walcott, C. M., Scheemaker, A., & Bielski, K. (2010, July). A longitudinal investigation of inattention and preliteracy development. *Journal of Attention Disorder, 14*(1), 79–85.

Wallentin, M. (2009, March). Putative sex differences in verbal abilities and language cortex: A critical review. *Brain and Language, 108,* 175–183.

Wang, J.-J., Bi, H.-Y., Gao, L.-Q., & Wydell, T. N. (2010, October). The visual magnocellular pathway in Chinese-speaking children with developmental dyslexia. *Neuropsychologia, 48*(12), 3627–3633.

Wang, S. H., & Baillargeon, R. (2008). Detecting impossible changes in infancy: A three- system account. *Trends in Cognitive Sciences, 12*(1), 17–23.

Wang, S., & Gathercole, S. E. (2013, May). Working memory deficits in children with reading difficulties: Memory span and dual task coordination. *Journal of Experimental Child Psychology, 115*(1), 188–197.

Wanzek, J., Roberts, G., Linan-Thompson, S., Vaughn, S., Woodruff, A. L., & Murray, C. S. (2010, March). Differences in the relationship of oral reading fluency and high-stakes measures of reading comprehension. *Assessment for Effective Intervention, 35*(2), 67–77.

Wawryk-Epp, L., Harrison, G., & Prentice, B. (2004). *Teaching students with reading difficulties and disabilities: A guide for educators.* Saskatchewan, Canada: Ministry of Education.

West, C. K., Farmer, J. A., & Wolff, P. M. (1991). *Instructional design: Implications from cognitive science.* Englewood Cliffs, NJ: Prentice Hall.

Wolter, J. A., Wood, A., & D'zatko, K. W. (2009, July). The influence of morphological awareness on the literacy development of first-grade children. *Language, Speech, and Hearing Service in Schools, 40,* 286–298.

Wright, B. A., Bowen, R. W., & Zecker, S. G. (2000). Nonlinguistic perceptual deficits associated with reading and language disorders. *Current Opinion in Neurobiology, 10,* 482–486.

Yamada, Y., Stevens, C., Dow, M., Harn, B. A., Chard, D. J., & Neville, H. J. (2011, August). Emergence of the neural network for reading in five-year-old beginning readers of different levels of pre-literacy abilities: An fMRI study. *NeuroImage, 57,* 704–713.

Yang, Y. F. (2010). Developing a reciprocal teaching/learning system for college remedial reading instruction. *Computers & Education, 55,* 1193–1201.

Yeatman, J. D., Rauschecker, A. M., & Wandell, B. A. (2013, May). Anatomy of the visual word form area: Adjacent cortical circuits and long-range white matter connections. *Brain and Language, 125*(2), 146–155.

Yeung, H. H., & Werker, J. F. (2009, November). Learning words' sounds before learning how words sound: 9-month-olds use distinct objects as cues to categorize speech information. *Cognition, 113,* 234–243.

Yopp, H. K., & Yopp, R. H. (2000). Supporting phonemic awareness development in the classroom. *The Reading Teacher, 54,* 130–143.

Yurick, A., Cartledge, G., Kourea, L., & Keyes, S. (2012). Reducing reading failure for kindergarten urban students: A study of early literacy instruction, treatment quality, and treatment duration. *Remedial and Special Education, 33*(2), 89–102.

Zimmerman, F. J., & Christakis, D. A. (2005). Children's television viewing and cognitive outcomes: A longitudinal analysis of national data. *Archives of Pediatric and Adolescent Medicine, 159*(7), 619–625.

Zoccolotti, P., De Luca, M., Di Pace, E., Gasperini, F., Judica, A., & Spinelli, D. (2005). Word length effect in early reading and in developmental dyslexia. *Brain and Language, 93*(3), 369–373.

# Index

## CORWIN
A SAGE Company

The Corwin logo—a raven striding across an open book—represents the union of courage and learning. Corwin is committed to improving education for all learners by publishing books and other professional development resources for those serving the field of PreK–12 education. By providing practical, hands-on materials, Corwin continues to carry out the promise of its motto: **"Helping Educators Do Their Work Better."**